SUPPLEMENT TO THE HANDBOOK OF MIDDLE AMERICAN INDIANS
Volume 3 Literatures

SUPPLEMENT TO THE HANDBOOK OF MIDDLE AMERICAN INDIANS

VICTORIA REIFLER BRICKER, General Editor

VOLUME THREE

LITERATURES

MUNRO S. EDMONSON, Volume Editor

With the Assistance of Patricia A. Andrews

UNIVERSITY OF TEXAS PRESS, AUSTIN

Requests for permission to reproduce material
from this work should be sent to:
    Permissions
    Box 7819
    Austin, Texas 78713
LIBRARY OF CONGRESS CATALOGING
IN PUBLICATION DATA
Main entry under title:
Literatures.
    (Supplement to the Handbook of Middle Ameri-
can Indians ; v. 3)
    Bibliography: p.
    1. Indian literature—Mexico—Addresses, es-
says, lectures. 2. Indian literature—Central
America—Addresses, essays, lectures. I. Ed-
monson, Munro S. II. Andrews, Patricia A.
III. Series.
PM3051.L57 1985   897'.4   85-3361
ISBN 0-292-77593-8

Reprinted by permission of the Smithsonian In-
stitution Press from Smithsonian Contributions to
Anthropology, No. 19 (1975), *The Great Tzotzil
Dictionary of San Lorenzo Zinacantán*, p. 17;
No. 23 (1977), *Of Cabbages and Kings*, pp. 372–
373; No. 25 (1980), *Of Shoes and Ships and Sealing
Wax*, pp. 208, 215–216; all by Robert Laughlin.

Grateful acknowledgment is also made to the fol-
lowing for permission to reprint previously published material as cited in the text: Cambridge
University Press for material from *Ethnography of
Speaking*; Harvard University Press for material
from *Chamulas in the World of the Sun*; Instituto
de Asesoría Antropológica para la Región Maya,
Asociación Civil, for material from a Writers'
Workshop program pamphlet; Instituto de Inves-
tigaciones Históricas for material from *Tlalocan*;
Mouton and Co. for material from *Meaning in
Mayan Languages*; Princeton University Library
for material from the Robert Garrett Collection of
Manuscripts in the Indigenous Languages of
Middle America.

To our eagles flying
One sleep ahead

THELMA D. SULLIVAN

FERNANDO HORCASITAS

ALFREDO BARRERA VÁSQUEZ

CONTENTS

GENERAL EDITOR'S PREFACE

The aboriginal literatures of Middle America received little attention as such in the *Handbook of Middle American Indians*. An article on the Precolumbian literatures was tucked away in one of five archaeological volumes (M. León-Portilla 1971). Narrative folklore was assigned to the social anthropology volume (Edmonson 1967). And bibliographic chapters on native prose sources appeared in the last of four ethnohistorical volumes (Gibson 1975; Gibson and Glass 1975). While useful and informative, the treatment of the native literatures of Middle America could not, in the space allotted to it in the *Handbook*, even begin to do justice to the richness and variety of the verbal arts in the region.

In this volume, we sample that richness and variety by considering, at greater length than was possible in the *Handbook*, literatures representing five Middle American Indian languages: Nahuatl, Yucatecan Maya, Quiche, Tzotzil, and Chorti. The first three literatures are exceptionally well documented for both the Classical and Modern variants of their languages. The literatures of many languages, such as Tzotzil and Chorti, are oral, not written, and in only a few cases do we

have enough recorded examples to permit description of their genres and styles. We hope that the treatment of literatures in this volume will give ethnographers and linguists the incentive to collect texts representing the full range of functional categories so that in the future there will be sufficient information on the literatures of other Middle American languages to justify additional volumes with this theme.

Our decision to devote a volume of the *Supplement to the Handbook of Middle American Indians* entirely to literatures coincides with an increasing interest in this subject in the scholarly community. The first issue of a new journal, *Latin American Indian Literatures*, appeared in 1977, and the first annual meeting of LAILA/ALILA (Latin American Indian Literatures Association/ Asociación de literaturas indígenas latinoamericanas) took place in April 1983. In addition, several sessions organized by linguists at the annual meetings of the American Anthropological Association in December 1982 were concerned with the stylistic characteristics of American Indian formal speech. There is, then, a growing consensus that Native American literatures have *literary*, as well as historical, cultural, and linguistic value. The five literatures represented here illustrate some of the dimensions of that concern.

V.R.B.

SUPPLEMENT TO THE HANDBOOK OF MIDDLE AMERICAN INDIANS
Volume 3 Literatures

1. Introduction

MUNRO S. EDMONSON

To the east and west, the boundaries of Anahuac are clear: the coasts of the world's two largest oceans. To the north and south, the frontier zones are deeper and less well defined, but if the deserts and jungle were more penetrable than the seas, they were nonetheless formidable obstacles to travel and contact among the native peoples. Geographic circumstances gave to their cultures a high degree of autonomy. Not only was the Land between the Waters largely independent of the rest of humanity; its peoples were also in great measure independent of each other. This separatism is particularly profound in matters of the spirit.

The present volume is an introduction to the spiritual culture of this area. It is perforce focused upon the two best-known currents of that culture: the relatively unitary literary tradition of the Nahuas and the relatively segmentary one of the Mayas (in this case Yucatec, Quiche, Tzotzil, and Chorti). It remains for me to place these central aspects of the subject in perspective.

The literature of even a simple society presents us with a great deal of contextually defined specificity and hence heterogeneity. And the societies and literatures of Anahuac are not simple. The playful and sophisticated word games of the feast of the *baktun*, the "strong throat" gossip of Tarascan women, the stoic but passionate lament of the Toltec exiles, the "whistle speech" ribaldry of Mixtec and Zapotec gallants, the elegantly insulting song of the women of Chalco to Axayacatl, the courtly honorifics of a Tzotzil ceremonial visit, and the engaging nonsense of Yucatecan children's stories point up the wealth of diversity to be encountered in any one of these stratified, urbane, and complexly articulated cultures. People pun, they riddle, they insult each other obscenely, they declaim, they mourn, they sing, they preach, they pray—they talk, ceremoniously and incessantly.

Theirs is a literature of priests, of curers, of peasants, of warriors, of merchants, of housewives, of lovers, even of orphans and slaves. But it is also true that their tradition included self-conscious and fully professional literary artists: they had and to a large extent still have orators, poets, minstrels, theatrical impresarios, directors, actors, musicians, costumers, mask-makers, clowns, story-tell-

1

ers, prophets, prayer-makers, scribes, illustrators, and engravers. They were very much aware of style—or more accurately of styles (suggesting that unofficially at least they even had critics)—and could manipulate literary modes in parody and satire as well as for elegance or solemnity.

These are literatures shaped in a polyglot world in which people were ever aware of the foreigners in the next town, or even in their midst. Enemies as well as friends were inevitably objects of interest, and generated literary reactions from derision to imitation. Thus we get Nahuatl poems "in the style of" different towns, Toltec songs in Quiche and Yucatec, Nahuatl myths in Mixtec and Otomi, Otomi songs in Nahua, Tarascan dramas in which people of different villages, times, and cultures are depicted. The Spanish conquest added a further international flavor, and traditional native literature came to be decorated with Spanish and Latin phrases and figures. Dramas are widespread in which centurions, pharisees, Moors, conquistadores, and revolutionaries jostle Quetzalcoatl, the Monkey Twins, Montezuma, Deer, and Jaguar. The postconquest literatures are undeniably complex, but the preconquest literatures were too.

Oaxaca is a world apart. Lying between Tenochtitlan and the Mayan cities but sealed off by its mountains; speaking a welter of tongues unrelated to either Nahua or Maya, and sadly neglected by chroniclers and historians, it has been the seat of a semi-autonomous civilization for at least as long as the better-known areas to the north and east. Like those of all the rest of Anahuac except for the Nahuan and Mayan, Oaxacan historical literature is largely lost to us, and we are left with what can be collected from oral sources. What can be done from full documentation of a largely oral literature is exemplified in the treatment of Tzotzil in this volume, and we have a good beginning on Oaxaca, particularly in Zapotec and Mixtec. Despite the difficulty and diversity of the Oaxacan languages, we may yet hope to obtain a much more complete and enriching

view of their ancient, lively, and strategic world. The myths, legends, tales, and word play we already have are tantalizing. We need their oratory, ritual, poetry, and drama as well.

The borderlands of Anahuac are also distinctive and also poorly documented: the Fish Country of Michoacan to the west, the tropical Huaxteca to the northeast, and the ill-defined territories of the barbarian Chichimeca to the north. In the far southeast lie the lands of the Pacific Corridor, familiar territory to the Nahuas and to a number of their predecessors from Mexico and Guatemala at least as far south as northwestern Costa Rica. All of them participate in various ways in the common traditions of Anahuac. The Tarascans built pyramids but rounded their corners. Huastecs spoke a Mayan language but didn't wear pants. Some Chichimecs learned Huastec, Otomi, or Nahuatl but not agriculture. The southerners of the Pacific Corridor spoke languages related to Nahuatl, Zapotec, Maya, and even Sioux, but constituted small and scattered enclaves in comparison with the centralized kingdoms to the north.

One particularly characteristic literary feature of Anahuac may be considered here in order to document the fact that, while its boundaries are not precisely drawn, it did have them. The element I have selected is couplet poetry.

Couplet poetry is general to the languages of Anahuac. It has been documented in most of the Mayan languages: Cakchiquel, Chol, Chontal, Chorti, Chuh, Huastec, Ixil, Jacaltec, Kanhobal, Kekchi, Lacandon, Mam, Pokomam, Quiche, Tojolabal, Tzeltal, Tzotzil, Yucatec, and Zutuhil. It also occurs in Huave, Mixe, Zoque, Popoloca, and Totonac. Among Utoaztecan groups, it is attested in Nahuatl, Huichol, Cora, Tarahumar, Tepecano, and Yaqui. It is widespread in Otomanguean literatures as well. I have examples from Villa Alta, Ixtlan, and Valley Zapotec; Mixtec; Trique; Chinantec; and Chatino in the Oaxaca area and from Jonaz Chichimec, Mazatec, Otomi, and Pame in the north. I have also found it in Tlapanec, Tequistlatec, and Seri among the Hokan languages, and in Tarascan. I have scanned enough North American Indian poetry to suppose that the couplet form is rare to nonexistent there. Nor, to my knowledge, are the North American scansions represented in Middle American poetry.

A certain confusion is perhaps inevitable in the scansion of poetry. Even a simple poem has many levels of resonance or potential resonance, and different hearers may both hear and sense different things in it.

The problems may be illustrated with a shaman's chant of the Macro-Chibchan speaking Chiripo of Costa Rica:

kusuala dža-kaebia

baebatala dža-kaebia

kauutala dža-kaebia

baegruala dža-kaebia

dederuala dža-kaebiua

hagnama pagle i-saible no-ite

iuibli (no-)katate

iuimasia no-iua

hagnama no-kaebisu

imalor tongarte no-kaebisu

With the magic stone I cure;

With the (?) stone I cure;

With the end of the stone I cure;

With the (?) stone I cure;

With the seagull stone I cure thee.

The fever leaves the house;

The fever escapes;

The mother of fever departs;

The fever is cured;

The little girl is cured

(Lehmann 1920:1:340; my translation)

At a purely syllabic level the chant presents a number of repeated syllables in an orderly pattern, suggesting at least three superimposed scansions. Since all of these elements are also syntactic, the syllabic scansions themselves are also syntactic. At least two additional syntactic scansions may also be discerned. All of these elements have meaning and hence all of them are semantic as well. But an additional three semantic

scansions derive from the juxtaposition of synonymous and complementary expressions. Thus the following scansion levels may be detected:

syllabic	aaaaabbbbb	a: *dža-*
		b: *no-*
	aaaabccbdd	a: *-a*
		b: *-ua*
		c: *-te*
		d: *-su*
	abbaaxxxxx	a: *-uala*
		b: *-tala*
syntactic	aaaaaxxxaa	a: *-kaebi-*
	xxxxxabbax	a: *hagnama (pagle)*
		b: *iui-*
semantic	aaaaabbbbx	a: 'stones'
		b: 'fever'
	xxxxxaaaxx	a: 'departure'
	xxxxxxxaxa	a: 'mother: daughter'

Note that the chant is clearly divisible into two stanzas, the first addressed to the patient and the second to her mother. And the mother is even personified as the disease!

As a matter of judgment, the predominant scansion seems to me to be aaaaa; bbbaa—but in any case the characteristic aabbcc...nn scansion of Anahuac is spectacularly absent. At the same time, stanzaic poetry appears to be late, atypical, and European-derived in Anahuac.

From the far northwestern frontier territory I shall cite the text of the Creation Song of the Arizona Pima:

a. *Tcuwutu Makai tcuwutu nata miakuka*

b. *Nyuita hasitco-onyi!*

c. *Sikalamu nata miakuka.*

d. *Tcuwutu Makai tavaku nata miakuka,*

e. *Nyuita hasiyaña!*

f. *Tapinyimu nata miakuka.*

g. *Tcuwutu Makai tcuwutu nata*

h. *Himlo,*

i. *Humutco-o.*

j. *Tcuwutu Makai tavaku nata.*

k. *Tcuwutu tapa sihaitconyoka-ana*

l. *Tavaku tapa sitco mamatcu-u.*

a. Earth Magician is to make the world.
b. Behold what he can do!
c. Round he is to make it.
d. Earth Magician is to make the mountains.
e. Heed what he has to say!
f. Smooth he is to make them.
g. Earth Magician makes this world
h. Larger,
i. Enlarged.
j. Earth Magician makes the mountains.
k. Into the earth the Magician glances;
l. Into its mountains he may see.

(Russell 1908:206)

Redundant as this text is, in performance it is much more so. The twelve lines cited are expanded into fifty-five: ababcb, ababab, defe, ababcb, ababab; gghhhi, gghhhi, jjhhhi, gghhhi, gghhhi; kl. Since all the lines are repeated verbatim in this pattern, this is the syllabic scansion of the song. Scanning just the text, there are additional patterns of scansion at the syntactic and semantic levels:

syntactic	axxaxxaxxaxx	a: *Tcuwutu Makai*
	axxbxxaxxbxx	a: *tcuwutu* b: *tavaku*
	axaaxaaxxabb	a: *nàta* b: *tapa*
	abaabaxxxxxx	a: *miakuka* b: *nyuita*
semantic	abcabcaddaaa	a: 'earth: mountain' b: 'see:hear' c: 'round: smooth' d: 'larger: enlarged'
	xxxxxxxxxxaa	a: 'glance:see'

The scansion of this Pima poem is in every way different from that of the poetry of Anahuac. As it is performed, the semantic scansion is: ababcb, ababab, abab, ababcb, ababab; aacccc, aacccc, ddcccc, aacccc, aacccc; aa (stanzas are separated by semicolons, substanzas by commas). There are thus two sestets, a quatrain, two sestets in the first stanza; five sestets (each of a couplet and a quatrain) in the second; and one couplet in the third. Neither the pattern of verbatim repetition nor the triadic structure of the sestets nor yet the stanzaic organization fits the pattern of the poetry of Anahuac.

The common elements of Nahua and Mayan literature constitute our best indicators of the literature of Anahuac. Both peoples set great store by speech, identifying it with spiritual virtues and power for both good and evil. People, gods, and spirits (including animal spirits) speak, and they do so with artifice and consequence. The Word of the gods is responsible for creation; the words of Hunac Ceel destroyed Mayapan; the words of shamans heal; the words of formal insult (*albures*) curse, defy, and destroy. To be a speaker is not just a talent: it is a formal, public, and ceremonial office. North America had its orators and talking chiefs, but in Anahuac the speakers were given specialized and esoteric training. They were the elite. They were assisted by scribes, equally specialized, who wrote, painted, or carved texts, maps, mnemonic and stylized books, monuments, murals, votive vases, and talismans. Thus words were remembered—in traditional puns, proverbs, riddles, clichés, and formulas—and in writing.

What was remembered was history. It differed from the episodic calendar-stick records of North Americans as the calendar of Anahuac differed from theirs. Tied to a cycle of fifty-two years within still larger cycles, these annals or chronicles were organized into theologically self-conscious histories, justified by legend and myth, and conferring the dynastic authority of the past upon the present or aspiring rulers.

In oral and in written form, and in various admixtures of the two, we have inherited the myths of the multiple creations, the Earth and Water Monsters, the Hero Twins, the Lord of the Mountain, and intertwined with them the themes of more ancient and more recent narrative folklore: coyote and rabbit stories, *nahual* and ghost and witchcraft stories, stories of buried treasure, omens, and portents. The tales explain the world as it is (why volcanoes erupt, where corn came from, why animals and foreigners can't speak properly), warn about what it may become (tales of prophecy, divination, illness, death, and doom), or sometimes merely amuse (how stupid can a Huiteco or an Otomi get?).

In a special category are the stories of the Toltecs, constituting a specific and even datable diffusion from the Nahuas to the Mayas during the Postclassic period. These include the characteristic Toltec origin myth of the four ancestors, the diaspora of the Toltecs, and the legends of Quetzalcoatl. They may stand as cautionary examples of the mutual influence of the peoples of Anahuac on each other from the most ancient times, documentable in this instance in literary terms from the tenth century on.

Not only a dramatic tradition, but specific dramas are widely shared in the region. The Flying Pole Dance ranges from at least Guatemala to the Huaxteca, and the Dance of the Elders is found from Nicaragua (Huehuence) to Michoacan (Viejitos). Plays of the Life of Christ are documented not only in Nahuatl and at least eight Mayan languages but in Mangue, Mixe, Zoque, four Oaxacan languages, Totonac, Otomi, Pame, Matlazinca, Tarascan, Cora, Tepehuan, Mayo, Yaqui, and Tarahumar as well. Plays of the Conquest (of the Moors, of Mexico, of Guatemala, or of all of them at once) are scarcely less widespread. The drama of Anahuac was in varying degrees ritual, but it included both farce and tragedy, historical commemoration and mythopoeic syncretism even before it ingested the histories of the Jews, the Romans, and the Spaniards. Actors were elaborately costumed and masked, and their performances incorporated music, dance, and poetry, often in the context of prayer and sacrifice, feasting, drinking, sports, acrobatics, and games.

Enough has been said to indicate the presence of a common poetic tradition. The power of the word was so great that it was only very rarely taken lightly, and while we can distinguish informal from formal speech, much the largest part of all discourse was and is formal. When it is, it is in semantic couplets, and hence poetry. The scope of poetry is correspondingly great. It includes songs (of love, war, philosophical reflection, curing, poverty, death, rejoicing, or fun), but it also includes prayer, incantations, history, narrative, sermons, legal documents, and arguments, in short, all but the briefest and most casual of expressions.

Linked by the coastal territory of the eastern Nahua—Nonoalco—the Mayas and the Nahuas have had a closer historical relationship than the distance between their major centers would suggest. There has nonetheless been ample room for diversity, as is documented by the chapters in this volume. I leave it for the readers to decide for themselves where the quintessentially Nahua, Yucatecan, or Tzotzil flavor lies. For myself, I see justice in the characterization of the Zapotecs as the Italians of the New World, voluble, excitable, extroverted, and expressive. The bloody Nahuas on the other hand have an extraordinary penchant for lachrymose self-pity, and take refuge in bright colors, the delicate aromas of flowers, and fatalistic sentimentality—in a word, Weltschmerz. The Quiche were clearly the dramatists of Anahuac par excellence, hiding behind the mask an Old Testament sense of guilt and duty. The self-effacing punctilio of Tzotzil courtesy may have similar roots, but the manner of its expression has something almost Japanese to it. The Yucatecans have a certain crafty dignity, sophisticated and worldly wise, but reserved and unsurprised at the world's wickedness. "Greeks of the New World" isn't bad: they were certainly as quarrelsome. The Otomi strike me as the original cigar-store Indians, rigid, stolid, stern, and unemotional. Among themselves, however, they wear a totally different face, engaging in sprightly and witty word play and bawdy jokes and stories. The aptness of these particular characterizations may be challenged, but these are certainly among the differences in style and spirit of the languages of Anahuac.

While this introduction has been mainly concerned with boundaries, it must be conceded that in the larger sense, literature has none. The purpose of this book will have been served if it helps Anahuac to make its own conquest by expressing to a broader world its distinctive spiritual realities and concerns.

2. Nahuatl Literature

MIGUEL LEÓN-PORTILLA

1. INTRODUCTION. The expression "Nahuatl literature" is used here in its broadest ethnohistorical and cultural meaning. It thus embraces the totality of expressions of highly diverse themes, periods, and places transmitted in Nahuatl, considered to be the classical language of the Mexican plateau, or in one of its ancient or modern variants. In this work I shall deal primarily with the products of the Prehispanic tradition, many of them written down in the Latin alphabet by virtue of contact with the Spanish. I set this time limit for reasons of space as well as because of the obvious need to date these materials. Despite the fact that the culture of the Nahua peoples has been affected more or less violently several times since the Spanish conquest, Nahuatl has continued in use not only as a daily means of communication, but also in some instances as a literary vehicle.

Because of the volume and variety encompassed by this view of Nahuatl literature, it is useful to commence with a few specific ques-

Note: This chapter, including all quoted material, has been translated from Spanish by Munro S. Edmonson.

tions: What realms of culture have been reflected in the literature in Nahuatl? How and in what social milieus were they created and transmitted? How have they been preserved and how are they studied and disseminated today? Do the modern Nahua communities have access to the literature composed by their ancestors, and is literary creativity continuing among them?

1.1. CULTURAL CONTEXTS OF NAHUATL LITERATURE. It is apparent upon examination that Nahuatl literature has been produced on the basis of Prehispanic Mesoamerican culture. Though it has its own identity, it also contains similarities to other Mesoamerican literatures, for example, that of the Mayas. Thus the deepest substrate in Nahuatl literature is that of Mesoamerican civilization, not only of the Postclassic period but also of earlier periods.

I understand Mesoamerican civilization in terms of an ethos or sum of values, beliefs, sociopolitical and economic institutions, and other traits shared by the various peoples who have lived together in the geographical environment that produced this civilization. It being impossible to describe this ethos

7

here, I refer the reader to a characterization of it which I consider to be very largely correct (Edmonson 1967). Despite external cultural influences, elements of this ethos can be observed in the literary productions of the Colonial and Independence periods.

In addition, most of the examples of Nahuatl Colonial literature display the stamp of Spanish culture and of the introduction of Christianity. This is manifest in the great majority of the documents produced at that time.

The extreme state of decline of some Nahua groups during the Colonial and Modern periods has tended to suggest that they eventually lost completely their talent and ability in literary creation. Ethnological research and spontaneous but direct contacts with certain communities show that this is not always the case. Some groups have preserved texts through oral tradition, and some have even put into written form the fruit of their own inspiration (Aquino Ch. 1973a; 1973b; 1973c; 1973d; Chino L. 1974; Horcasitas 1968; Horcasitas and Ford 1979; Joel Martínez Hernández et al. 1980; Santos V. 1975a; 1975b). In a few cases, some of these works have been published. In theme and form of expression, most of them show clearly the influence of the mestizo culture of Mexico and sometimes also that of foreigners. The non-Mesoamerican impact on them is also clear in the frequent loan words and changes of expression in the dialects in which they are produced.

1.2. ORIGINS AND MODES OF TRANSMISSION. Prehispanic tradition has given us large numbers of Nahuatl texts: religious (hymns, songs, sermons, prayers . . .), records of the past (myths, legends, annals . . .), probably designed to be publicly declaimed or chanted on particular occasions. The sources tell us of two kinds of transmission of these compositions. The first, systematic and if you will sometimes sophisticated or even esoteric, took place particularly in the centers of higher education (the *calmecac*) and perhaps also wherever members of the noble class (*pipiltin*) foregathered. Our sources (*Códice*

florentino: fol. 159r; *Coloquios de los doce*; fol. 34v; Durán 1867–1880:2:229) make it clear that the sages and priests made use of *amoxtli* ('books') and *amatl* ('papers') to facilitate this kind of systematic transmission. What was put into writing in what we now know as "native codices" was a record of what the sages and priests wished to remember, or at least functioned as an aid and complement to systematic oral transmission. On the hieroglyphic writing used by the Nahuas, and particularly on its capacities as a medium of expression, see the works of Charles E. Dibble (1971:322–332) and Henry B. Nicholson (1973:1–43).

There was another form of transmission of some works, for example, hymns and religious songs. This was more broadly aimed at the *macehualtin*, the common people of the various *calpulli* or wards, and was probably begun in the *telpuchcalli* ('young men's houses') attended by the sons of commoners. We also know from other evidence (*Códices matritenses*: fol. 259r) that there were priests whose job it was "to teach the people the holy songs throughout the wards. They put forth calls for the peasants to come together so that they could learn the songs well."

Some distinctions must be introduced with regard to the form of composition and origins of the works that have come down to us. Some songs included in the compilations are definitely attributed to a *cuicapicqui*, or songmaker. Thus we know the names of a certain number of these poets who lived in the leading principalities or kingdoms of the central part of Mexico during the fourteenth to sixteenth centuries (Garibay 1953–1954:2:373–390; M. León-Portilla 1978b).

The great majority of compositions, in verse and prose alike, are of unknown authorship. Such compositions as mythical tales and historical annals must be attributed to groups of priests and sages, custodians of the tradition and art of hieroglyphic writing.

An examination of the available documentation furthermore convinces us that a high percentage of the literary products was in one way or another the work of individuals or groups belonging to the nobility. A very few exceptions allow us to conclude that we have before us the work of a commoner. As in the cultures of classical antiquity, the literature of the Nahuas carried with it a rich burden of meanings and beliefs supporting the identity, norms, and sense of direction of the group, and reinforcing its social and political organization. Such works were carefully preserved and enriched by members of the ruling class in the various communities, principalities, or states (*Códices matritenses*: fols. 158v–159r). This appears to have occurred not only among the Mexicas but also among other groups contemporary with them: Tetzcocans, Chalcas, Tlaxcaltecas, etc., and even very likely in the earlier periods of Tecpanec, Culhuacan, and Toltec hegemony.

We also owe many of the works traceable to the centuries of Spanish rule to descendants of the ancient lords or chiefs. Nonetheless, we find various kinds of written works in the Colonial period—letters, historical accounts, and others—which are the work of individuals who did not come from the old ruling class (M. León-Portilla 1977; 1978a: 13–39; Anderson, Berdan, and Lockhart 1976).

In the traditions and other productions collected in the Modern period, including those whose authors are known to us, the distinction of social class loses its importance in many cases. Some of the Modern works composed in different variants of Nahuatl are due to people who continue to regard themselves as custodians of ancient tradition, while others appear to spring from the individual inspiration of persons of no particular distinction in the Indian community.

1.3. PRESERVATION, RECOVERY, STUDY AND DIFFUSION OF NAHUA LITERARY WORKS. As has already been described several times (Garibay 1953–1954:2:21–88; M. León-Portilla 1966:8–22), we owe to the efforts of some surviving Indian scholars and to the parallel zeal of several humanist friars of the sixteenth century the recovery of at least a part of the literary wealth conceived and expressed in Nahuatl. It is well known that few of the Prehispanic books escaped the

destruction that followed the conquest. As far as the central region is concerned, there remain to us as a sample the books that make up what is known as the Codices of the Borgia Group. Despite everything, the production of other codices or pictographic manuscripts continued, preserving in greater or lesser degree their Prehispanic purity, tradition, and style. Some examples are the *Codex Borbonicus*, the *Tira de la peregrinación*, the *Mapas de Cuauhtinchan*, and the Codices *Xolotl, Tlotzin,* and *Quinatzin*. More than two hundred pictographic manuscripts with hieroglyphic inscriptions of direct relevance to the history of ancient Mexico have come down to us, sometimes accompanied by glosses in Nahuatl at times with some kind of literary value. In the large majority these contain elements of genuine Prehispanic tradition (Glass 1975).

Besides all these native books, the recovery efforts of knowledgeable natives and humanist friars included the recording of many texts preserved by oral tradition. In the Prehispanic period the education in the *calmecac* (the centers where the *pipiltin* were primarily prepared) included the memorization of a broad spectrum of texts. After the conquest, Nahua priests, sages, and other surviving *pipiltin* made it possible in one way or another for many of the texts they knew to be transcribed in Nahuatl, taking advantage of the Latin alphabet. In some cases this task was accomplished by the Indians themselves reducing these texts to alphabetic transcriptions (Garibay 1953–1954:2:222–266). In others, as in the undertakings of Andrés de Olmos and Bernardino de Sahagún, the recovery and transcription were the result of the combined effort of Indian informants and Spanish priests (Edmonson 1974:3–15). More than a few samples of the various literary genres described below thus came to be included in various manuscripts. In some of these, to be sure, the alphabetic representation of Nahuatl is accompanied by hieroglyphics and pictures following the Indian tradition, as for example in the *Historia tolteca-chichimeca*.

9

Particularly from the last third of the sixteenth century on, other forms of literary production appear, many with historical content, thanks to Nahuas, most of them descendants of *pipiltin*, writing on their own account and for various purposes. In some cases, as in that of the native chronicles (Castillo 1908), the intent appears to have been to preserve a body of data. In others, the aim appears to be linked to economic or social considerations. Such is the case with those who write to support particular demands or claims addressed to the Spanish authorities. In any event, those who continued to be involved in this have left many works in which ancient accounts, sometimes copied literally, appear beside the ruminations of those who collected and used them.

Stretching the concept of literature to the maximum, many other compositions also from the Colonial period may be placed beside those of the types already mentioned. These include various kinds of correspondence of the descendants of both nobles and commoners, and a broad range of legal writs, wills, inventories, acts of sale or donation, municipal records, *cofradía* registers, petitions, complaints, and ordinances, as well as other texts with religious content: hymns, songs, dramatic compositions, comedies, sacramental autos, sermons, confessionals, devotionals, and Christian catechisms. Some works of these last sorts were printed in Mexico City or, less often, Puebla. From this period too come more than fifteen *Artes* or grammars, beginning with that of Olmos, completed in 1547 but only published in the last century (1875). Outstanding among the grammatical and lexicographic contributions are those of Alonso de Molina, author of two *Vocabularios* (1555; 1571b) and an *Arte de la lengua mexicana y castellana* (1571a). Also deserving of special mention are the contributions revealing a penetrating knowledge of Nahuatl and of correct expression in that language, the works of three distinguished Jesuits: the mestizo native of Tetzcoco, Antonio del Rincón (1595); Horacio Carochi (1645); and Ignacio Paredes (1759).

1.4. REEVALUATION AND STUDY OF THESE TEXTS. Toward the end of the nineteenth century and particularly in the twentieth there finally began the rediscovery and study of this body of materials, including the few known Prehispanic codices, the various hieroglyphic and painted manuscripts prepared after the conquest, the many genres of texts in the Latin alphabet but still in Nahuatl, and finally the copious documentation that continued to be produced for various reasons throughout the era of New Spain. Pioneers in the study of these works were Rémi Siméon, Daniel G. Brinton, Francisco del Paso y Troncoso, and Eduard Seler. Those who later continued this kind of study from a humanist standpoint include the outstanding figures of Walter Lehmann, Charles E. Dibble, Arthur J. O. Anderson, and, in Mexico, Angel María Garibay K. and Wigberto Jiménez Moreno, who have trained new groups of investigators.

1.5. NAHUA WORKS OF INDEPENDENT MEXICO. From the period of Mexico's independence to the present time derive rather more copious compositions than might be supposed, published or collected in various forms. Let me begin by mentioning some proclamations, such as those put out by Carlos Ma. de Bustamante under the title *La Malinche de la Constitución*, published in Mexico in 1820 (Horcasitas 1969:271–278), or the manifestos that Emiliano Zapata addressed to other revolutionary contingents in April 1918, also in Nahuatl (M. León-Portilla 1978a). Research carried out by both ethnologists and ethnolinguists, on the other hand, is responsible for the bulk of the texts that can be said to sample Nahuatl oral literature. As Fernando Horcasitas and Sara O. de Ford (1979) have shown, the variety of the texts obtained is very great. Most are samples of the oral tradition that yet survives in the Nahua communities of Morelos, Veracruz, Puebla, Tlaxcala, Oaxaca, Tabasco, Guerrero, the state of Mexico, Hidalgo, Michoacan, San Luis Potosi, Durango, the Federal District, and the Republic of El Salvador.

The texts sometimes reveal antecedents in the Prehispanic or Colonial periods. In terms of content they can be classified as myths, historical legends, etiological tales, moralizing stories, and other forms in which the influence of literary inventions from very distant cultural areas is at times clearly perceptible (Horcasitas 1978:177–209). Besides the evidence of oral narrative, various *cuicatl* or songs have been successfully collected and in some cases published, including some by known authors and others anonymous.

Relatively recently a number of periodical publications in Nahuatl have likewise appeared whose pages have included narratives, legends, tales, poetic compositions, and essays. The following may be remembered as a sample: *Mexihkayotl* ("Mexicanism"), published in 1946 by the Sociedad Pro Lengua Náhuatl Mariano Jacobo Rojas; *Mexihkatl Itonalama* ("Mexican Daily"), thirty-one issues of which I know to have appeared, all in 1950, thanks to the efforts of Miguel Barrios E.; and *In Amatl Mexicatl Tlatoani* ("The Mexican Speaker"), publicity organ of the Centro Social y Cultural Ignacio Ramírez, which appeared in the town of Santa Ana Tlacotenco, Milpa Alta, D.F., in 1975.

To all of these kinds of literature one must add the numerous publications of translations into Nahuatl of a variety of texts ranging from the New Testament in different modern dialects, messages like the one that President Lázaro Cárdenas produced in 1937, under the title of *Itlahtol in mexihcayo tlalnantecuhtli tlacatecatl Lazaro Cardenas intechcopa in Mexihcayo altepeme* ("Address of the chief, governor of the Mexican country, directed to the towns of Mexico"). Among the works translated and published in Nahuatl, some may be considered unexpected. An example is *Lecciones espirituales para las tandas de ejercicios de San Ignacio, dadas a los indios en el idioma mexicano* by a priest of the bishopric of Puebla de los Angeles, Puebla, 1841. Another is a version in the Nahuatl of the San Luis Potosi Huaxtec area of Virgil's fourth *Eclogue* (Martínez 1910). In recent years, under the auspices of the Secretaría de Educación Pública the collection and in several instances publication of poetic composi-

tions, tales, and other sorts of narrative has been achieved in various modern Nahua dialects (A. León-Portilla 1980).

From what has been said, one should not necessarily suppose that there is now a renewed literary florescence in any of the modern variants of this language. The situation is uncertain in this respect, and there are those who think that these kinds of spiritual products will become increasingly rare in the Indian communities that still exist in the country. Recognition of this situation leads us to pose the question of what the literature of their ancestors and the personal creativity of some of their members mean to the modern communities.

1.6. MODERN NAHUA COMMUNITIES AND LITERATURE. There are groups among whom both traditional and individually creative works are listened to with pleasure, either in the bosom of the family or in certain celebrations in which everybody participates. By way of example, one may mention certain performances that have been produced before the assembled community for many years: the *Dances of Coatetelco* (Horcasitas 1980), the so-called *Legendary Cycle of Tepoztecatl* (González Casanova 1976), and other forms of the dances of the conquest or evocations of historical events like the battle of May 5, 1864, against the French. These performances confirm that in some communities the force of tradition survives despite everything.

On the other hand, the modern Nahua communities have virtually no access to the literary works of their ancestors, Prehispanic or Colonial. Publications of this sort mainly manage to reach the academic and urban communities with an interest in native literatures; in the circuits of native groups they are rarely seen. Nor has access to this literary heritage been provided to its heirs through the schools. In only a few cases known to me have some teachers attempted to make examples of the ancient literature available to the rest of the community, as in Santa Ana Tlacotenco, Milpa Alta, D.F., cited above. In this light one is tempted to think that it is the moral duty of those of us who study ancient and modern Nahuatl literature to make it available to those who still keep alive in one or another variant the language of the ancient Mexicans.

2. GENRES BASED ON PREHISPANIC TERMINOLOGY. Examination of a considerable number of works plausibly attributable to Prehispanic tradition leads to the distinction of two major sorts of literary genres. On the one hand are the *cuicatl* 'songs, hymns, poems.' On the other are the *tlahtolli* 'word(s); discourse, narrative.' If one wished to compare them to the literary products of the Indo-European languages, with all the appropriate limitations of the comparison, one might say that the *cuicatl* would correspond to poetry, complete with rhythm and measure, while the *tlahtolli* would be comparable to prose. But above and beyond comparison, it is of interest to specify the major features of the *cuicatl* and the *tlahtolli*, as is done below. The various genres that are included within the range of variation of each of them are then discussed in sections 3 and 4.

2.1. STRUCTURE AND FEATURES OF THE *cuicatl*. The characteristics and structure of the literary genre of the *cuicatl* have been relatively little studied. I shall here follow particularly the observations of Garibay (1953–1954:1:59–106) and of Frances Karttunen and James Lockhart (1980). The outstanding features of the *cuicatl* genre are as follows:

(a) Distribution of their texts in a number of specific groupings of words, sometimes in true paragraphs. The manuscripts contain various indications of these groupings. Karttunen and Lockhart (1980:16) have identified these as "verses": "the basic entity of Nahuatl poetry is what we call the verse." In considering these groupings in the *cuicatl* we shall designate them simply as *units of expression*.

(b) Various kinds of rhythm and meter; presence of nonlexical elements in the *cuicatl* as possible indicators of rhythm.

(c) Stylistics. This includes the internal structure of the units of expression, and their external structure with regard to other units of the same *cuicatl*; also the characteristic resources of this genre of Nahuatl compositions, such as parallelisms, *difrasismos*, and correlations of certain phrases.

2.1.1. UNITS OF EXPRESSION. A number of sixteenth-century manuscripts include transcriptions of various *cuicatl*. The main ones are *Cantares mexicanos*, the *Romances de los señores de la Nueva España* (Garibay 1964), the *Historia tolteca-chichimeca*, and the *Códice florentino*. The *cuicatl* that they include appear in units or groupings separated by dots and space, and sometimes also by the sign that indicates a new paragraph or by an indentation of the lines that follow a line preceded by dots and space and beginning with a capital letter.

These units of expression vary considerably in length. In a few cases they consist of a single line; in others of two, three, or more. Another element which also appears to be important in separating the units is the presence of syllables devoid of lexical content which appear to be exclamations or interjections: *aya*, *iya*, *huiya*, *ohuaya*, and others, at the end of a number of units. There are also *cuicatl* in which the nonlexical syllables are inserted into the text and sometimes fused with other words. In another source, *Anales de Tlatelolco*, the only element permitting recognition of the boundaries of the units of expression of the *cuicatl* is precisely this nonlexical or exclamatory expression.

Bearing in mind these indicators, one must wonder about the adequacy of translating these *cuicatl* into European languages by converting them into verses and stanzas that fracture the units of expression that appear in the manuscripts.

Certainly the examination of the *cuicatl* often permits identification of such specific stylistic devices as parallelism or the repetition of the same thought at the end of the various parts of the same *cuicatl*, which may be taken as a basis for dividing the components of its text in a particular way. Units of expression have been thus divided into specific lines or "verses" which have parallel semantic content or which appear to constitute a unitary phrase or utterance that as a sort of coda or conclusion may be considered the natural ending of the poem. Based on precisely this sort of support, various translators of the *cuicatl*—including Garibay and myself—have divided the "units of expression" of the *cuicatl* as "verses" and "stanzas."

As I complete the present study, I wish to acknowledge that in preparing paleographic transcriptions and translations of the *cuicatl*, if one wishes to follow the manuscripts strictly, one should preserve the units of expression that they present. Even if in some cases this should impede emphasis on parallelisms and other features characteristic of this literature, it would imply maximal fidelity to compositions from a cultural ambience very different from that of the European languages.

To show the more obvious differences between the two forms of paleographic transcription and translation, I offer the text of the first unit of expression of a *cuicatl* from the beginning of the *Romances de los señores de la Nueva Espana* (fol. 1) without introducing any change whatever into its unit of expression, and then as Garibay has it in his edition of this manuscript:

Tla oc tocuicaca tla oc tocuicatocan in xochitonalo calite zā ya atocnihuani catliq̃ y ni quinamiqui can niquitemohua ya yo ca q̃on huehuetitlan ye nicā non ohuaya ōhuaya.

Let us sing then; let us follow the song within the flower light and heat, O friends. Who are they? I find them; there where I seek them thus; there next to the drums; they are here already. Ohuaya, ōhuaya.

Let us look now at the formal presentation Garibay makes of this text:

Tla oc toncuicacan
tla oc toncuicatocan
in xochitonalo calitec, aya

antocnihuan
Catlique?
in niquic namique
canin quintemohua
quen on heuhuetitlan,
ye nican ah. Ohuaya ohuaya.

Cantemos ahora
ahora digamos cantos
en medio de la florida luz del sol
oh amigos.
¿Quiénes son?
Yo los encuentro
en donde los busco:
allá tal cual
junto a los tambores.

Let us sing now;
Now let us tell songs
Amid the flowery light of the sun,
O friends.
Who are they?
I find them
Where I seek them—
There, wherever,
Next to the drums.

(Garibay 1964:1)

As one can see, the division into "verses" introduced by Garibay into what constitutes a unit of expression in the original manuscript is guided by a criterion which in this case is easily perceived. To divide the text into lines or "verses" he has paid attention to the parallelism or complementarity of meaning that exists between some phrases. It should be noted nonetheless that parallelism is not all that frequent in the units of expression of the *cuicatl*, and the possibility of leaning on metrical criteria for establishing such divisions is problematic.

2.1.2. TWO TYPES OF ANNOTATION. While some points have been established, there are many uncertainties about the existence of meter in the *cuicatl*. In this connection we must not overlook two kinds of annotation that appear repeatedly in the manuscripts.

13

One has already been mentioned: the exclamatory nonlexical syllables. The other, which is less frequent, appears before the first unit of expression of the *cuicatl* or is inserted between the units of the poem. Here is an example of this sort of annotation from the *Cantares mexicanos* (fol. 39v):

Tocoto tocoti, auh ynic ontlantiuh cuicatl, toco toco tocoto ticoticotico ticoticoticoti toco toco tocoti.

'Tocototocoti, and when the song is about to end, toco toco tocoto ticoticotico ticoticoticoti toco toco tocoti.'

In folios 40r and 40v, other units of expression are followed by annotations of the same sort, albeit different ones. All of them, however, make use of the four syllables *ti*, *to*, *co*, and *qui* in various combinations. Some *cuicatl* provide us with additional information. A song attributed to Hernando de Guzmán, hence postconquest, in describing the genre *cococuicatl* 'song of the turtledoves', adds the words 'the tune'. Then, as if to explain which tune goes with this *cuicatl*, he adds *cototiqui titi totocoto*. Eight units of expression further on, at the beginning of folio 50v, we read:

Yc ome huehuetl ['with two drums'] *titoco titoco titocoto titiquiti tiquititi titiquiti.*

Guzmán's extremely long poem (sixty units of expression, ending on folio 52v with the Latin word *finis*) includes eleven other similar annotations. All but the last one indicate how many drums will sustain the tune of the *cuicatl*, and contain notations always in combinations of *to*, *ti*, *co*, and *qui*.

Another note on folio 7r of the same manuscript makes a number of points about the syllables which appear to have marked the tune:

Here begin the songs which are called true *huexotzincayotl*. They relate the deeds of the lords of Huexotzinco. They are divided into three parts: songs of lords or eagles (*teuccuicatl*; *cuauhcuicatl*), flower songs (*xochicuicatl*), and songs of privation (*icnocuicatl*).

And the drum is sounded thus: they finish one word [or group of words?] and fall on the next word [or group of words?] with three *ti*'s, or one may begin with a single *ti*. And one repeats the same thing until the beat of the drum sounds within it again. One holds one's hand still, and when it is halfway done, beats the edge of the drum rapidly again. This will be seen at the hands of one who knows how to beat it. This song was played once recently in the house of don Diego de León, lord of Azcapotzalco. The player was don Francisco Plácido, in 1551, on the Nativity of Our Lord Jesus Christ.

Garibay (1965:xxxviii–xl) has noted, "it is obvious that this is a matter of indicating the measure or rhythm of music." The same author admits the possibility that each of the syllables mentioned could have corresponded to a note within a pentatonic scale accepted by various students as that of native music. Accordingly, *ti* would correspond to the octave *do*; *qui* to *la* natural. According to Garibay again, "it may be conjectured that the initial *do* was not noted." This would complete the pentatonic scale alluded to.

A different interpretation is that of Karl A. Nowotny (1956) who identifies from *Cantares mexicanos* 758 different arrangements of the syllables involving the consonants *t* and *c* (*qu-*) and the vowels *i* and *o*. He considers that these are indicators of different rising and falling tones. He further indicates that the most complex combinations of these syllables accompany certain *cuicatl* composed in the Colonial period.

For my part, I shall note that the extensive poetic work of the celebrated Sor Juana Inés de la Cruz (1648–1695) includes a *villancico* (Christmas song) which includes a composition of her own in Nahuatl, described by her as a *tocotin* (Juana de la Cruz 1969:187–188):

Los mexicanos alegres
también a su usanza salen . . .
y con las cláusulas tiernas
del mexicano lenguaje,

NAHUATL LITERATURE

en un tocotin sonoro
dicen con voces suaves . . .

The happy Mexicans
Also appear as is their wont . . .
And in the tender phrases
of the Mexican language,
In a sonorous *tocotin*
And in soft voices say . . .

Following this introduction comes a twenty-four-line song, from which I shall copy the first four lines:

Tla ya timohuica
totlazo Zuapilli
maca ammo, Tonantzin
titechmoilcahuiliz . . .

If you are going,
Our beloved Lady,
No, dear Mother of ours,
Do not forget us . . .

In classifying her composition as a *tocotin*, Sor Juana shows that she knows the notation in the syllables *to, co, ti, qui* that accompanied some of the *cuicatl* of the Prehispanic tradition in the early Colonial period. When she refers further to "a sonorous *tocotin*," she confirms what we know from the native texts about musical accompaniment and song, an expression of these poems. Not being able to fathom the comparison of the metrics of Sor Juana's *tocotin* with that of the *cuicatl* that are preceded by a similar notation, we have at least recorded this interesting testimony of the great seventeenth-century poet.

By way of conclusion concerning these notations, I should indicate that they appear especially with those *cuicatl* which had the character of mime or dramatic performance, intoned to the music of the drum (*huehuetl*).

Let us now return to the other nonlexical elements which, as we have seen, also have an effect on the units of expression of the *cuicatl*. We have already said that they sometimes appear intrusively, incorporated into one of the words (the lexical material) of the

verses. In other cases they go at the end of a sentence or utterance or at the end of a unit of expression of the *cuicatl*, as though concluding it. It should be noted further that there are compositions in which the nonlexical words themselves are shared with other units of expression or even with all of them within a given *cuicatl*.

A list of the more frequent of these nonlexical syllables includes: *a, ah, ya, aya, iya, huiya, ohuaya, ahuaya, ohuaye, ahue, ohue, ohuia, ohuiya, lili, aylili, tanlalala, ayao, yehuaya* (or *yeehuaya*).

When these nonlexical syllables appear as independent elements, whether within a unit of expression or at the end of it, their function may be of a metric order, but in many cases they may likewise be factors or elements imparting emphasis to the preceding expression. In cases in which they modify words intrusively, it is very important to identify their presence, both for reasons of meter and to avoid erroneous readings and interpretations. Thus the syllable *ya* added to a verbal form could lead to an erroneous understanding of the corresponding verb tense. Another example of possible error is the intrusive *a* attached to nouns like *xochitl*, suggesting a compound *xochitla*, meaning not just 'flower' but 'abundance of flowers'. Other examples of nonlexical syllables incrusted in the text of compositions are to be found in the following units of expression. The nonlexical syllables are in boldface type:

Nicamanaya nicmanaya xochicacahuatl maya onihuaya yeichan nopiltzin Moteuczomatzi o **ancayome**

I offer, I offer the flowery water of cacao; may I go to the house of our prince Moteuczomatzin!

(*Cantares mexicanos*: fol. 36v)

Zan teoaxochioctla yc yhuintic yeoncan totoatepan **aya** *quaxomotlaya . . .*

Only with the flowery divine liquor, drunk there on the bank of the bird water, (the warrior) Quaxomotl . . .

(Ibid.: fol. 55v)

15

2.1.3. RHYTHM AND MEASURE. The question should be raised of whether there is a direct relation between the metrics of the *cuicatl* and the nonlexical syllables (*ohuaya, huiya, aya*, etc.). We have seen that the other notations using *ti*, *qui*, *to*, and *co* appear to indicate how the *huehuetl* should be played. The problem nonetheless remains, since besides not knowing the precise musical value of these notations, we have also been unable to establish what relation they may have to the internal rhythm of the *cuicatl*.

Two main attempts have been made to correlate the exclamatory nonlexical syllables. The first was by Garibay (1953–1954:1: 60–67), according to whom they play an important role in the distinctive rhythm of different *cuicatl*.

(1) He first describes as the oldest form of metric organization in Nahuatl the structuring of accented and unaccented syllables in an order of three accents. He offers an example taken from the *Anales de Cuauhtitlan* from an ancient mythical tale. I offer below another passage from the same text, presented in three separate lines, the better to show its metric structure:

Ómpa antláminázque
noyúhqui in Míctlanpa teotlálli
yýtyc antláminázque

You should shoot thither;
So too toward the place of the dead, the broad earth,
You should shoot into it.

(*Anales de Cuauhtitlan*: 3)

(2) Another mode of rhythmic organization is structured with accented and unaccented syllables in an order of two accents. Garibay also judges it to be of "very ancient origin." This is the example he offers:

Óncan tónaz, óncan tláthuiz
óncan yézque, áyamo nícan

There the sun will appear; there there will be light;
There shall we be: here no longer.

(Garibay 1953–1954:1:60–67)

It is very probable that the preceding example may contain a linguistic assimilation of the *e* of *yezque* to the *a* of *ayamo*. In another example from the sacred hymn of the *Totochtin* we also find nonlexical syllables:

Macáiui/ téutl/ mácoc/ yé cho/ cáia . . .

Let it not be thus; he made offering to the god; now he weeps . . .

(*Códice florentino*: 1: fol. 143r)

I shall merely indicate the other three types of rhythm perceived by Garibay in the *cuicatl*, in which nonlexical syllables may likewise function as rhythmic complements. There are (3) series of six syllables with just two accents, the accented syllable being preceded and followed by an unaccented one; (4) series of two hemistichs (similar to the alexandrine of Castilian literature); and (5) a combination of hemistichs involving structures of types (3) or (4).

Despite the preceding specifications, Garibay (1953–1954: 1:64) recognizes that "it is not always possible to adjust the text to metrics." In his judgment the irregularity perceived in a particular *cuicatl* can be explained as an artifice introduced by the songmaker, or as a consequence of bad transcription by an unskilled scribe.

The other approach to the metrics of the *cuicatl* is exemplified by Karttunen and Lockhart (1980). They consider that it is necessary to take into account the length of the syllables or else the length of the feet composed of the words and even the exclamations (nonlexical syllables) of these compositions. They mean feet in the classic sense: "any part of two, three, or more syllables which make up and by which one measures a verse in those compositions in which attention is paid to quantity of temporal length in pronunciation" (Real Academia Española 1970:1020–1021). After analyzing various examples from the extant collections of *cuicatl*, they reach this conclusion:

It happens repeatedly: a verse appears very promising at the outset and disappointment soon follows. Often one finds a pair of equal phrases or even four or five of them at the beginning of a poem, as in our example, and then it decays into great irregularity, at least looked at in the same terms. There is no doubt that equal phrases were a stylistic resource in Nahuatl poetry, but we still don't see how they can be the basis of metric organization within the verse.

(Karttunen and Lockhart 1980:30–31)

So Karttunen and Lockhart then concentrate their attention on the feet they consider identifiable in the *cuicatl*. Presenting several examples, they note the existence of some which, using the Greek terminology, can be described as *dactylic feet*, that is, composed of three syllables, the first long and the other two short. After analyzing the dactylic feet present in various compositions, they admit that further along in the same *cuicatl* what appears to be its proper measure is sometimes very quickly lost:

We are aware that each poem may have its own metric scheme, and the instructions for the drumbeats seem to imply that this may occur in the middle of a verse.

(Ibid.: 33)

Thus, like Garibay, these investigators admit that there remains much to be clarified about the metric structure of the phrases and units of expression of the *cuicatl*.

2.1.4. STYLISTICS. The description of the most salient stylistic features of these compositions can be made from two perspectives: on the one hand paying attention to the elements that make up each unit of expression of a *cuicatl*, and on the other including the units presented in the text as they interrelate in making up a single poem. I shall begin with the broader perspective, which may help to identify what is generally characteristic of these poems in their broadest structure.

2.1.4.1. INTER-UNIT STRUCTURE. We have already seen that there are various kinds of indications in the manuscripts that permit us to distinguish fairly clearly where a unit of expression begins and ends within a given *cuicatl*. Often a set of units is preceded by a line or lines of text in different letters which may be taken to be a description or title of the *cuicatl*. In other cases the separation is introduced by a single word in Spanish or Nahuatl. Thus in *Cantares mexicanos* (vol. 4), the word *otro* ('another') appears between two dashes, signaling that the *cuicatl* that follows belongs like the preceding one to the group of *chalcayotl* ('songs of the things of Chalco').

Other types of breaks are established in both the *Cantares mexicanos* and the *Romances de los señores de la Nueva España* by means of a numeral. In fact in the latter of these manuscripts, which is divided into four parts, the scribe used the numbers 1 to 14 in both the first and the second parts to distinguish what he judged to be twenty-eight different *cuicatl*. In the much briefer last two parts the breaks are limited to four in each poem, indicated by the corresponding numerals. Thus the *Romances* record thirty-six different *cuicatl*.

Besides these more explicit divisions, both the *Romances* and the *Cantares mexicanos* contain others, consisting in simply a wider blank space than that which exists between the lines. This kind of separation sometimes occurs within the group of units under the same title or number. In many cases it can be affirmed that it is a matter of different *cuicatl* grouped together under a fairly general title because of their similarities. In *Cantares mexicanos*, for instance (fols. 16v–26v), there are nineteen of these separations, apparently indicating a collection of twenty *cuicatl*. The title preceding them indicates what they have in common:

Here begin what are called straight songs which were raised in the palace in Mexico and also on the mainland of Acolhuacan. With them they made sorrow depart from the lords.

Notwithstanding the presence of these various kinds of notation, students of the *cuicatl* must sometimes decide for themselves which units of expression must really be taken to make up a single poem. Karttunen and Lockhart show in their examination of the *Romances* twenty-eight examples of eight units of expression or of multiples of eight. This appears to mean that compositions in four pairs of units were pleasing to the *cuicapicqueh*, or songmakers.

Paired groupings within the collection of units making up a *cuicatl* are thus a first characteristic feature. The fact that pairing is manifested primarily through variations on the same theme leads us to recognize that, rather than a lineal development of ideas or arguments, the *cuicatl* contains convergent processes of approach aimed at showing from different angles whatever is the key subject of the composition.

As an example I give here an analysis of the content of the eight units of expression of a *cuicatl* from *Cantares mexicanos* (fols. 18r–v) on the war of Chalco carried out by the Mexicans. A few words of invitation to eagles and ocelots mark the beginning of the *cuicatl*. In the same first unit the central concern of the song is expressed: "The shields clash, it is the encounter to take prisoners . . ."

The second unit, besides including the last of the preceding phrases as a refrain, enunciates from a new angle the theme of the Chalco war: "They scatter over us, the flowers of battle rain over us, the god is happy with them."

The third and fourth units, likewise paired, are further abundantly metaphorical descriptions of what war is. The third proclaims: "Now it boils there, now the fire twists and billows. Glory is acquired, the renown of the shield. Over the rattles the dust rises." In the fourth unit we read: "The flower of war shall never cease, there it is on the riverbank, there the flower of the ocelot opens its petals, and the flower of the shield . . ." And the refrain, agreeing with the third unit, reiterates: "Over the rattles the dust rises."

In the fifth and sixth units this approach is followed up, adding depth to the theme of the flowers of war. First we are told: "The pungent flower of the ocelot: that is where it falls, inside the plain, it comes to delight us.

Who wants it? Here is prestige, glory." The sixth unit is paired with the preceding: "Deformed flowers do not bring happiness; the heart flowers have been attained on the plain, at the side of war, there have the nobles gone forth. Here is prestige, glory."

Two final groupings, the seventh and eighth, end the *cuicatl*. In both the approximation to the central theme attains fulfillment. In lively images the war of Chalco and Amecameca becomes visible to us. In the seventh unit we hear: "With the shields of the eagles are intertwined the standards of the ocelots. With the shields of quetzal are mixed the standards of water bird feathers; they billow, they reverberate these. They have come to a stand, those of Chalco and Amecameca. The war swirls and clamors." The last unit of the *cuicatl* closes the poem and is paired with the preceding one: "The arrow cracked, the obsidian shattered. Those of Chalco and Amecameca stood forth. The war swirls and clamors."

Although there are many structural differences in the body of *cuicatl* that have been preserved, our analysis of the interrelation of the units that make up the preceding poem reflects something very characteristic of these poems generally: successive paired approaches to the matter to which attention is to be drawn lead step by step in a strong flow of metaphor to the final contemplation of the key object: in our example, war, what is first said to be "the pleasure of the god," is now seen as an intermingling of banners and shields where the arrows break and the knives shatter amid dust that covers everyone, where the enemies, those of Chalco and Amecameca, arise, against whom the war undertaken by the Mexicas swirls and clamors furiously. Admittedly, a great deal remains to be specified about the structuring of units in a *cuicatl*.

2.1.4.2. INTRA-UNIT STRUCTURE. I have dealt with one form of parallelism between the paired units of a single poem. The concept of parallelism can be employed again in application to the very frequent use of phrases of related connotation appearing

18

within the units. The *cuicatl* analyzed in section 2.1.4.1 provides examples of this. Thus in its second unit we find: "They scatter over us, / the flowers of battle rain over us." In this case the parallelism is strict enough that the two phrases have the same subject. The third unit gives us another example: "How it boils there, / now the fire twists and billows." In this case the second phrase amplifies the image of the fire, boiling and raging. The second of these two parallel phrases makes explicit how glory is attained in war: "Glory is acquired, / the renown of the shield." By way of complement, contrast, diminution, or reference to a third reality, the frequent parallelisms within the units of expression are a stylistic attribute shared by the Nahuatl poems with those of other literatures of the ancient world, as for instance in the case of the Hebrew psalms.

Two other stylistic elements should be mentioned. One is what Garibay (1953–1954: 1: 19) describes as *difrasismo* (diphrasis), which he defines as "pairing two metaphors which together give a symbolic means of expressing a single thought." To illustrate this I shall adduce the very *difrasismo* that Nahuas used to express an idea akin to our 'poetry': *in xochitl, in cuicatl* 'flower and song'. Precisely a long composition is included in *Cantares mexicanos* (fols. 9v–11v) in which various songmakers are invited by Lord Tecayehuatzin of Huexotzinco to discuss and elucidate what in the last analysis is meant by *in xochitl, in cuicatl*.

It should be noted that although the use of *difrasismos* is frequent in the *cuicatl*, it may perhaps be more so in certain forms of *tlahtolli* 'sets of words, discourse, narrative'. I shall therefore limit myself here to two more examples. The first is from *Romances*:

Chalchihuitl on ohuaya in xihuitl on in
motizayo in moihuiyo, in ipalnemohua
ahuayya oo ayye ohuaya ohuaya.

Jades, turquoises: thy clay, thy feathers,
Giver of life.

(Garibay 1964: fol. 42v)

The interest of this example takes off from the fact that it interrelates two different kinds of *difrasismo*. On the one hand we have the words *chalchihuitl* and *xihuitl* 'jades, turquoises' which together evoke 'something precious'. On the other hand *mo-tiza-yo, mo-ihui-yo*, possessed forms of *tiza-tl* 'clay' and *ihui-tl* 'feather', are evocations of the color white for warriors' dress, of which the feathers are the decoration. *Tizatl* and *ihuitl* together evoke war. The sense of the double *difrasismo* is to assert that struggle and confrontation are *par excellence* a precious thing.

In this additional example, the learned Nezahualcoyotl appears, reflecting on the only thing that can be a source of power on earth:

Ma oc ye xiyocoya in Nezahualcoyotzin auh ca
huelichan aya ipalnemoa ni zan itlan conan-
tinemi ynipetl ynicpalli zan co ya mahmatinemi
in tlalticpac in ilhuicatl ayahue.

Think, Nezahualcoyotl, only there can be
the house of the Giver of life; only there can
he be taking his mat and throne. Thus only
one carries the earth, the heaven.

(*Cantares mexicanos*: fol. 17r)

Here the well-known *difrasismo* is composed of *petlatl* 'mat' and *icpalli* 'throne'. To occupy the mat and throne was to exercise command: to carry the earth, the heaven.

Since I shall later amplify what has been said about *difrasismo* in relation to the *tlahtolli*, I shall here attend to another feature, which is much more characteristic of the *cuicatl*. This consists in the use of a set of images and metaphors which actually reveal the indigenous origin of this kind of expression. Although the themes of the *cuicatl* are variable, many images appear and reappear in the larger part of the corpus of this poetry. The most recurrent of these evoke the following: flowers and their attributes, such as the opening of their petals; a great flock of birds; likewise and particularly butterflies; also within the animal kingdom, eagles and ocelots. A separate set is made up of the symbolic color spectrum. From the vegetable

19

kingdom and apart from the flowers already mentioned, certain garden plants appear frequently: salvia, and corn, as seed, ear, plant, and human food. There is also mention of *teonanacatl*, 'the flesh of the gods' (hallucinatory mushrooms), and *ololiuhqui*, the narcotic 'morning glory seed', as well as tobacco smoked in cane tubes and clay pipes, and foaming cacao sweetened with honey, which is served to nobles.

Precious objects are also symbols, including all sorts of precious stones: *chalchihuitl* 'jades, jadeites' and *teoxihuitl*, turquoise-colored stones, as well as the precious metals, both yellow and white, as nuggets or bracelets, and likewise the various musical instruments: the *huehuetl* 'drums', *teponaztli* 'slit log drums', *tlapitzalli* 'flutes', *ayaeachtli* 'tambourines,' and *oyohualli* 'rattles'. Now and again places of pleasure and wisdom show up: *xochicalli* 'flower houses', *tlahcuilolcalli* 'painting houses', and *amoxcalli* 'book houses'. Metaphors of war, some of which have been mentioned, also include 'smoke and haze', 'water and fire', 'sharpened obsidian', bringing to mind a living sense of war.

Every set of categories that has been mentioned could be specified by enumerating its subsets. To name only one example, the *cuicatl* mention, among other birds, the *xiuhtototl* 'turquoise-colored bird', *quecholli* 'red-feathered bird', *teocuitlacoyoltototl* 'golden-yellow rattle bird', *zacuan* 'bird with gold and black feathers', *elotototl* 'cornfield bird', *tzinizcan* 'another bird with fine plumage', *huitzitzilin* 'precious hummingbird', *cocoxqui* 'multicolored pheasant', and *tlauhquechol*, identified by some as a parrot and by others as a flamingo.

Symbolism in the realm of colors is equally extensive and varied. The song that initiates the *Anales de Cuauhtitlan* exemplifies interesting variants of the correlation of colors with cosmic directions. There greenish blue connotes the east; white, the region of the dead, the north; yellow, the direction of women, the west; and red, the land of thorns, the south. The colors appear also to qualify and enrich the meaning of things which are themselves symbolic, so that to specify the color of flowers, birds, garments, and other objects gives the image a double significance. By these and other less frequent means the songmakers expressed the essence of their craft.

2.2. STRUCTURE AND FEATURES OF THE *tlahtolli*. The distinction between *cuicatl* ('poetry') and *tlahtolli* ('prose'), as previously stated, is that *cuicatl* are 'songs, hymns, poems', while *tlahtolli* means 'word(s), discourse, narrative'.

Tlahtolli include what we should now call myths, legends, annals, chronicles, histories, and tales. They also constitute part of the distinctive *huehuehtlahtolli*, the 'ancient word', discourses communicating the high points of moral norms and guidance to human beings in their progression on earth.

To say that the *tlahtolli* have a structure similar to what we call prose in other literary contexts is fairly simplistic, as much so as assigning the *cuicatl* to the genre of poetry. There is, however, a contrast between the two.

2.2.1. UNITS AND NARRATIVE TONE. We have seen that in *cuicatl*, rather than the lineal development of a theme, we often find the components to be so many convergent approximations to the same matter. At times this will be a matter of amplification, at others, of contrast or specification, illuminating particular details, but generally there will be a recurrence of the idea or image upon which attention seems to be fastened. In the *tlahtolli*, on the other hand, it is more difficult and even unnecessary to keep track of the units of expression (not indicated in the manuscripts), while the narrative tone implies a lineal development to the sense of successive words.

Like the *cuicatl*, the *tlahtolli* show an inclination toward structuring pictures or scenes that seem to superimpose themselves on one another. Nonetheless, the difference lies in the fact that while the perspectives in the *cuicatl* return to the subject expressed in the first unit, in the *tlahtolli* imagination and memory come into play to introduce sequences, sometimes altering space and time. I will mention three texts as examples of this form of structure. One, which describes itself as a *nenonotzalli* ('narrative'), is included in the *Códice florentino* (Book 7: fols. 3r–7r): *in ye huehcauh ic tlanonotzalia huehuehtqueh in inpiel catca* 'a narration which the elders who kept it related in ancient times'. The account hinges on a meeting of the gods while it was still night in Teotihuacan, to return a sun and moon to the sky. Another account included in the *Florentino* (Book 3: fols. 9r–23r) has as its theme *In ihtolloca in Quetzalcoatl* 'the history (what was told) of Quetzalcoatl'. A third is *In ihtlatollo Nezahualcoyotzin* 'the compilation of words about Nezahualcoyotl', the lord of Tetzcoco, from the *Anales de Cuauhtitlan* (fols. 34–54). I shall analyze the superimposition and sequence of meanings in the first of these three examples.

A first scene establishing temporal and spatial references introduces us to the theme of the account, showing us a preoccupation of the gods which was to matter greatly to human beings:

It is said that when it was still night, when there was still no light, when it was not yet dawning, they got together, the gods called upon each other there in Teotihuacan. They said, they said to each other: "Come, O gods! Who will take it upon himself? Who will take charge of it? Who will make light? Who will make it dawn?"

(*Códice florentino*: Book 7: fol. 3r)

The gods, seeming concerned and questioning from the outset, are the figures who will maintain the sequence and meaning that give unity to the account. Apart from the assembled gods—Ehecatl, Quetzalcoatl, Tezcatlipoca, Totec, Tiacapan, Teyco, Tlacoyehua, Xoyocotl, and others—two other divine personages appear as extremely important speakers and actors, Tecuciztecatl and Nanahuatzin, who are to offer themselves to make it possible for a new sun to shine and to make it dawn. In a second scene, superimposed on the first, the offer of each is heard, as the assembled gods are seen talking and asking

what is going to happen. The third scene does not imply a change of place nor a gap in time: it is still night, there in Teotihuacan. The personages are also the same, but there is a lineal sequence of events. The narrator enjoys contrasts:

Then they start to do penance. The two fast for four days, Nanahuatzin and Tecuciztecatl. It is then too that the fire is lit. Now it burns there in the divine hearth . . .

Everything with which Tecuciztecatl does penance is precious: his spruce boughs are quetzal plumes, his rolls of grass are gold, his spines of jade . . .

But Nanahuatzin's spruce boughs are all just green cane, new shoots in handfuls of three, all tied together to make nine. And his rolls of grass are just real slivers of pitch pine; and his spines too are real maguey thorns. And what he bleeds with them is really his blood. His copal is in fact what has been scraped up . . .

(Ibid.: Book 3: fol. 9r)

The same setting of Teotihuacan shapes another sequence of scenes. The text records what happens when four days have passed, during which the fire around which Tecuciztecatl and Nanahuatzin have done penance has gone on burning. The gods speak again, urging Tecuciztecatl to throw himself into the fire to emerge transformed into the sun. The event in the same sacred space shows the frustrated attempts of the arrogant god Tecuciztecatl, who is unable to consummate the fire sacrifice. As in the ritual penance, the action of the sore-covered Nanahuatzin is very different. He soon "concludes the thing," burns in the fire and is consumed.

A transition scene shows us the eagle and the ocelot also entering the fire. That's why the eagle has black feathers, and the ocelot, who was only half-singed, has black spots.

Marking the thread and fate of the story, the assembled gods return to the forefront. They keep watch and discuss the direction where the sun is to rise. Those who keep looking in the direction of the color red make good on their word. In the direction of the

21

color red, the east, the sun is seen. The scene is completed by the appearance of Tecuciztecatl, transformed into the moon and also coming from the direction of the color red, following the sun.

Superimposed images, always in the same sacred space, continue to the end of the account. The sun and moon shine equally bright. The gods have to put a stop to that:

Then one of those lords, of the gods, comes running out. He goes and wounds with a rabbit the other's face, Tecuciztecatl's. Thus he darkened his face, thus he wounded his face, as is seen even now . . .

(Ibid.)

The following scene shows us that the attempted solution was not the complete answer. Although the moon now shone less, it and the sun were still together. Again the gods are concerned:

How are we to live? The sun isn't moving. Are we perhaps to cause a disordered life for the *macehuales*, for the human beings? Let the sun be strengthened by means of us, let us all die!

(Ibid.)

The picture of the primordial sacrifice of the gods, who make life and the movement of the sun possible with their own blood, is destiny fulfilled and an anticipation of what the *macehuales*, the human beings, are to do. The god Ehecatl puts the other gods to death. In a discrepancy reflecting an internal dialectic in the world of the gods, Xolotl, the double of Quetzalcoatl, resists dying. He flees from Ehecatl who is going to kill him, and again and again transforms himself, first into a double cornstalk, then into maguey, and finally into an axolotl, until in the end he is sacrificed.

The gods consume their offering of blood. That and the efforts of Ehecatl, the wind god, make possible the movement of the sun. When he arrives at the place where he hides himself, the moon then begins to move. Each will follow his own road. The *tlahtolli*, having

evoked and illuminated the sacred setting of Teotihuacan, ends by recalling that this is a story told from ancient times by the old men who had it in their charge to preserve it.

Like this one, other *tlahtolli* of Prehispanic tradition, in a wide range of variants but with an insistent presentation of ideas and images that unify and make sense, are likewise structured in superimposed scenes with semantic loadings until they attain full significance.

2.2.2. RHYTHM AND METER. In contrast to what happens with the *cuicatl*, the manuscripts do not give us any precise indication of different units of expression in the *tlahtolli*. Nor do we find in them the sorts of annotation that so frequently accompany the *cuicatl*, such as those that seem to relate to rhythm, or combinations of the syllables *ti*, *to*, *co*, and *qui* and occasional notes referring to the use of the drum, leading us to infer recitation to the sound of music. Nor do *tlahtolli* texts include the nonlexical syllables (*ohuaya*, *ahue*, *ohuia*, etc.) often found in the *cuicatl*.

While these differences are obvious, a reading of numbers of examples of the genres amply confirms their distinctiveness. Among other things the phrases of the *cuicatl* are usually briefer and syntactically less complex. And further, while one or more metric structures can often be identified in *cuicatl*, this is infrequent in *tlahtolli*.

As examples of *tlahtolli* with some kind of perceptible metric structure, one may cite passages of texts from the history of Quetzalcoatl (*Códice florentino*: Book 3: fols. 9r–23r), or from those dealing with the earliest ethnic and cultural origins of the Mexica (ibid.: Book 10: fols. 140r–150r). Nonetheless, in cases like these one may wonder whether such narratives are a particular kind of *cuicatl* rather than *tlahtolli*.

2.2.3. STYLISTICS. To show some characteristic features in the stylistics of *tlahtolli* I shall analyze two very different compositions. The first is part of the *huehuehtlahtolli* collected by Sahagún (*Códice florentino*: Book 6). The second is from *In ihtolloca in*

Quetzalcoatl 'the history of Quetzalcoatl' in the same manuscript. Both can be considered classic products of this Prehispanic literature.

In the *huehuehtlahtolli* I shall analyze (*Códice florentino*: Book 6: fols. 63v–67r), a *tecuhtlahto* or 'leading judge' addresses the people of the city in general, after the recently elected *huey tlahtoani* 'supreme governor' has given his first speech to admonish them and tell them the path to follow. The *tecuhtlahto* exalts above all the importance of what the *huey tlahtoani* has said, he exhorts the people to reflect and to ask themselves who each member of the community is, and he insists that they should be aware of their own limitations. Thus they can all better appreciate the significance and importance of those who govern by the gods' design. The *huey tlahtoani* is father and mother of the people; he knows and reveals some of what the gods have communicated to him; he has them all in his charge. If there are misfortunes in the city, hunger, scarcity, and threats from the outside, it will be up to the *huey tlahtoani* to satisfy the needs of the public, ordaining war when necessary, seeing to it that there is an abundance of supplies both for humans and for the gods, who thus make life on earth possible. He insistently concludes his speech by reiterating that it is the duty of the people to take into account the words of the *huey tlahtoani*, obey him, and respect him as a father and mother who provides all that is good.

Analyzing the stylistic mechanisms of this *huehuehtlahtolli* we find many of those found in *cuicatl* to be used frequently, such as *difrasismos* (see section 2.1.4.2). To show the kind of *difrasismo* used in *tlahtolli* I shall focus on the main ones and indicate their meanings:

ca yz tonoc in tiquauhtli, in ocelotl

You who are here, you eagle, you ocelot

This expresses the idea of man as a warrior. As a necessary complement, the *tecuhtlahto* immediately refers to the women in another *difrasismo*:

Auh in ticueie, in tihuipile

And you too, owner of the skirt, owner of the blouse

Mention of feminine garments is an obvious designation of women, underlining the fact that the speech is directed to men and women equally. The text continues:

In mixpan quichaiaoa in chalchiuhtli, in teuxiuhtli

Before you he strews jades, turquoises

What the *huey tlahtoani* has scattered in speaking before the people is a reality as precious as jades and turquoises. A parallel *difrasismo* follows immediately:

Ca otlapouh in toptli, in petlacalli

Because he has opened the chest, the trunk

The supreme governor, in speaking to the people of what the gods have revealed to him, has made manifest what was obscure, secret. Using another two parallel *difrasismos* he makes his point more explicit:

In tlatconi, in tlamamaloni, in inpial, in innelpil

What he has in his charge, what he is burdened with, what he is tied to (what is kept)

The series of parallelisms used in this *huehuehtlahtolli* is quite rich. Sometimes the same *difrasismo* reappears modified by different morphological elements, as in:

In titlatquitl, in titlamamalli

You are the burden, you are what is carried on his back

As this describes the condition of the people governed, so certain attributes of the *huey tlahtoani* are very important:

In ihiio, in iten, in itlatol

His breath, his lip, his word

And to summarize what a good *huey tlahtoani* is for the people, two more . *difrasismos* are immediately counterposed:

23

Ye nelli monantzin, y, ie nelli motahtzin, in ticnoquauhtli, in ticnocelotl

Truly (he is) your revered mother; truly (he is) your revered father, thou (who art) a poor eagle; (thou who art) a poor ocelot.

On the other hand, those who do not revere him who governs, who is the "mother and father" of all, will receive punishment from on high:

At ie iz huĩtz in iquahtzin, in itetzin totecuyo?

Perhaps there will not fall (upon you) the stick, the stone of our lord?

Another consequence of the punishment imposed by the gods will be misery and want:

At noço in icnoiotl in ayaçulli, in tatapatli tonmottaz?

Will it be privation, the old cloak, the patched cloak that you will have to know?

Another *difrasismo* reiterates the precariousness of the governed:

Cuix oytla mopan mito in topan, in mictlan?

Will it be because of you that something was said there, above us, in the land of the dead?

The weakness of the *macehualtin*, the common people, is almost mocked:

Cuix te mopan teutl qualoz, cuix te mopan tlaloliniz?

It is by you that the (sun) god is eaten (eclipsed); is it from you that the earth moves (quakes)?

Weak as they are, the *macehualtin* are exposed to many dangers:

Cuix ixpolihuiz in cuitlapilli, in atlapalli?

Perchance the tail, the wing (people) will perish?

Finally I shall cite another set of *difrasismos* referring this time to the *huey tlahtoani* who, in order to guide the people, defend and pre-

serve their existence, must often undertake a sacred war:

Ca teuatl, ca tlachinolli in quipitztoque, in quiyocuxtoque in totecuiioan, inic vel mani tlalli ca teatlitia, ca tetlacualtia, ca tetlamaca in topan in mictlan

Because the divine water, the fire (war) have they gone to foment, to place our lords so that the land remain thus; drink is to be given; food is to be provided; it should be given to those (the gods) who are over us, in the land of the dead (in the beyond).

It is in the *huehuehtlahtolli* that *difrasismos* are most abundant. In narrative these stylistic devices are not lacking, but they are less used. Besides *difrasismo* there are also numerous other sorts of parallel expression. Parallel expression is also frequent in other kinds of compositions, like the history of Quetzalcoatl, to which I now turn. Of the various chapters of this legend, I shall focus on one that deals with some of the portents that were brought about in Tula by the sorcerers who had come to tempt Quetzalcoatl. The object is to emphasize some of the parallel expressions in this text:

Quilmach iztac cuixi tlatzontechtica, mintinenca, patlantinenca, mocanauhtinenca, in inpan tulteca amo veca

It is said that a white hawk was going along with its head pierced by an arrow; it was gliding; it was going up, near the Toltecs, not far . . .

(*Códice florentino*: Book 3:fol. 18v)

While the parallel phrases specify what was happening to the hawk, whose presence was an omen, it is also perceptible how it is reiterated by parallelism that the bird was nearby, over the Toltecs, and not far from them as its flight approached the earth. Let us look at another example from the same story:

Quil centetl tepetl itoca çacatepetl tlataia, in ioaltica, veca necia, inic tlatlaia in tlecuecallotl veca ieoaia . . .

They say a mountain named Zacatepetl was burning in the night; it was seen at a distance; thus it was burning; the flames rose in the distance . . .

(Ibid.)

Going on then to describe the reaction of the Toltecs to this and other portents, the text uses parallel expression to render still more vivid the description of what was happening next:

Aoc tlatlacamamanca, aoc yvian ieloaia . . .

One was no longer in tranquility; people no longer found themselves at peace in their houses . . .

(Ibid.)

The parallelisms in this text and in many other narratives or in the *huehuehtlahtolli*, and generally in the many *tlahtolli* of Prehispanic tradition, are so numerous that they spring up almost constantly. They must be said to be a characteristic feature of the genre.

A final notable stylistic feature of the *tlahtolli*, though related to parallelism, deserves separate treatment. It consists in the frequent attribution of a series of different predicates to the same grammatical subject or object. Often the predicates are made up of diverse verbal structures, but each may be described as a convergent phrase in which each action is referred to the same topic. This kind of expression is so frequent in the *tlahtolli* that it can be called one of the most characteristic attributes of their style. Here are some examples:

In tlacatl, in tlatoani, in mitznotza, in mitztzatzilia, in momatca in mitzmaca, in mixpan quitlalia, in mixpan quichaiaoa in chalchiuhtli, in teuhxiuhtli . . .

The lord, he who governs, he who calls upon you, he who raises his voice for you, in your name, he gives to you; he places (things) before you; he scatters jades, turquoises . . .

(*Códice florentino*:Book 6:fol. 68v)

This very frequent structuring of the style of the *tlahtolli* can be better appreciated through other examples of different origins and contents. Let us look first at the following fragment of the history of Nezahualcoyotl from the *Anales de Cuauhtitlan*, describing how the Tecpanecs of Azcapotzalco put to death his father, Lord Ixtlilxochitl of Tezcoco:

Auh yniquac onmic Yxtlilxochitzin, niman ye quinhualpehualtia [yn pipiltin] yn onyohuac yn temaquixtique yn tetlatique yn oncan quauhoztoc, yn yehuatzin Huahuantzin, Xiconocatzin, Cuicuitzcatzin. Niman ye quinhuicatze yn Quamincan texcalco quimotlalico oc oncan cochque. Niman ye quinhualehuitia, quinquixtico Teponazco tlatzallan, çan quintlatlatitihuitze yn pipiltzitzinti yn Neçahualcoyotl, yn Tzontecochatzin, niman quimonaxtico yn Yztacalla Nextonquilpan.

And when the Lord Ixtlilxochitl died, then (the princes) came to undertake it; when the night had passed, they rescued (Nezahualcoyotl) and hid him there in the cave in the woods, in Cuauhoztoc, those (called) Huahuantzin, Xiconocatzin, and Cuicuitzcatzin. Then they came to leave Tetzihuactla; they approached Chiauhtzinco. They proceeded toward the rocky spot of Cuamincan. There they came to place him; they still slept there. They happened to arise at once, and happened to leave for Teponazco. There they soon went to find them in a depression, the little princes Neżahualcoyotl and Tzontecochatzin. Then they went on to approach Iztacalla Nextonquilpan.

(*Anales de Cuauhtitlan*:fol. 35)

The better to perceive the structure of this text, it is useful to isolate the particular subjects for which several things are predicated. The implicit subject at the beginning, which I have indicated in brackets, is the *pipiltin*, the princes of Tetzcoco who rescued Nezahualcoyotl after his father's murder. Several lines further on the names of the three *pipiltin* who pulled this off are given: Huahuantzin, Xiconocatzin, and Cuicuitzcatzin. It is these three personages who are the plural subject of a number of subsequent assertions.

Now let us address the predicates involved, first noting that quite precise time references are given at two places in the text.

The first specifies the time of the event to be recounted: "when Ixtlilxochitl died." From other sources we know that this happened in 4 Rabbit or 1418, when Nezahualcoyotl was sixteen. The other temporal reference is given below. What the princes did occurred "when the night had passed," that is, on the day following the death of Ixtlilxochitl. Aside from these indications of time, we find only the repeated use of the particles *niman ye* 'immediately' to link together the various phrases that cumulatively express the attributes of the subject, which is the princes.

I shall emphasize too that just as time indicators are introduced, so too others of a spatial type are inserted, from which the places are indicated where the actions attributed to the princes who have rescued Nezahualcoyotl are taking place.

I list below the various predicate phrases (sometimes sentences) that have as their common subject the princes who saved Nezahualcoyotl. It will be seen that they constitute a sequence. In successive steps they tell us what the princes did:

. . . (the princes) came to undertake it,
they rescued,
they hid,
they came to leave,
they approached,
they proceeded,
they came to place him,
they slept,
they happened to arise,
they happened to leave,
they went to find them,
they went on to approach . . .

The series of predicates is basically composed of verb forms following a temporal sequence, but this is not always true of the use of cumulative predicates in the *tlahtolli*.

Sometimes they have a convergent character, as in the following example from the chapter of the history of Quetzalcoatl. After describing the various portents that occurred at Tula:

Auh çatepan onnenca illamato, papannamacaia, quitotinenca: ma amopatzin.

And at once a little old lady was walking along there. She was selling flags, she was going along saying, "Here are your little flags!"

(*Códice florentino*:Book 3:fol. 19r)

Here the cumulative predicates have a convergent rather than a temporal character. Three predicates are attributed to the subject, the *illamato* 'little old lady,' ordered by increasing specificity rather than time.

With or without temporal sequencing, this kind of convergent accumulation is also found in relation to objects, whether direct, indirect or circumstantial:

8-Acatl xihuitl yca. Inic quitlamaceuique yn imaltepeuh in chichimeca . . . yn tepetl cotoncan, Petlazoltepec, Tzouac Xillotepec, quauhtli ichan, ocelot ichan, yn ichimal in itlahuiz yn imauh yn itepeuh chichimeca, y tepilhuan yn tlatlauhqui tepexioztoc yntenyocan, inmachiyocan yn auixco yn tepeixco . . .

In the year 8 Reed (it also happened). Thus they obtained lands, their city, the Chichimecas . . . Cotoncan hill, Petlazoltepec, Tzouac Xillotepec, the House of the Eagle, the House of the Ocelot, (the work) of their shield, of their arms, their water, their mountain (their city), of the Chichimec princes, in the cave of the red canyon, the place of their fame, of their model, next to the face of the water, on the surface of the mountain . . .

(*Historia tolteca-chichimeca*:fol. 32r)

Here the direct object "lands" is enriched by a number of following attributes: where the lands were, how they were acquired, the city and shrine that they made possible, the fame that accrued to the Chichimecs as a consequence, etc.

The final example involves accumulation with respect to a circumstantial complement of time:

Auh zan no ypan ynin xihuitl [4-Acatl, 1431], *ypan Izcalli, in yquac huey yihuitl quichihuaya . . .*

And only then too, in this year, 4 Reed, in the (twenty-day) month of Izcalli, when they were celebrating a great feast . . .

(*Anales de Cuauhtitlan*:fol. 47)

Spelling out the specified time proceeds step by step with increasing explicitness.

Accumulation of predicates occurs in other literatures, but it is a quite characteristic feature of Prehispanic Nahuatl literature. The combination of these with parallelisms and *difrasismos* in many of the *tlahtolli* makes them immediately recognizable as Nahuatl. Reproduction of these features in translation may make Nahuatl texts sound strange or even exotic, but it is only by such translation that one can attempt to convey to the reader the characteristic syntax and style of ancient Nahuatl expression.

3. GENRES OF *cuicatl*. *Cuicatl* can be subdivided into a fairly large number of species or subtypes on the basis of themes, annotations, and other references.

On the one hand, we may establish the type of *cuicatl* by thematic analysis: a war song, invocation to the gods, memorial of a hero or famous person, celebration of friendship, etc. Furthermore, some *cuicatl*, as we have seen, bear indications that help establish whether they were chanted to a particular musical accompaniment. The manuscripts also contain references not only to music but to the themes of particular dances, ballets, or other kinds of acting, which help to classify the *cuicatl*.

On the other hand we have other references and notes that tell us explicitly what type a particular composition belongs to. We find such references in various of the books of the *Códice florentino*, particularly in the descriptions of the ceremonies celebrated in each twenty-day month (Book 2), or in the discussion of the attributes and fates associated with the calendric sign *Ce Xochitl* '1 Flower' (Book 4: fol. 18r). There are also similar references, albeit fewer, in other works that include *cuicatl*, such as the *Anales de Cuauhtitlan* and the *Historia tolteca-chichimeca*. I have already referred to the notes in *Romances de los señores de la Nueva España* and *Cantares mexicanos*. The latter contains many more of these notes than some of the other sources.

From such references and notes it is possible to understand the poetic distinctions drawn by Prehispanic thought itself. The principal categories below follow the terminology of the ancient songmakers. The fact that a large majority of the various classes of *cuicatl* were accompanied by music and dance must be taken into account in understanding the meaning of these compositions in their own cultural and social setting.

3.1. *Cuicatl*, MUSIC, AND DANCE. Analysis of Book 2 of the *Códice florentino*, together with the pictographs in such codices as the *Borbonicus* registering the ceremonies throughout the eighteen months of the solar year, makes plain the integration of song, music, and dance as a ritual act of the greatest importance for all members of the community. This is so true that we find in the terminology used to describe the ceremonies a number of words compounding the root of *cuicatl* with words relating to the dance. In the description of the celebration of the feast of Tlacaxipehualiztli we are told:

Niman ic peoa in cuicanolo, mitotiaya in telpuchtequioaque . . .

At once they begin, they do the dance with song [*cuicanolo*], the young warriors dance . . .

(*Códice florentino*:Book 2:fol. 24r)

Other words of similar structure include: *cuicanocoa* 'to dance to the sound of song', *cuicomana* 'to make a song offering', *cuico-yanoa* 'to harmonize a song with a dance', *cuecuechcuicatl*, described by the chronicler Diego Durán as a "ticklish dance," or songs and dances "of loose women and lewd men" (Durán 1867–1880:2:230–231). Describing feasts and celebrations in which dance played a leading role, Durán reiterates the close association of dances and songs:

The youths took great pride in knowing how to dance and sing well, and being guides to the others in the dances. They prided themselves on keeping time with their feet and responding to the tempo with their bodies in the shaking they use, and with their voices in time, because their dances were not only governed by the beat, but also by the rises and falls that the song makes, singing and dancing together. For which songs they had poets among them who composed them, giving each song and dance a different tune, as we do with our songs, giving the sonnet, octava rima, and tercet their different tunes to sing them, and so with the others. Thus they had these differences in their songs and dances, for they sang some calmly and seriously, which the lords danced and sang and in the great solemnities and of great authority; they sang them with great measure and tranquility. There were others of less gravity which were dances and songs of pleasure . . .

(Durán 1867–1880:2:230)

Such differences in the rhythm and the close relationship that existed between song, music, and dance imply a series of distinctions in these kinds of expression. I shall limit myself here to the principal and best-documented ones.

The chronicler Toribio de Benavente Motolinía divides dances into two types, each with subtypes which he recognizes and of which other authors also speak:

In this language of Anahuac, dance or ballet has two names: one is *macehualiztli* and the other *netotiliztli*. The latter properly means dance of joy with which the Indians gladden and take pleasure in their feasts, as with the

leading lords in their house and in their marriages, and when they dance thus they say *netotilo*, they dance; *netotiliztli*, ballet or dance. The second and main name for dance is *macehualiztli*, which properly means merit: *macehualo* means deserve; they held this dance to be a meritorious work, just as we say one earns merit in works of charity, penance, and the other virtues . . . And these dances were performed in the general feasts and also the particular ones of their gods, and they did them in the plazas. In these they not only called upon and honored and praised their gods with vocal songs, but also with the heart and feelings of the body, in order to do which well they had and used many commemorative acts, like shakes of the head, of the arms, and of the feet, as they worked with their whole bodies to call upon and serve the gods . . .

(Motolinía 1971:386–387)

While other data confirm what Motolinía says, there are sources in which the distinction between *macehualiztli* and *netotiliztli* seems at times to have less importance. A text of the informants of Sahagún describing what was appropriate to the day *Ce Xochitl* '1 Flower' in the *tonalpohualli* or 260-day astrological calendar, speaks of the celebrations directed by the *huey tlahtoani*, involving various kinds of dance and song to the sound of instrumental music. Although it initially uses the word *macehualiztli* 'dance of merit', it later uses the verb *onmitotiz* 'there he'll do the dance', from the same root as *netotiliztli* 'with which the Indians gladden and take pleasure'. It may be supposed that the strictly religious was not altogether absent from the dances of joy, nor animation and happiness from the dances of merit.

In the various compilations of *cuicatl* we have examples of *macehualiztli* or *netotiliztli*. Thus the so-called "Twenty Sacred Hymns of the Gods" included in an appendix to Book 2 of the *Códice florentino* are related to ceremonies in which the *macehualiztli* had the principal place. This can be seen from the title at the beginning of the "Hymns":

*Nican mitoa in incuic catca in tlatlacateculo
inic quinmauiztiliaya inin teupan ycan in çan
quiiaocac.*

Account of the songs that were said in honor
of the gods: in the temples and outside of
them

(*Códice florentino*:Book 2:fol. 131r)

Directed to Huitzilopochtli, Huitznahuac
Yaoutl 'the Warrior of the South', Tlaloc,
Teteuinnan 'the Mother of the Gods', Chi-
malpanecatl 'He Who Is Born over the
Shield', Ixcozauhqui 'He of the Yellow Face'
and 'Lord of Fire', Xochipilli, Ayopechtli,
Cihuacoatl, Xippe Totec, and other deities,
these hymns or *cuicatl* are basically related to
the celebrations that took place in each of the
eighteen months during the solar year. Consequently, these compositions were true
teocuicatl 'divine songs, songs of the gods'.

We encounter other designations in relation to the songs and dances arranged by the
huey tlahtoani, for example, those for Ce
Xochitl '1 Flower':

Then the *tlahtoani* decided, he asked what
kinds of songs were to be sung (which were
known by the following names), perhaps
cuextecayotl 'song in the mode and fashion of
the Cuextecas', *tlaoancacuextecayotl* 'in the
manner of drunk Cuextecas', *huexotzincayotl*
'in the mode of those of Huexotzinco', *ana-
huacayotl* 'in the mode of those of Anahuac,
those of the coast', *oztomecayotl* 'according
to the usage of the Oztomeca merchants',
nonoalcayotl 'like the Nonohualcas', *cozcate-
cayotl* 'according to those of Cozcatlan', *metz-
titlancalcayotl* 'in the fashion of those of
Metztitlan', *otoncuicatl* 'Otomi song', *cuata-
cuicatl* 'like the Cuacuatas (inhabitants of
Matlatzinco)', *tochcuicatl* 'rabbit songs',
teponazcuicatl 'to the sound of the slit log
drum', *cioacuicatl* 'songs in the mode of
women', *atzozocolcuicatl* 'as girls with only
one lock of hair sing', or perhaps an *ahuilcuicatl* 'song of pleasure', *ixcuecuechcuicatl*
'song of tickling', *cococuicatl* 'turtledove
song', *cuappitzcuicatl* 'arrogant songs', *cua-
teçoquicuicatl* 'bleeding songs' . . .

(*Códice florentino*:Book 4:fol. 18r)

Almost all of the above designations occur
as well in the *Cantares mexicanos* or the *Romances de los señores de la Nueva España*.

In the *Romances* there are notations like
these:

De Atlixco [note written thus in Spanish]
'from Atlixco' (fol. 8r)

Chalcayotl tlahtocacuicatl 'song of lords in
the mode of Chalco' (fol. 9r)

Huexotzincayotl tlahtocacuicatl 'songs of lords
in the mode of Huexotzinco' (fol. 10r)

*Canto en alabanza de Axayacatzin, rey de
México y de Nezahualpiltzintli de Tetzcuco y
Chimalpopoca de Tlacopan* [annotation in
Spanish] 'song in praise of Axayacatzin, King
of Mexico and of Nezahualpiltzintli of
Tetzcuco and Chimalpopoca of Tlacopan'
(fol. 12v)

*Vevemotecuzomatzin cuando lo de los huexo-
tzincas* [thus in Spanish] 'Motecuzomatzin
the Elder at the time of the Huexotzincas
affair' (fol. 31r)

The *Cantares mexicanos* has many more
examples of the genres mentioned in the
Códice florentino. Two are *cuextecayotl* 'in
the mode of the Cuextecas', one entitled
Tlapapal cuextecayotl 'In the multicolored
fashion of the Cuextecas' (fols. 36r–37r), and
another is called a *yaocuica cuextecayotl* 'war
song in the Cuexteca fashion' (fols. 65r–66r)
Further on other units of expression declare
that those who are fighting are Cuextecas,
drunk on the liquor of war:

the fire [war], *aya*, shakes with power; there
is our flower, *ah*; we are Cuexteca; we have
come shouting; the god finds pleasure in
the shields . . . with flowery liquor one
gets drunk, *aya*; there is the place where
the Cuexteca dance, *aya*; in Atlixco,
yyayaa . . .

(*Cantares mexicanos*:fol. 65r)

There are various examples of *otoncuicatl*
'Otomi songs' as well, so called either because they were translated from Otomi, because they were chanted in Otomi style, or

because they bore some relation to the military rank of *otomitl*. *Cantares mexicanos* contains several examples. One of them, called *Xopan cuicatl otoncuicatl tlamelauhcayotl* 'Song of the green time, Otomi song, in the straight manner' (fols. 2r–2v), deals with the singer's visit to Xochitlalpan 'the Land of Flowers', where sadness is dispelled in the fullness of day, light, heat, and the generous gifts of him who brings rain and does so much to make life possible. Another note indicates the next song: *oc ce tlamelauhcayotl* 'another to the same tune, in the straight manner' (fols. 2v–3r). Another *cuicatl* follows, with the title *Mexica otoncuicatl otomitl* 'Another Otomi song of sorrow' (fols. 4v–5r). A note in Spanish appears to be addressed by the anonymous Indian scribe to the friar interested in the collection:

Ancient songs of the native Otomis who used to sing at parties and weddings, turned into the Mexican language, but keeping to the juice and soul of the song, the metaphoric images they uttered. As Your Reverence will understand better than I, with my scant talent, they flowed with reasonable style and beauty, so that Your Reverence may take advantage of them and squeeze them into your schedule as may be convenient, as the good teacher Your Reverence is.

(Cantares mexicanos:fol. 6r)

From the context one presumes that this note refers precisely to the preceding *otoncuicatl*. Garibay (1953–1954:1:320–373) dedicates a chapter to a detailed study of what he calls "Otomi poems."

Another paragraph in Nahuatl introduces the songs in Huexotzinco style and explains their nature:

Here begin the songs that are called authentically *huexotzincayotl* 'in the manner of Huexotzinco'. In them are told the deeds of the Huexotzinca lords who were in power. They are divided into three kinds: *teuccuicatl* 'songs of lords' or *cuauhcuicatl* 'eagle songs', *xochicuicatl* 'flower songs', and *icnocuicatl* 'songs of privation'.

(Cantares mexicanos:fol. 7r)

The songs that follow this note are separated under these three rubrics (fols. 7r–15r)

Other songs in the *Cantares mexicanos* are also preceded by the word *huexotzincayotl* (fols. 6v, 28r–28v, 79r–80r). As Garibay (1965:cxii) notes, the songs of this genre are of high quality poetically and in terms of lofty thought. Among them is the "dialogue of flower and song," in which a number of songmakers participated, meeting in the house of Tecayehuatzin, lord of Huexotzinco, toward the end of the fifteenth century to clarify the meaning of *in xochitl, in cuicatl* 'flower, song', poetry and symbolism (M. León-Portilla 1961:126–137).

For reasons of space, I shall simply list other song types recorded, whether named for provenience or style of delivery: *chalcayotl*, three examples (fols. 3v–4v, 31v–36r, 72v–74r), *matlatzincayotl* (53v), *tlaxcaltecayotl* (54v, 83r), *chichimecayotl* (69v–72v), together with *teponazcuicatl* 'songs to the sound of the slit log drum' (26r, 31r–31v), *teuccuicatl* 'lords' songs' (73r–74r), *cococuicatl* 'turtledove songs' (74v), and others coinciding with the *Códice florentino* listing.

Among these various kinds of song "the *tlahtoani* decided and requested which one would be sung" (*Códice florentino*:Book 4: fol. 18r), and by implication, also danced. Since the classification we have discussed derives from Prehispanic tradition, it may be considered to show both the origin of these compositions and their modes of performance in the ceremonies in relation to instrumental music and dance.

To specify more precisely each of the subtypes mentioned, we should need far more adequate knowledge of the musical accompaniments and the rhythm and movements of each dance. While some works exist on music and dance in Prehispanic Mexico (Mendoza 1956; Martí 1961; Stevenson 1968), the subject continues to present many obscurities. The field is open for a much more detailed study of the available documents (codices, Nahuatl texts, chronicles) providing information on the songs that were performed to the accompaniment of music and dance.

3.2. THEMATIC CLASSES OF *cuicatl*. Reference has already been made to the *teocuicatl* 'divine songs' collected in the "Twenty Sacred Hymns of the Gods" (*Códice florentino*:Book 2:app.). There are other references to this preeminently religious genre as well, implying exaltation of the attributes of the gods, and various kinds of supplication or seeking favors of them. A significant allusion to them occurs in the *Códice florentino* itself in relation to the practices of the *calmecac*, the centers of higher education:

[the students] learned the songs there, those that were called *teucuicatl* 'divine songs', following what was written in their books [*amoxtoca*].

(*Códice florentino*:Book 3:fol. 39r)

Anyone interested in pursuing further study of the twenty hymns mentioned is referred to the works of Seler (1904) and Garibay (1958). In the *Cantares* can be found many others which because of their close relationship to the divine should be considered with this subgenre.

Let us now consider other thematic classes of songs. From the notes in *Cantares mexicanos* and *Romances de los señores* it can be said that a rather broad range of matters is treated in the songs. On the basis of these notes, the best defined subtypes are as follows:

Yaocuicatl, cuauhcuicatl, ocelocuicatl 'war songs, eagle songs, ocelot songs'.

Xopancuicatl, xochicuicatl 'songs of the time of verdure, flower songs'.

Icnocuicatl 'songs of privation' and also poems of philosophical reflection.

Cuecuechcuicatl, ahuilcuicatl 'tickling songs, songs of pleasure'.

Each of these is described below.

3.2.1. WAR SONGS. Conquests and struggles with other peoples are recorded in *yaocuicatl, cuauhcuicatl,* and *ocelocuicatl*, which also glorified famous captains or Mexican victories in general. They were often accompanied by acting, music, and dance in commemorations and celebrations. There are samples of them not only in *Cantares mexi-*canos and *Romances de los señores* but also in *Anales de Tlatelolco*. The latter includes, among others, a song recalling the war between the Tenochcas and Tlaltelolcas (fol. 25r). Another *yaohcuicatl* records the defeat of the Mexica at the hands of the Tecpanecs in Chalpultepec (*Anales de Cuauhtitlan*:fol. 17).

I shall allude to only a few of the many war songs collected in *Cantares mexicanos*: the *melahuac yaocuicatl* 'genuine war song' among the compositions chanted in Chalco style (fols. 31v–33v), the *cuauhcayotl* 'in the mode of the eagles' in which the central figure is the young prince Tlacahuepan who lost his life in war (fols. 36v–37r), the collection of songs from folios 64r–66v, including *Yaoxochicuicatl* 'Flowery song of war' and *Yaocuicacuextecayotl* 'War song in the Cuexteca mode'. A particularly interesting composition attributed to Aquiauhtzin, a songmaker from Ayapanco, near Amecameca, is entitled *In Chalca Cihuacuicatl* 'Song of the women of Chalco'. This poem, which compares war to a siege with a sexual flavor, is treated in some detail below.

3.2.2. FLOWER SONGS. *Xopancuicatl* 'songs of the time of verdure' and *xochicuicatl* 'flower songs' may be considered equivalent terms, as Garibay (1953–1954:1:87) has noted. In two different places in *Cantares mexicanos* the same song appears, once (fol. 68r) with the heading *xopancuicatl* and again (fol. 64v) with that of *xochicuicatl*. Sometimes these poems sing of the good there is on earth: friendship and love, the beauty of flowers, the delights of poetry. At other times the flower songs take on a sad tone, evoking bitterness and even death. The metaphors that have been referred to in dealing with the *cuicatl* in general may perhaps be more frequent here than in other works. Thus we find many references to flowers and their attributes; birds and butterflies; symbolic colors; things that produce pleasure, like tobacco, or foaming chocolate sweetened with honey; precious objects (also symbolic): jades and turquoises, bracelets and necklaces, pictures and musical instruments.

Examples of *xochicuicatl* and *xopancuicatl* are numerous in *Cantares mexicanos, Romances de los señores*, and other manuscripts. A number of the *otoncuicatl* 'Otomi songs' belong to the genre of *xopancuicatl* and are found in *Cantares mexicanos* (fols. 2r–4v). Other examples of the genre in *Cantares mexicanos* include a *xopancuicatl* described as a warning song, a call to reason to those who failed to distinguish themselves in battle (fol. 6r), a long *xochicuicatl* which may well be considered a collection of poems (fols. 9v–12r), a *totocuic* 'bird song' referring to Totoquihuatzin, lord of Tlacopan, actually another *xochicuicatl* (fol. 30v), as well as a series of songs headed by one or the other of the two genre names (fols. 52v–53r, 60r–64v, and 68r–69r). There are other *cuicatl* in the same manuscript not preceded by either name which nonetheless belong to this subtype in terms of content.

From *Romances de los señores* I shall cite only *De Nezahualcoyotzin*, a *xopancuicatl* addressed to the learned lord of Tetzcoco, of whom it says:

Amoxtlacuilol yn moyollo, tocuicaticaco ic tictzotzona in mohuehueuh, in ticuicanitl xopan cala itec, in tonteyahultiya, yao, yli yaha ilili lili iliya ohama hayya ohuaya ohuaya

A book of songs your heart; you have come to sing; you sound your drum; you are a singer within the house of verdure; there you delight the people.

(Garibay 1964: fols. 38r–38v)

In large part these are songs of lyric tone, relatively numerous in the manuscripts. It may be added that some poems of the Colonial and Modern periods also belong to this subtype.

3.2.3. SONGS OF PRIVATION. *Icnocuicatl* 'songs of privation' or of meditation and quest in the philosophic manner, are perhaps the best evidence of the intellectual development attained in ancient Mexico. Often attributable to *cuicapicqueh* 'songmakers' or *tlamatinimeh* 'scholars', sometimes known by name, they provide a setting for many of the questions of those who in other times and places have been considered philosophers. We find in them questions about the brevity of existence, the riddles of human destiny, rectitude and evil in human behavior, the instability of life, death, the beyond, and the possibility of approaching, knowing, and speaking with divinity, the Giver of life, the Master of the here and now, he who is like the night and the wind.

Among the relatively numerous compositions expressing this kind of concern, I shall choose a few which I consider representative. In various cases the names of the authors have been preserved: Tlaltecatzin of Cuauhchinanco, Tochihuitzin Coyolchiuhqui, Nezahualcoyotl, Cuacuauhtzin of Tepechpan, Nezahualpilli, Ayocuan Cuetzpaltzin, Aquiauhtzin of Ayapanco, Xayacamachan of Tizatlan in Tlaxcala, and Cacamatzin of Tetzcoco (see section 3.2.5).

Probably one of the best-known *icnocuicatl*, since it occurs both in *Cantares* (fols. 30r–30v) and in *Romances* (fols. 7r–8r), is by Tlaltecatzin of Cuauhchinanco. The matter on which he fixes his attention is the contrasting reality of how much is pleasant to him on earth and what he knows with certainty: that one day he will have to go away forever to the land of the dead. The hope that this will at least occur without violence ends the meditation. Following the units of expression indicated in the manuscript, here is my translation of this text:

I only grieve, I say, that I not go there to the place of the fleshless. My heart is a precious thing; I, I alone am a singer; golden are the flowers I have, *ye oo o iya iya*. Now I must—now I must abandon it; now I contemplate my house; the flowers remain in a row. Are great jades perhaps, spreading plumages, are they perhaps my price, *o o*? With this I shall have to go away; sometime it will be. There I shall go alone; I shall have to be lost, *ay yoo ahuiya*.

I surrender myself, my god, Giver of life. I say, let me go! Let me be wrapped like the dead, me the singer. So be it. Can anyone take possession of my heart, *ayo*?

Only thus shall I have to go off, my heart

covered with flowers. The jades will remain tumbled together—the precious bracelets that were skillfully worked. Nowhere is its model on earth. So be it, and may it be without violence.

(Cantares mexicanos:fol. 7v)

At the same time that concern and questioning about the inevitability of death crop up in the icnocuicatl, we also find examples of deep inquiry into the mystery of divinity. In Romances de los señores (fols. 19v–20r) there are a number of cuicatl which can be attributed to Nezahualcoyotl and which have as their central theme doubt and anguish over being unable to dissipate the mystery of the divine. The translation again is confined to the units of expression set apart in the manuscript.

Are you, are you true? Someone perhaps has gone astray, Giver of life. Is this true? Is it perhaps not, as they say? Let not our hearts hold torment, yehua, ohuaya, ohuaya!

All that is true, they say that it is not true. The Giver of life just shows himself to be arbitrary. Let not our hearts hold torment, yehua, ohuaya, ohuaya!

Only he, the Giver of life. Was I never afflicted then, ohuaya? Not ever, ohuaya, ya? Do I perhaps know happiness beside the people, ohuaya, ohuaya?

(Romances:fol. 19v)

On the basis of icnocuicatl like these and references from other manuscripts, I have been able to prepare a study of Prehispanic Nahuatl thought (M. León-Portilla 1963; 1966). The analysis of these forms of thought in which problems are posed about the origin and destiny of the world and humanity, the mystery of the beyond and the divine, appears to justify the application of the concept of philosophy to the thought of the tlamatinime, the scholars of ancient Mexico.

3.2.4. SONGS OF PLEASURE AND TICKLING. This genre is documented in the Códice florentino, which specifically mentions ahuilcuicatl 'songs of pleasure' and cococuicatl 'songs of turtledoves', as well as by the well-

informed chronicler Durán, who alludes to cuecuechcuicatl as a "ticklish dance" proper to "loose women and lewd men" (Durán 1867–1880:2:230–231). Cantares mexicanos includes some compositions bearing the same designation.

An example of cococuicatl is found on folios 74v–77r of the manuscript of Cantares. From the context we can infer that here the turtledoves are women of pleasure, or as they are also called ahuianimeh 'gladdeners'. An important feature is that alongside expressions that can be characterized as erotic there also appear reflections on themes frequent in the songs of privation, as in this example:

Aya noquich in acaxochitl o ypan nomati, ymac non cuetlahuix nech ya cahuaz.

Xochicuahuitl cueponi a, on quetzalli xelihui a, ca ye conitlotia nicnihuia, ca ca ya nopilohua, ho ho ma ye ic ayao ohuaya ohuaya ninocaya.

My man considers me like a red wildflower. In his hand I must wither; he will abandon me.

The flower tree opens its blossoms; the quetzal plumes are scattered. I only make my friends dance, my nephews, ho ho ma ye ic ayao ohuaya ohuaya ninocaya.

(Cantares mexicanos:fol. 76r)

These turtledove songs are worthy of further study, as are other related songs in which, as Garibay has noted (1968:64–70), several ahuianimeh debate about their pleasures and misfortunes. Let us look now at another example with a known author, entitled In Chalca cihuacuicatl 'Song of the women of Chalco'. It bears the following note:

In tlatlalil chalca in quimopapaquiltilico in tlatoani in Axayacatzin, çan oc o yehuatzin oquimmopehueli in çan cihuatzintin.

Composition of the Chalcas with which they came to delight Axayacatzin, only him who had conquered them and not [conquered] the little woman.

(Cantares mexicanos: fols. 72r–73v)

The identification of the maker of this song we owe to the chronicler Chimalpahin in his *Seventh Relation*, folio 174v (Chimalpahin 1889). He tells us that those who appeared before the ruler of Tenochtitlan went to chant in his honor a song composed by Aquiauhtzin of Ayapanco, near Amecameca (b. ca. 1430; d. post 1490). The song is a challenge by the women warriors of Chalco to Axayacatzin (who prided himself on his military feats) to show his manhood before them: those who provoke it to love and pleasure. According to Chimalpahin's account, the Chalcas who sang this composition in the palace of Axayacatl won the victory with neither shields nor arrows. Axayacatl was so delighted that:

. . . he much wanted—he was delighted with the song of the women of Chalco. So he made the Chalcas come back again; for all the nobles he asked them to perform the song . . .

Thus Axayacatzin ordered, and so they gave him the song . . . In the year already told (13 Cane, 1469) Lord Axayacatl made this song his property . . . because truly the song of the women of Chalco was very marvelous, and thanks to it the city of Amecameca which today is just a small town won renown.

(Chimalpahin 1889: *Septième relation*: fol. 176r)

The units of expression of this poem present a clear sequence of thought. First of all there appears the invitation of a woman of Chalco to her companions, exhorting them to seek and cut flowers, but specifically "of water and fire," an evocation of war. In this case it is to be an erotic siege. Here is the challenge: "Little companion, you, Lord Axayacatl, if you are truly a man, here you can exert yourself." The woman of Chalco uses her weapons: "Perhaps you shall not go on? Go on with force? Make erect what makes me a woman . . ." The siege continues: "Perhaps you are not an eagle? An ocelot?" Finally Axayacatzin will desire to achieve his pleasure. In metaphors frequent in other songs,

the siege is transformed into victory, surrender, sleep and rest. The erotic images are expressive in themselves:

. . . I have come to give pleasure to my flowery vulva, my little mouth, *yya oohuia*.

I desire the lord, little Axayacatl. Look at my flowery picture, look at my flowery picture: my breasts, *oohuia*.

Will your heart perhaps fall in vain, little Axayacatl? Here are your little hands; now with your hands take me: let us have pleasure, *aayyaha*.

On your mat of flowers where you are, little partner, little by little give yourself to sleep; stay quiet my little baby, you, Lord Axayacatl, *yao, ohuaya*.

One sees what Durán means when he speaks of lewd songs and ticklish dances.

3.2.5. AUTHORS. In most cases it is impossible for us to identify the author of a particular *cuicatl*. Furthermore, it appears certain, especially in the case of the *teocuicatl*, the sacred songs or hymns, that we owe them to groups of native priests and sages who had been transmitting and enriching them from one generation to the next. As in other ancient literatures, there is no basis for trying to find particular authors with recoverable biographies in most areas of Nahuatl literature.

A section of the *Códices matritenses*, in describing priestly functions, contains two important references to *cuicatl*. On the one hand (fol. 259r), we are told that priests called *tlapixcatzin* 'keeper, preserver' had the duty of teaching the people of their *calpulli* ('wards') the *teocuicatl* 'divine songs', carefully seeing to it that the texts remained unaltered. The other reference is to a priest called Epcohua *Tepictoton* 'Mother-of-Pearl Serpent', a title of Tlaloc and of the *tepictoton*, little figurines also related to rain. His job involved examining and approving songs:

The tonsured priest of Epcohua Tepictoton. His job was as follows: he took care of song matters. When someone was composing songs, they were told to him so that he might present [them, and] he could give orders to the singers to come and sing at his house. If anyone composed songs, he gave his verdict about them.

(*Códices matritenses*:fol. 260r)

The biographies of some of these songmakers are partially known, predictably enough when they were both songmakers and nobles, some of them very famous. Garibay takes note of them briefly in his *Historia* (1953–1954:2:373–390) and in an appendix to his edition of the *Romances* (1964: 220–239). In *Trece poetas del mundo azteca* (M. León-Portilla 1967), I have worked out the biographies and collected the works of a few other important people of Precolumbian Mexico.

Five of them come from the Tetzcoco area: Tlaltecatzin of Cuauhchinanco, a singer of pleasure, women, and death who lived in the fourteenth century; Nezahualcoyotl, more than thirty of whose poems are preserved (b. 1 Rabbit [1402], d. 6 Flint [1472]); Cuacuauhtzin of Tepechpan, a singer of love betrayed who died in the middle of the fifteenth century; Nezahualpilli, learned governor and successor to Nezahualcoyotl (b. 11 Flint [1464], d. 10 Reed [1515]); and Cacamatzin, who witnessed the arrival of the Spanish (b. ca. 2 Rabbit [1494], d. 2 Flint [1520]).

Four more are natives of Tenochtitlan: Tochihuitzin Coyolchiuhqui, son of Itzcoatl and lord of Teotlatzinco (d. ca. middle fifteenth century); Axayacatl, the *huey tlahtoani* of Tenochtitlan (d. 2 House [1481]); Macuilxochtzin, daughter of the famous Tlacaelel (who also lived in the fifteenth century); and Temilotzin, a captain defender of Tenochtitlan and singer of friendship (d. 1525).

Four songmakers can be identified with the area of Puebla and Tlaxcala: Tecayehuatzin of Huexotzinco, who organized the famous debate on the meaning of "flower and song" (b. second half of the fifteenth century; d. beginning of the sixteenth); Ayocuan Cuetzpaltzin, a famous sage, native to Tecamachalco and a contemporary of Tecayehua-

tzin; Xicotencatl of Tizatlan, governor of one of the four Tlaxcalan chiefdoms, who witnessed as an old man the coming of the Spanish; and, finally, Chichicuepon, an unlucky plaintiff from Chalco, who lost his life defending his lands, and left us a single song.

I shall mention briefly seven more, concerning whom I have another work in preparation: Aquiauhtzin of Ayapanco, author of the "Song of the women of Chalco"; Moquihuix of Tlaltelolco, who lost his life in the war against Tenochtitlan in 7 House (1473); Totoquihuatzin of Tlacopan (fifteenth century), author of festive and philosophic poems; Xayacamachan of Tizatlan in Tlaxcala, who speaks of the houses of picture books, contemporary and friend of Tecayehuatzin of Huexotzinco; Teoxinmac of Tenochtitlan, composer of several songs of privation before the death of Tlacahuepan (ca. 1494); Tetlepanquetzaltzin of Tlacopan, who witnessed the conquest and who wrote war songs as well; and Oquitzin of Azcapotzalco, also a witness of the confrontation with the Spanish and author of a number of *xopancuicatl* 'songs of the time of verdure'.

4. GENRES OF *tlahtolli*. As we have seen, *tlahtolli* differ from *cuicatl* among other things in the structure of their units of expression, and particularly in their stylistics. I shall now consider the subtypes of *tlahtolli*. As with the *cuicatl*, I shall take into account the terminology derived from Prehispanic tradition.

From a general standpoint we may set to one side what would be called *narrative* in European languages. On the other side we find a number of subtypes, among others the *huehuehtlahtolli* 'ancient word', didactic or hortatory expositions of ancient religious doctrines, morals, or behavior. Likewise distant from narrative are other *tlahtolli* describing, normatively or informationally, cultural institutions (commerce, markets, professions) and fields of knowledge (animals, plants, pharmacology, medicine, the calendar, fates, etc.).

4.1. NARRATIVE. The *Códices matritenses*

(fol. 122r) tell us that narrators (*tlaquetzqueh*) were people involved in repeating ancient traditions or other kinds of stories. The word derives from the same root as *quetza* 'stand up, elevate, erect, manifest'. A narrator, then, was one who elevated his subject and made it clear. Another derivative of the same root is *tlaquetzalli*, translated by Molina (1571b) as 'fable, fairy tale', which we can understand more broadly as narrative.

We can see that the transmission of legends, stories, and all sorts of tales was valued:

Tlaquetzqui, the narrator, has wit, says things cleverly, is like an artisan of lip and mouth. A good *tlaquetzqui* is of tasteful words, happy words. He has flowers on his lips. In his words tales abound; in correct speech, flowers bloom from his mouth. His *tlahtolli* is tasteful and happy like flowers. His is the *tecpillahtolli* 'noble language' and careful expression.

(*Códices matritenses*:fol. 122r)

The *tlaquetzqueh*, storytellers of ancient Mexico, attracted the attention of the people, elevating and disseminating all manner of stories, from the actions of the gods to the deeds of the ancestors, warriors, sages, nobles, and supreme rulers. It is interesting that the word *tlaquetza* with the sense of narrating or recounting a recollection remains current in many of the modern Nahuatl dialects spoken in different regions of Mexico.

Various subtypes of *tlaquetzalli* can be specified. First there are the *teotlahtolli* 'divine words', recalling the actions of the gods and the origins of the world and of human beings. Then there are *in ye huehcauh tlahtolli* 'words of ancient times' or also *ihtoloca* 'what is said of something or someone', speeches or tales, sometimes legendary, sometimes more fully historical.

Finally there are what are called by the long name *tlamachiliz-tlahtolzazanilli* 'oral relations of what is known', evocations of real or imaginary events passing from mouth to mouth and comparable to fables, fairy tales, and certain kinds of stories. In fact, in modern dialects of Nahuatl the word *zazanilli* bears a connotation similar to 'story'.

4.1.1. DIVINE WORDS. A great many Nahuatl texts exemplify *teotlahtolli* and are comparable to a certain degree to epic tales or to the stories of the genesis of all things to be found in sacred books in the cultures of classical antiquity. Bearing in mind that the various Mesoamerican peoples participated in a common heritage, it is not surprising to find narratives in the *teotlahtolli* similar to texts in other languages. In Maya, for example, as in Nahuatl, there exist similar accounts of the cosmic ages, the culture hero Kukulkan (Quetzalcoatl), the land of the dead, and various other themes.

The Nahuatl *teotlahtolli* deal mainly with origin myths, culture heroes, and legends. Narratives of cosmic and divine origins are preserved in the *Florentino* and the two *Matritense* codices, the *Anales de Cuauhtitlan*, and the manuscript known as *Leyenda de los soles*. Some (e.g., *Anales de Cuauhtitlan*: fol. 2) tell of the ages or suns that have existed; others (*Códices matritenses*:fols. 161v–163r), of the age in which we live. The latter relates the creation of the fifth sun in Teotihuacan, the journey of Quetzalcoatl to the land of the dead, in search of the bones of the men of prior generations, and the rediscovery of corn at Tonacatepetl, the Mountain of Our Sustenance.

The *teotlahtolli* about the learned priest Quetzalcoatl, sometimes considered a god or a name for the supreme deity, sometimes a culture hero, are of great interest. He plays a fundamental role in the *toltecayotl* 'the collected works of Toltec culture'. Tales of Quetzalcoatl are included in the *Códice florentino* (Book 3:fols. 9r–23r) and *Anales de Cuauhtitlan* (fols. 3–7). These are among the most expressive and beautiful narratives of the Nahua peoples.

Legends and tales of the gods and other legendary personages include many texts on the gods of rain, wind, the fields, war, etc. The *Leyenda de los soles* contains several of these tales, such as the one about the ball game played by the *tlaloqueh* 'rain gods' with Huemac, the last lord of Tula. Huemac, whose extravagances are described in the *Historia tolteca-chichimeca* (fols. 4–7), among other places, is a good example of a legendary personage, as is Mixcoatl, sometimes held to be the father of Quetzalcoatl.

Stylistically speaking, a common feature of all of these kinds of *teotlahtolli* is the sense of detail produced by multiple descriptions used to express a fact or an idea from highly varied viewpoints. On the other hand, native expression sometimes attains subtle abstractions through the reference to concrete elements—flowers and songs, face and heart, quetzal crests, jades and precious stones. Much of what has been said of the style of *tlahtolli* in general applies to the *teotlahtolli* in particular.

Another kind of text belonging to this subtype deals with the universe of the gods, religion and human fate. Outstanding among the sources of such texts are the "Primeros memoriales" of the *Códices matritenses*, containing descriptions, probably learned by heart in *calmecac* or priestly schools, of ceremonies, sacred ritual, the attributes of the various priests by rank, the characteristic costumes of the principal gods, the clothing, food, drink, and pastimes of the lords. There are other aspects as well, always relating to the world of the gods or of the nobles who were their representatives on earth.

The study of the various *teotlahtolli* helps us to understand the awareness the Nahua themselves had of their ties to the universe of the gods, their world view, and the religious beliefs and principles governing their social, religious, and political organization.

4.1.2. WORDS OF ANCIENT TIMES. This category was known as *in ye huecauh tlahtolli* 'words of ancient times', or as *ihtoloca* 'what is said of something or somebody' or *tlahtollotl* 'sum and essence of the word', understood as a collection of discourses dedicated to recalling the past. These historical texts are relatively abundant. They are often postconquest "readings" of what had been written in the old codices. In other cases they are systematically memorized oral traditions communicated to native scribes, with or without the participation of the friars interested in Prehispanic antiquities.

To assess the development leading in the Colonial period to the alphabetic transcription of the *xiuhamatl* 'papers of the years', I shall refer to some of the historical codices of the central region. Because these are codices put together after the conquest, one can see in them how, little by little, the use of letters was imposing itself upon that of hieroglyphics and pictures. A first group of manuscripts registers dates, numbers, and other elements basically by means of glyphs placed beside the pictures, e.g., the *Tira de la peregrinación*, the *Códice en cruz* and the first three *Mapas de Cuauhtinchan*. Codices including Nahuatl glosses, from single words to fuller texts, are more numerous. Among them are the so-called *Mapa de Sigüenza*, the *Lienzo de Tlaxcala*, the *Anales de Tula*, the codices *Moctezuma*, *Azcatitlan*, and *Mexicanus*, and those of the Tezcocan group: the codices *Xolotl*, *Tlotzin*, and *Quinatzin* and the *Tira de Tepechpan*. There are also codices with Spanish glosses, like the *Telleriano-Remensis* and the *Mendoza* (*Mendocino*).

Other manuscripts, like the *Códice Aubin*, the *Historia tolteca-chichimeca*, the *Códice Cozcatzin* and the *Manuscrito mexicano, número 40* in the Bibliothèque Nationale in Paris, list the years with their corresponding glyphs and further contain pictures, all of this accompanied by a full Nahuatl text in Latin letters. In fact in these documents the Nahuatl text is primary, and extremely rich in historical content.

Finally we find "readings" in Nahuatl of codices of which the pictures and all but a minimum of the glyphs have failed to survive, e.g., the *Anales de Tlatelolco*, the *Leyenda de los soles* of 1558, the *Anales de Cuauhtitlan*, and various sections of the *Florentino* and the two *Matritense* codices. Something similar can be said of at least sections of the Nahuatl chronicles of Alvarado

Tezozomoc (1949), Castillo (1908), and Chimalpahin Quauhtlehuanitzin (1889; 1965). There are also very early Spanish translations of some of these "readings in Nahuatl" of native codices, such as García Icazbalceta (1941:209–239).

Actually the sequence of changes in the mode of transmission of histories had antecedents in the period of Prehispanic autonomy. In the centers of education next to the temples, the pictures and hieroglyphics of the codices were the objects of "commentaries," also a kind of "readings," which had to be systematically memorized. Thus, long before the conquest, history was transmitted in a double fashion: through the codices and through systematic oral tradition.

The accounts of the *ihtoloca* deal with the origin, splendor, and ruin of the Toltecs, ways of life of the different Chichimec groups, and the establishment of the lordships in different parts of the central plateau—Cholula, Culhuacan, Chalco-Amecameca, Aculhuacan, Tlaxcala, Tecamachalco, Cuauhtinchan, and others in the Puebla region, and of course in the Valley of Mexico. A special place is occupied by the migration of the Mexica, the confrontations they had on the way, their arrival at Tenochtitlan, their subjection at Azcapotzalco, their victory over their former conquerors, the alliance with Tetzcoco and Tlacopan, and the development and splendor of Tenochtitlan and its conquests in very distant regions.

Other parallel *ihtoloca* exist, dedicated to others of the kingdoms that have been mentioned—Culhuacan (Chimalpahin 1958), Tetzcoco or Azcapotzalco (*Anales mexicanos*). Another group of Nahuatl documents are in the Archives of the National Museum of Anthropology of Mexico: the *Anales antiguos de México y sus contornos* and the *Anales de México y Tlatelolco*. Composed after the conquest, these works in part are additional examples of "readings in Nahuatl" of codices.

Like other Mesoamerican peoples, the Nahuas were concerned with knowing the measure of time and fate; they had in their own way a deep sense of history. The texts that have escaped destruction allow us to become acquainted with their viewpoints about their own past.

4.1.3. IMAGINATIVE PROSE. The Nahuatl term *zazanilli* covered tales, fairy tales, and stories and is still used in that sense today. Let us now examine some *tlahtolli* that exemplify imaginative prose. Some of these are inserted into other genres. Various brief didactic tales occur in some of the *huehuehtlahtolli*, and others in *teotlahtolli* by way of complement or illustration. It is more common to encounter them in *ihtoloca*, that is, in histories. Such tales were very likely preserved by oral tradition.

Fernando Alvarado Tezozomoc, who "read" in Nahuatl and transcribed the contents of a number of codices, some genealogical, included some of these tales in his *Crónica mexicayotl* (1949). Although related to historical or legendary events, *zazanilli* are presented as more ornate narratives, evoking particular events in livelier colors and sometimes in a fantasy mode, as in the tale of how Lord Huitzilihuitl was able to take to wife the princess Miahuaxihuitl, daughter of Lord Ozomatzintecuhtli, ruler of Cuauhnahuac (Alvarado Tezozomoc 1949:90–95).

There are examples of *zazanilli* in the ensemble of texts given to Bernardino de Sahagún by his informants. I shall cite three. The first concerns a coyote grateful to a man for saving him from a *cincoatl* snake that was about to kill him (*Códice florentino*:Book 11:fols. 8r–8v). Another describes the attributes of a fantastic animal called *ahuitzotl*, which lived near the water and trapped and drowned anyone it could, in a sacrifice related to the rain gods (ibid.:fols. 33v–34r). A final one depicts how the Nahuas hunted monkeys (ibid.:fols. 15r–16v).

Tales like these are the Prehispanic antecedents to the abundant narratives of the contemporary Nahuas. Both the perception of detail and the way the plot is spun give good evidence of the very richly creative and expressive Nahua imagination.

4.2. THE ANCIENT WORD. Among all the *tlahtolli*, the *huehuehtlahtolli* 'ancient word' is the subtype in which striving for preciosity of expression is most perceptible. Various things touching upon the most ancient traditions were communicated with an abundance of metaphors and parallelism. In preciosity, the *huehuehtlahtolli* can only be compared with some of the *icnocuicatl* of Nezahualcoyotl and other learned men. Elegance as a characteristic attribute of the language of these texts can be explained in terms of their origins and aims. Sahagún, to whom we owe the largest collection of *huehuehtlahtolli*, has a clarifying prologue to them in the *Códice florentino*. He begins by asserting that all nations "have looked to the learned and powerful to persuade, and to men eminent in moral virtues . . ." There are examples, he tells us "among the Greeks, Romans, Spanish, French, and Italians . . ." He adds:

The same was customary in this Indian nation, and more particularly among the Mexicans, among whom learned, virtuous, and enterprising speakers were held in high esteem, and they elected high priests, lords, leaders, and captains from among them, however low their destiny may have been. These ruled the republic, led the armies, and presided over the temples . . .

(*Códice florentino*:Book 6:prologue)

And the texts Sahagún collected in Book 6 of the *Florentino* were indeed the work of "learned speakers, virtuous and enterprising." He titled Book 6 as follows:

On the rhetoric, moral philosophy, and theology of the Mexican people, where there are curious things touching upon the subtleties of their language and very delicate things touching upon moral virtues.

In the *calmecac* and temples this form of rhetoric, so much prized not only by the Nahua but also in Mesoamerica generally, was perfected and transmitted to the young students. The thirteenth of the rules observed in the *calmecac* refers precisely to this:

Cenca vel nemachtiloia in qualli tlahtolli.

They were carefully taught good language, good speeches.

(*Códice florentino*:Book 3:fol. 39r)

The apprenticeship in the *calmecac* in careful forms of speech, *tecpillahtolli* 'the noble language', and the systematic memorization of the *huehuehtlahtolli* transformed the students into the kind of men described by Sahagún as "learned speakers, virtuous and enterprising." Thus, particularly among the members of the upper class of *pipiltin*, it was a common thing to encounter people who, besides expressing themselves elegantly and precisely, could recite the most appropriate *huehuehtlahtolli* for a given circumstance as occasion demanded. Those who transmitted these *huehuehtlahtolli* to Sahagún were already elderly, having memorized them in the *calmecac* before the conquest. Thanks to a note at the end of Book 6, we know the year when the collection was completed:

It was translated into the Spanish language by the aforesaid father Fray Bernardino de Sahagún, after thirty years of its being written in the Mexican language, this year of 1577.

(*Códice florentino*:Book 6:fol. 215v)

If it had been thirty years since the *huehuehtlahtolli* were transcribed, we must conclude that that occurred in 1547, or only twenty-six years after the seizure of Mexico-Tenochtitlan. Other *huehuehtlahtolli* had been collected earlier, between 1533 and 1536, by Olmos, and have also come down to us, albeit with some interpolations to adapt them to the missionary purposes of certain friars who did not cavil at using them in education of the natives as texts of elevated moral content. Perhaps because of these interpolations, there were those even in the sixteenth century who doubted that they were authentic derivations from ancient wisdom. Sahagún reacted to this with a certain indignation:

In this book it will be very clearly seen that what certain rivals have alleged, that everything written in these books before and after

39

the present one is fictions and lies, they are saying as bigots and liars, because what is written in this book is beyond human understanding to make up, nor could any man living fake the language it is in. And all educated Indians, were they asked, would agree that this is the very language of their ancestors and the works they composed.

(*Códice florentino*:Book 6:prologue)

There are thirty-nine *huehuehtlahtolli* in Book 6, and one must add another score scattered in various places in Books 3, 4, 5, 9, and 12. Another two are in the *"Primeros memoriales"* (*Códices matritenses*:fols. 61v–65v). Twenty-nine, including some of those collected by Olmos, have been published in Nahuatl with a summary version by Fray Juan Bautista (ca. 1600).

Bautista's collection shows fairly frequent interpolations and other kinds of modification: no less than five of the twenty-nine can be considered late compositions, specifically designed for evangelization of the natives. That the others are basically Prehispanic is nevertheless unquestionable. As Bautista himself notes at the end of his edition, they show that:

Almost universally all the people of these Indies have a natural eloquence, so that it is easy for them to orate and to plead their blessings and ills, as if they had learned and drunk in all the rules and colors of rhetoric all their lives in agreement with the art, particularly the Mexicans . . .

(Bautista ca. 1600:fol. 92r)

Besides the *huehuehtlahtolli* collected by Olmos and Sahagún, another group of compositions has been published by Garibay (1943). In large part they are on various forms of salutation, farewell, and dialogue, and allow one to make out that they are products of the Colonial period, inspired, perhaps, by examples of the "ancient word." Garibay believes the collection to be by Carochi, author of the excellent grammar of 1645. As far as we know, other *huehuehtlahtolli* texts are merely copies, with variations, from those of Olmos

and Sahagún, including the one described by Georges Baudot (1978): as "unknown," but which was published by Bautista (ca. 1600: fols. 35r–41v).

The themes of the *huehuehtlahtolli* maintain a close relation to the condition or status of the people uttering them. While Sahagún recognizes that people "of low station" could be educated in the art of speaking, the analysis of the *huehuehtlahtolli* forces us to conclude that, with some exceptions, they were recited by nobles or by people who enjoyed special prestige in some ways. We thus encounter such discourses by the *huey tlahtoani*, by royal officials, priests, judges, captains, and others, or by leaders of the *pochteca* or merchants, a group which had attained a very important rank in the society of the Nahua peoples. In many of the *huehuehtlahtolli* we find attempts to inculcate in the people that it is the destiny of the nobles to keep and transmit the ancient wisdom, to carry the people on their shoulders, and to feed the gods with the blood of captives seized in the sacred war. Such ideas confirm not only that these discourses were the speeches of nobles but also that among their aims was the reinforcement of the status of the ruling group.

By virtue of the rank of the person speaking, the following classification of *huehuehtlahtolli* can be established:

Speeches directed to the people by the *huey tlahtoani*, the supreme ruler, and the replies of royal officials.

Speeches calling upon a god or gods by the *huey tlahtoani*, some other royal official, or a high-ranking priest.

Speeches by high-ranking officials directed to the *huey tlahtoani* in various circumstances, and his replies.

Speeches by a father or mother to a son or daughter and their corresponding replies.

Speeches of parents to children on such occasions as weddings, the birth of a grandchild, etc., and the corresponding responses.

Speeches of the *ticitl* 'midwives' to the newborn and the parents and relatives.

Speeches of ambassadors in particular instances.

Addresses of the leaders of the *pochteca* and various other merchants on different occasions, and the corresponding replies.

Speeches of the fathers, priests, and teachers to children entering school, and the corresponding replies.

Speeches given when someone had died, whether a supreme governor, a noble, or a person of lesser importance.

This first classification shows the great variety of circumstances in which the ancient word was heard. Focusing upon the semantic content of these discourses I here adopt the classification of Josefina García Quintana (1978:61–71):

Religious: by priests and addressed to the gods.

Ritual: by priests and other dignitaries in a wide range of religious ceremonies.

Courtly or noble: by the *huey tlahtoani*, royal officials, ambassadors, and other leaders, dealing with social and political life, legal rules, and the world view of the Nahuas.

Specialist: by midwives, doctors, merchants, and other professionals.

Familiar: by parents to children in a variety of situations. García Quintana (1978:66) includes here "those of everyday use, both among the nobility and among artisans and commoners, including formulas of politeness, words of consolation, advice, announcements, etc."

Literary: teaching models of the noble and careful style of speech.

Popular: folk wisdom: auguries, superstitions, and proverbs.

Christian: postconquest missionary works produced by the friars for evangelization but inspired by the ancient compositions.

Obviously the themes of these literary compositions are highly varied. The esteem in which the Nahuas themselves held the "ancient word" is seen in the efforts they made to preserve it. It is interesting that as late as 1600, the *huehuehtlahtolli* were the only Prehispanic works published even in part by Bautista (ca. 1600). Some of the *huehuehtlahtolli* themselves insist on their great value as the legacy of the ancestors. A

father exhorting his son to lead a moral life alludes to this:

You who are my son, you who are my boy, listen to these words; place them inside your heart; write there this word, these two words that our ancestors left spoken to us, the elder men, the elder women, the revered, the admired, those who were wise on earth. Here is what they gave us, what they entrusted to us, the ancient word (*in huehuehtlahtolli*), that which is bundled, that which is kept, that which is in the mat trunk . . .
(*Códice florentino*:Book 6:fols. 93r–93v)

While we are here appraising the "ancient word" as a legacy of wisdom, in other cases it appears to reflect an eagerness to justify the nobles' destiny of rule. In this instance, a *huehuehteuctlahto*, an aging royal official, addresses the *huey tlahtoani*. The nobles are descended from Quetzalcoatl. Hence it is determined—it is their destiny—that they be the lords, the rulers:

O lord, O you who rule, our lord. Here is the tail, the wing [the people], that here takes, that here appropriates, that truly here grows rich, [that] rejoices with what is due to it, that receives such a spark from your precious word . . .

Here also are appropriated some of your breath, precious word, the noble children of our lords, those of their lineage, precious realities, jades, bracelets, his noble children, his deeds, the descendants of Quetzalcoatl, those who have his skill, his enchantment. For this have they come to live; for this they were born, which is what is assigned to them, which is their deserts; it is the mat, the chair of rule [power]; it is they who carry it, who bear the burden of the world. Thus then came they to life, were born, were created, when it was still dawn; it was arranged, it was determined that they should be lords, that they should govern . . .
(*Códice florentino*:Book 6:fol. 67v)

By evoking the tie of the nobles to Quetzalcoatl, *Topiltzin* 'Our Son, Our Prince', he who is of our lineage, the *huehuehtlahtolli* reaffirms with symbolism and refinement that the destiny of the heirs of the Toltec lord is likewise to rule. As Sahagún notes, there is nothing better than reading and study of the *huehuehtlahtolli* for assessing what the ancient Mexicans were like:

extremely devout toward their gods, extremely zealous about their republics, among themselves very urbane; toward their enemies very cruel; toward their own, humane and strict . . . and I think that from these virtues they obtained the empire . . .
(Sahagún 1956:9:53)

4.3. OTHER FORMS OF *TLAHTOLLI*. Among the non-narrative *tlahtolli*, a special place is occupied by the *in tonalli in tlatlahtolloh* 'disquisitions on fates', diagnostics delivered from interpretation of the *tonalamatl* 'the book of fates'. Another subtype is *nahuallahtolli* (from *nahualli* 'witch, curer, diviner'), the esoteric language used by sorcerers and magicians for their incantations and exorcisms.

Both genres are very remote from anything we classify today as literature. But these *tlahtolli*, like the others we have examined, are profoundly rooted in the Nahua world view. There are two reasons for not bypassing fates, spells, and exorcism here. One is that all them were important forms of expression in ancient Mexico. The other is that despite our modern point of view, swollen as they are with symbols and meaning, they are by their very nature part of the *tlahtolli* and thus deserve inclusion.

It being impossible to include here a detailed analysis, those interested are referred to the sources.

On the *in tonalli in tlatlahtolloh* 'disquisitions on fates', see Book 4 of the *Códice florentino*. It is strange that little has been done on these divinatory texts. Shortly before the conquest, the *tonalpohualli* 'count of fates' was included in the *tonalamatl*, as in the *Codex Borbonicus* and the *Tonalamatl de Aubin*. Perhaps the best commentary on the *tonalli* giving the fates of all 260 days is that of Jacinto de la Serna (1900:328–398).

An important source on the *nahuallahtolli* is Hernando Ruiz de Alarcón (1900; 1983; Coe and Whittaker 1983). Brother of the famous dramatist, and endowed priest of Atenango, he was able to collect numerous spells and exorcisms from a wide area of the northeastern part of modern Guerrero. As he says, it was not his aim

to make a detailed investigation of the natives of this land, which would require a very long work and many subdivisions, and I don't know what such a work might be useful for today. I do claim to know how to break the trail from the ministers to the Indians so that between the two sets of principles they may readily come to a knowledge of this depravity, so that they may better attempt its correction, if not its cure . . .
(Ruiz de Alarcón 1900:129)

A study of this genre of *tlahtolli* containing oaths, exorcisms, spells, and sorcery has been published by Alfredo López Austin (1967). The best advice to those who wish to learn more is to refer to the sources, as with the other *tlahtolli* we have considered.

Other subtypes, equally distant from narrative, relate to specialized professionals: texts concerning medicine (*Códice florentino*: Books 10–11; *Códice Badiano* [Cruz 1964]), or merchants (*Códice florentino*:Book 9). One may assume that others on legal precedent, religious doctrine, etc., were similarly memorized in the appropriate schools.

5. CONCLUSIONS. The various kinds of *cuicatl* 'poetry' and *tlahtolli* 'prose' considered here are all products of Prehispanic tradition. Of some we know by reason of particular songs or narratives that they were composed in the fifteenth or early sixteenth century, just before the conquest. The date of composition of the *cuicatl* can be better specified when dealing with the works of known authors: in addition to the documentable fifteenth-century songmakers, we have, for instance, one of the fourteenth century: Tlaltecatzin of Cuauhchinanco.

It is likely that some of the "Twenty Sacred Hymns of the Gods" may be of considerable antiquity, some of them composed perhaps in the days of the hegemony of Culhuacan if not before, in the Toltec period. Further thought should be given to the "ancient words" (*huehuehtlahtolli*), modified perhaps by the interests of Mexico-Tenochtitlan during the Mexica period, but which may have originated several centuries before the first ruler of that city was enthroned.

It is certain that Indians who survived the conquest are responsible for the preservation of almost all of these works. Among the earliest works of the Colonial period on Nahuatl literature, the compilations, transcriptions, and sometimes translations done by these Indians—former priests, teachers, and students, like those of the Holy Cross College in Tlatelolco—are outstanding. Alone, or together with some of the friars, they dedicated themselves to saving these evidences of their spiritual life for a variety of reasons.

Beyond this task of recovery, the Indians continued to produce *cuicatl* and *tlahtolli*, although often with new themes. First came astonishment at the unheard-of things it was their lot to witness. The lamentations over the conquest and the texts of the "visions of the vanquished" speak to us of this. Later on, chroniclers like Alvarado Tezozomoc and Chimalpahin were to write in Nahuatl about the past of their people on the basis of such documents and traditions as they could bring together. Others, working beside the friars, were to be the authors of religious songs, dramas, and pious histories aimed at the conversion of the natives of the land.

Written expression in Nahuatl continued thereafter for highly varied reasons. In many cases there were only treatments of legal, social, or economic matters (Anderson, Berdan, and Lockhart 1976). Nonetheless, even in such documents, the ancient style, the familiar kind of rhetoric, the native art of speaking well, flower in spontaneous fashion. Native works of the Colonial period which today appear to us with a certain sort of literary value were produced almost by instinct, time after time contesting injuries and all kinds of violations of the rights of the indigenous people.

What has been said about literature in precontact times, when Nahuatl was still spoken in its classic form and as a lingua franca in a broad area of Mesoamerica, permits a partial vision of this literature and its variety of genres, here described in the terminology of Prehispanic tradition. Even if much of this literature was lost, the samples we do have (fortunately far from rare) permit us to get close to the preoccupations and day-to-day activities, world view and culture of one of the peoples whose track is most perceptible in the sphere of Mesoamerican civilization. Among other things, this explains why both in Mexico and in other nations of the new and old worlds, there is increasing interest in better knowing, studying, and appreciating these works, different, but, because they are human, of universal significance.

3. Yucatecan Mayan Literature

MUNRO S. EDMONSON AND VICTORIA R. BRICKER

1. PREFATORY NOTE. The death of Dr. Alfredo Barrera Vásquez on December 28, 1980, was a great loss to Mayan studies, and has robbed us specifically of an essay on the present topic which he had undertaken to write. It is with diffidence and deep regret that we attempt to substitute for him.

2. INTRODUCTION. It may well be that Yucatecan Mayan literature is the oldest in the Americas. It is even possible that it was the only American literature in the strict sense antedating the Spanish conquest. Its origins and early development involve a number of unsolved problems to which only speculative or partial answers can be given at present.

2.1. THE OLMEC QUESTION. The language spoken by the creators of Olmec culture on the Gulf Coast of Mexico and Izapan culture on the Pacific Coast of Guatemala has been much discussed. The continuities in calendar and writing systems would suggest that the answer may be a Mayan language, perhaps ancestral Yucatecan. Historical linguistic evidence suggests that it may have been proto-Mixe-Zoque (Campbell and Kaufman 1976). The temporal priority of Yucatec thus remains unproved, especially since placing Yucatec later than this horizon might also make Zapotec a contender for first place.

2.2. THE LANGUAGE OF THE CLASSIC PERIOD. There is increasing evidence that the language of the monumental inscriptions and painted vases of the Classic period may well have been proto-Cholan at least in some areas, while it remains probable that it was proto-Yucatecan in others. Further research is needed to specify sites and boundaries, but progress is being made.

2.3. THE CODICES. Four extant picture manuscripts with glyphic texts are all that remain of the formerly very extensive written literature of the Yucatecans. The earliest (and the only preconquest) one is the *Dresden Codex*. The *Madrid*, *Paris*, and *Grolier* codices are sixteenth century in date but may well be Colonial copies of precolonial books.

2.4. GLYPHIC LITERATURE. The earliest documented example of Yucatecan literature comes from the eighth century A.D. (J. E. S. Thompson 1937:192; 1950:197–199). Although the tradition of hieroglyphic writing in the Maya Lowlands dates back to the third century A.D., the oldest texts probably represent proto-Cholan, rather than proto-Yucatecan literature.

2.5. THE BOOKS OF CHILAM BALAM. The four centuries following the Spanish conquest of Yucatan saw the composition of fourteen books that are usually called the *Books of the Speaker of the Jaguar* (*Chilam Balam*). Written in Yucatecan Maya in Latin letters, these works have a highly varied content, much of it specifically literary. It is possible that some of the texts they include are transcriptions of glyphic originals; others are almost certainly derived from oral tradition, while still others were composed in their present written form at various times during the Colonial and early Republican periods. The extant copies are late, most of them dating to the nineteenth century, but some passages claim to record events as early as A.D. 672 and as late as 1848. The *Books* are mainly named for the towns in which they were found, and six of them are primarily literary works: those of *Chumayel* (Edmonson in press; Roys 1933), *Tizimin* (Edmonson 1982a), *Mani* (Craine and Reindorp 1979; Escalona Ramos 1935), *Chan Kan* (Hires 1981), *Kuua*, and *Tusik*. Others are medical (*Ixil*) or calendrical (*Tekax* [Gates 1935b] and *Nah*, both from Teabo). Five of them are lost (*Hocaba, Nabula, Telchac, Tihosuco,* and *Tixkokob*). Three other works have sometimes been called *Books of Chilam Balam* but shouldn't be: the *Xiu Chronicles* (*Chronicle of Oxkutzcab*) and *Chronicle of Calkini* (Barrera Vásquez 1957; Gates 1935a), and the *Notebook of Teabo*, a medical text. The *Book of Teabo* is another name for the *Tekax* (Barrera Vásquez and Rendón 1948).

The *Books of Chilam Balam* and a number of other Yucatecan documents are distinctive in having a cumulative and encyclopedic character. They have clearly been recopied many times from a variety of earlier sources, and the individual texts (or "chapters") are usually in no particular chronological order. Internal evidence and explicit Mayan dates usually make it possible to date them satisfactorily to the nearest *katun*, at least in the

Tizimin and the *Chumayel*, and the chronology of the history that follows leans heavily on those works. We have not attempted to cite every dated text, but rather to emphasize those with a salient literary value.

2.6. OTHER WRITTEN SOURCES. Aside from the *Books of Chilam Balam* there is a large body of other writings in Yucatec: land documents, chronicles, wills, medical works, songs, poems, and letters. These are cited as completely as possible in the sketch history that follows. There are also a number of documents in Spanish that may be relevant, but even when these are translations from Yucatec they have been excluded from the present account unless we possess the Mayan text.

2.7. ORAL LITERATURE. There is good reason to suppose that a substantial part of Yucatecan literature has always been oral. The texts on stone monuments now appear to have been primarily dynastic history, albeit with ritual implications. Those on vases or other small objects may have been mainly ritual and mythological. There is no way to know how much was written in codex form. The surviving examples are principally astronomical, ritual, and divinatory, but it seems extremely likely that histories and prophecies were also written on paper. It is striking that we have no dramatic texts written by natives of Yucatan from any date. Prayers, spells, proverbs, speeches, songs, riddles, and tales, as well as drama, ritual and otherwise, were predominantly oral forms throughout. There is no evidence that the Yucatecans ever attempted to write music. Most of what we know of these genres has been collected and transcribed by scholars in the present century, but it is beginning to be extensive.

3. CLASSICAL LITERATURE. Aside from the dynastic histories carved on the Classic monuments, we may conveniently begin Mayan literature with a myth: the myth of the *Hero Twins*. We have no Yucatecan text for this tale, but from vase paintings possibly as early as the Early Classic period, it appears that some version of it must have been known in the southern lowlands and in the Kekchi

area. At least some episodes appear to resemble closely the Quiche version in the *Popol Vuh* (Edmonson 1971).

The only surviving texts that purport to represent Classic Mayan literature are the chronicles: *The First Chronicle* (A.D. 672–1848 [Edmonson in press:Ch. 1]), *The Second Chronicle* (A.D. 711–1539 [ibid.:Ch. 2]), *The Third Chronicle* (A.D. 909–1618 [ibid.: Ch. 3]), and *The Chronicle of Nonoualco* (A.D. 948–1611 [Craine and Reindrop 1979: 138–140]). Laconic and contradictory, they tell us very little about either the history or the literature of the Classic period.

3.1. THE SEVENTH CENTURY. The *Tizimin* dates the beginning of *The First Chronicle* to 8 Ahau (A.D. 672–692). The *Chumayel* starts with 6 Ahau (A.D. 692–711). This is in any case a ritual rather than a historical date, and the chronicle records only "the appearance of the Chichen Itzas."

To give a sense of this ostensibly early text, we quote the beginning of it from the *Chumayel*:

The account
  Of the counted *katuns*
Of the appearance of the Chichen Itzas
  says this.
This has been written
  In this country—
What may have happened,
  What may be known
By anyone who may sense
  And may understand
The counting
  Of the *katun*.
In 6 Ahau occurred
  The appearance of the Chichen Itzas.
          (Edmonson in press: lines 1–14)

3.2. THE EIGHTH CENTURY. *The Second Chronicle* begins with the birth of the Sun Giants (*Pauah Tun*) in 4 Ahau (A.D. 711–731):

4 Ahau
  Was the name of the *katun*
When there occurred

The birth of the Giants
And the touring
  Of the lords.
          (Edmonson in press: lines 153–158)

The First Chronicle reports the arrival of the Xiu in 2 Ahau (A.D. 731–751) and notes the occurrence of an even *baktun* in 9.17.0.0.0 (A.D. 771):

And 13 Ahau
  Was the ordering of the mat.
          (Edmonson in press: lines 17–18)

3.3. THE NINTH CENTURY. *The First Chronicle* notes the movement of the Itza to Champoton in 1 Ahau (A.D. 869–889). The *Tizimin* version says:

Two hundred years
  Chichen Itza ruled.
Then it was destroyed.
  Then they went
To the settlement
  Of Champoton,
Where there were then
  The homes
Of the Itza,
  The gods who own men.
          (Edmonson 1982a: lines 39–48)

No less than fourteen dates carved on twelve of the buildings at Chichen refer to the years 866 to 886. There are no earlier dates at Chichen and only three later ones (J. E. S. Thompson 1937:186).

3.4. THE TENTH CENTURY. *The Third Chronicle* begins its count at 12 Ahau (A.D. 909–928) and records the destruction of Conil in 6 Ahau (A.D. 948–968
          [Edmonson in press: line 258]).
The Chronicle of Nonoualco describes the departure of the Toltec Xiu from Tula in 968:

The Toltec Xiu
  Had been established
To the west
  Of Zuyua for four *katuns*.

The place they came from
  Was Tula.
Holon Chan,
  The ruler,
Arrived in the country
  With his subjects
When the *katun* 8 Ahau
  Had already passed.
            (Craine and Reindorp 1979:138;
                  scansion Edmonson's)

The Second Chronicle notes "The Great Descent" in 4 Ahau (A.D. 968–987). Much has been made of the theory that there was also a "Little Descent," and that Yucatan was originally populated from two directions, but see Edmonson in press: line 166.

4. POSTCLASSIC LITERATURE. The last dated stone monument was erected in 10.6.0.0.0 (A.D. 1125), which is usually taken to mark the end of the Classic period, though it terminated at most sites at least a century earlier.

4.1. THE ELEVENTH CENTURY. *The Chronicle of Nonoualco* reports the arrival of the Tutul Xiu at Chacnouitan in 1047. This was probably in southern Veracruz, and, like the preceding "history," appears to be largely mythical.

. . . And *katun* 2 Ahau
In which the governor
  Of the Toltec Xiu
Came
  To Chacnouitan.
            (Craine and Reindorp 1979:138;
          interpretation and scansion Edmonson's)

4.2. THE TWELFTH CENTURY. *The Third Chronicle* reports the destruction of Izamal in 5 Ahau (A.D. 1086–1106) and the destruction of Chichen Itza in 1128:

. . . 1 Ahau
Were destroyed
  The remainder of the Itza at Chichen.
On the third measured *tun*
  In 1 Ahau

Was the destruction
  Of those of Chichen.
            (Edmonson in press: lines 272–278)

4.3. THE THIRTEENTH CENTURY. *The First Chronicle* records the destruction of Champoton in 8 Ahau (A.D. 1158–1204). *The Second Chronicle* places the destruction of Chichen Itza in 4 Ahau (A.D. 1224–1244). *The First Chronicle* appears to agree in the *Tizimin* version:

Forty years,
  Then they came
And established
  Their homes again;
Then they destroyed the road
  Of Champoton.
            (Edmonson 1982a: lines 83–88)

The Chronicle of Nonoualco dates the arrival of the Toltec Xiu at Uxmal to 1263 (Craine and Reindorp 1979:138).

4.4. THE FOURTEENTH CENTURY. *The Third Chronicle* reports a raid by cannibals in 5 Ahau (A.D. 1342–1362):

5 Ahau there came
  The foreigners who ate people,
And Foreigners without Skirts was their name.
            (Edmonson in press: lines 307–309)

The *Dresden Codex* probably belongs to this period or perhaps a century earlier. The original composition or parts of it may be earlier still.

4.5. THE FIFTEENTH CENTURY. *The First Chronicle* records the establishment of the Xiu in Uxmal in 8 Ahau (A.D. 1441–1461) in the *Tizimin* version. The *First* and *Second* chronicles record the fall of Mayapan in 1451, and the sequelae are detailed in the *Third*.

As cumulative histories, the *Chronicles* continue into Colonial times. *The First Chronicle* breaks off at 3 Ahau (A.D. 1618–1638) in the *Chumayel* and at 13 Ahau (11.16.0.0.0) or 1539 in the *Tizimin*, which nonetheless lists all the *katuns* down to 1848.

The Second Chronicle ends with 1539. *The Third Chronicle* breaks off at 3 Ahau (1618), but records no events after 7 Ahau (1579).

4.5.1. THE ACCOUNT OF THE KATUNS. Although the *First* (and earliest) *Chronicle* calls itself an "account of the *katuns*," and all three give scanty histories ostensibly beginning in the Classic period, the four earliest chronicles are best considered precursors to the *katun*-by-*katun* prophetic histories more properly so titled. These begin in *The Third Chronicle* in 12 Ahau (A.D. 1401–1421) and collectively the *Books* cover every *katun* to 11 Ahau (1824–1848). The earliest entry in the series is:

12 Ahau then got

Otzmal its *tun* period.

(Edmonson in press: lines 327–328)

This *Account of the Katuns* (*U Kahlay Katunob*) (Edmonson 1982a: Chs. 3–5, 7, 8, 10, 11, 13, 16–18, 23, 26, 35, 37, 41; in press b: Chs. 4–6, 8, 11, 16, 18, 19, 22, 25, 26, 28, 33, 35, 36, 38, 40, 45; Craine and Reindorp 1979: 116–122) thus blankets the history of Yucatan from the beginning of the fifteenth to the middle of the nineteenth century (A.D. 1410–1848). The relevant texts are contained in the *Chumayel*, *Tizimin*, *Mani*, and *Kaua* (Edmonson 1982a; in press; Craine and Reindorp 1979; Barrera Vásquez and Rendón 1948).

Because of the cumulative recopying of previous texts, a Yucatecan tradition which may well go back to Classic or even earlier times, there is an emphatically syncretistic quality to the literature of Yucatan. But it was a syncretism governed by mathematics, and by the specific mathematics of the Mayan calendar. The Maya are and were a ceremonious people, and they lived their lives by the numbers, predicting their history and then living it, on the assumption that fate was dictated by cyclical repetition. The most important cycles were those of the *uinal* (20 days), *tzol kin* (260 days), *tun* (360 days), *haab* (365 days), *katun* (20 *tuns*), *kin tun y abil* (52 *haabs*), *may* (13 *katuns*), and *baktun*

(20 *katuns*). *The Account of the Katuns* is a ritual and prophetic history that rephrases the events of Mayan history and fits them to divinatory (or sacred) time.

The chronicle of each *katun* specifies the city that seated the *katun*, its lord (or lords), the Jaguars (*Balam*), its fate (food and drink), and its ceremonies. It alludes to but does not describe the *Ceremonial of the Katun*, the ritual with which every *katun* ended, a drama in thirteen acts which was the political and religious focus of Mayan life in the Postclassic and Colonial periods. If you have never seen a *katun* ending ceremonial (and no one now living has), the *Account of the Katuns* is a particularly opaque and esoteric form of history. It does, however, indicate that the *Ceremonial of the Katun* had the same acts as the *Ceremonial of the May* (see section 5.1.1), and in the same order.

4.5.2. SERMONS. Like the Hebrews of the Old Testament, the Maya set great store by their prophets (*ah bobat*), who were designated Speakers (*Chilam*) to the Jaguar (*Balam*), and were thus the second-ranking religious and political officials of the state. Their prophecies were ceremonially announced five years (a quarter-*katun*) before the beginning of each *katun*. They were vague and hortatory homilies, and the earliest one we have is probably the *Sermon* of Ahau Pech for 2 Ahau, dated to 1495. It preaches an end to the civil war that followed the fall of Mayapan, forty-four years earlier:

The prophecy of Ahau Pech,

The great priest.

It is time

As the sun is rising,

My fathers,

That the face of the ruler will be lifted,

Perhaps soon

In the fourth part of the *katun* period.

(Edmonson in press: lines 433–440)

5. COLONIAL LITERATURE. The first Spanish entry into Yucatan occurred in 1507, and the Colonial period is generally dated from

the founding of Spanish Merida in 1542. Even discounting subsequent rebellions, the military conquest of Yucatan took notably longer than that of Mexico, Guatemala, or Peru. The literary conquest took longer still. As the most literate people of the New World, the Maya took to alphabetic literacy with an enthusiasm which has persisted to the present day.

Colonial Mayan literature documents in exquisite detail both the sophistication of Mayan culture and its stubborn traditionalism. Its continuity with the preconquest past is beyond dispute.

5.1. THE SIXTEENTH CENTURY. *The Account of the Katuns* was continued, covering the period from 2 Ahau to 7 Ahau (A.D. 1500–1599). The *Sermons* of Puc Tun, Xopan Nahuat, Tzin Yabun, and Kauil Ch'el (Edmonson in press: Chs. 9, 10, 13, 21) also appear to run from 2 Ahau to 7 Ahau (A.D. 1500–1599). The survival of the *Madrid*, *Paris*, and *Grolier* codices testifies to the continuation of the hieroglyphic tradition despite the onslaught of the Inquisition. Torn by an ongoing civil war between the western Xiu and the eastern Itza, the Mayas nonetheless maintained their traditional calendric ritual, which eventually outlasted the Spanish empire itself.

5.1.1. DRAMA. On the very eve of the conquest of Merida, in 1539, the Itza and the Xiu attempted to compose their differences by inaugurating a new calendar. The date was the end of 13 Ahau, the last *katun* of the cycle (the *may*), according to the Itza count. The Mayapan calendar was inaugurated first in that city by the Itza and slightly later in Merida by the Xiu. The *Ceremonial of the May* (Edmonson in press: Ch. 12) describes the Xiu celebration, an elaborate ritual drama in thirteen acts to inaugurate a new cycle, destined to coincide almost exactly with the period of Colonial rule (A.D. 1539–1824).

The *Ceremonial* began with a ritual circuit covering the whole of the modern state of Yucatan. This was followed by the seating of the *katun* and then that of the yearbearers,

and the ritual renewal of land titles (the pacing of the *katun*). Next were the dawn ceremonies, confirming titles to offices, and then the sacrifices, followed by a feast and the ritual examination of the lords. The "word" (fate) of the *katun* was announced and the lords did penance. There followed the commemoration, in this instance a reenactment of *The Fall of Mayapan* as a historical drama. The *katun* was then counted, and a farce was performed, in this case called *Centipedes and Gnats*. The Ceremonial ended with a *Sermon* (Edmonson in press: Ch. 12).

The opacity of the allusions to the *Ceremonials of the Katun* may be illustrated by this reference to the seating ceremony of Yaxal Chac as Jaguar in Merida in 1539:

Yaxal Chac
Was the face in the lordship.
Descended was the high fan;
Descended was the high branch
And the celestial
Incense.
Sounded was his drum;
Sounded was the rattle of the lord of 11 Ahau
(Edmonson in press: lines 1587–1594)

Many of the ritual symbolisms are even more esoteric.

The same period (A.D. 1539–1559) provides us with an oblique description of the *Ceremonial of the Haab*, the year's-end ceremony (Edmonson in press: Ch. 15). This ceremonial, rather than the medical text to which Roys awarded the title, could properly be described as the "Ritual of the Bacabs." Our description is largely concerned with insignia and personnel, and the sequential acts of the drama are not given.

Act 19 of the *Ceremonials of the Katun*, the *May*, and the *Baktun* was always a farce. A number of these are listed in the sixteenth-century dictionaries (Barrera Vásquez 1980): the Black Dance (Boox), Shaken Sticks (Hatz'-lam Che), Wide Open (Hech), Butterfly Dance (Pepem), Dance of the Gallants (Tzublal), Snake Poison (Zabanil), and Holding Hands Dance (Machlan Kab Okot). A number more are described as forbidden, presumably by the Church: the Monkey Dance (Maax Okot), Shading Tree (Booyal Che), Reeling Drunk (Naual), and Desire (Pochob). The last has been attributed to the fifteenth century and was still performed in Tinum in the 1920's (Barrera Vásquez 1980). All of the "forbidden" dances appear to have been erotic in character.

5.1.2. CHRONICLES. The Spanish invasion was well under way by 1539, and the introduction of the Mayapan calendar in that year marks the beginning of the Colonial period from the Mayan point of view (Edmonson 1976). Previous *katuns* had been counted by their ending dates. From 11 Ahau (1539–1559) on, they were counted by their beginnings.

A particularly interesting text dating to 1556 describes *The Building of the Pyramids*. It dates the completion of them to 11.15.0.0.0. A unique feature of the account is its use of rebus writing (5 for *ho* and 2 for *ca*):

181 Tz'uul	The midyear of the foreigners
A t. 5	At Merida [Ti Ho]
9 dik:	Was the ninth of December
2nhele	Of the yearbearers [*can hel e*].

(Edmonson in press: lines 1361–1364)

Besides the *Books of Chilam Balam* other cumulative histories were initiated in the sixteenth century: the *Chronicle of Calkini* (1557–1813), the *Chronicle of Yaxkukul* (1511–1553 [Juan Martínez Hernández 1926]) by Macan Pech, and the *Chronicle of Chac Xulub Chen* (1511–1562) by Nakuk Pech. There are also collections of land documents of lesser literary interest: the *Titles of Ebtun* (16th–19th c. [Roys 1939]), the *Mani Land Treaty* (1557 [Riese 1981]), the *Documents of Tabi* (1569–1821), and the *Land Documents of Sotuta* (1600 [Craine and Reindorp 1979]).

5.1.3. MYTH. A very elegant creation myth in the *Chumayel* (Edmonson in press: Ch. 20) called *The Birth of the Uinal* dates to 9 Ahau (1559–1579). It relates the beginning of counting time, the twenty sacred days of the *uinal*, to the appearance of *uinic* ('man, twenty'). Each of the day names is accounted for by a punning folk etymology, ending with Muluc:

On 6 Muluc
  Occurred the burial (*mucchahal*)
Of all caves,
  And this was before the awaking of the world.
This occurred
  By the commandment
Of our father
  Who is God.
Everything that there was not
  Was then spoken in heaven,
For there had been no stones
  And trees.
And then they went and tested each other.
  Then he spoke as follows:
"13 heaps
  And 7 heaps makes one."
    (Edmonson in press: lines 2133–2148)

The final equation is a neat summary of the central mystery of Mayan numerology and religion, reconciling unity and diversity, monotheism and polytheism.

5.2. THE SEVENTEENTH CENTURY. The Mayan literature of the seventeenth century forcefully illustrates the survival of indigenous tradition. Cumulative history continued to be written, and ceremonial drama reached its highest documentable peak outside of the art of the Classic period. Its content was predominantly historical (prophetic) and ritual (commemorative).

5.2.1. CHRONICLES. The *Account of the Katuns* continued into the seventeenth century from 5 Ahau to 10 Ahau (A.D. 1599–1697), as did the other chronicles and other documents mentioned in section 5.1.2. A parallel cumulative history was also initiated, the *Chronicle of Oxkutzcab* (1689). The *Parish Book of Cacalchen* (Breton 1919–1922) also belongs to this period.

The entry for the seating of the *katun* at Valladolid in 1658 reports the lordship of Yax Chuen:

A sun priest
  Seated
On the throne,
  On the mat,
In the jaguar robe
  And rattles.

(Edmonson 1982a: lines 4051–4056)

A long and somewhat deviant history, the *Annals of Bacalar*, is included in the *Tizimin* (Edmonson 1982a: lines 1549–2980) and the *Mani* (Craine and Reindorp 1979:98–115). It gives a year-by-year account of Itza history from 1593 to 1614, and contains a calendar correlation confirming Landa's: Sunday, July 16, 1555 = 13 Muluc 1 Pop. The *Annals* are deviant in that they present the history as though it were the history of *katun* 5 Ahau, which ran from 1598 to 1618, but the deviance was predicated on the theory that the "*katun*" 1593–1614 would repeat an equally fictitious "*katun*" 1541–1562, one calendar round or *kin tun y abil* (fifty-two years) earlier. This is the only Yucatecan instance of calendar round cyclic history on the record, but the Maya were constantly exploring their calendar.

5.2.2. DRAMA. The drama of the seventeenth century is represented by the *Ceremonial of the Baktun*, performed in Merida in 1618 at the start of *katun* 3 Ahau (Edmonson in press: Ch. 29). This extravaganza was in honor of the fact that the date marked the beginning of an even *baktun*: 12.0.0.0.0. It was a ritual drama in twenty acts because the *baktun* has twenty *katuns* in it. Act 17, the commemoration, was *The Birth of the Flowers*, a reenactment of the origin myth of the Xiu, a tale of Toltec origin. Act 19, the farce, was a comic morality play called *Envy and Spite*.

Because of the rarity of the occasion (the previous *baktun* ending, presumably celebrated in Mayapan, was in 1224, and there will never be another), the Mayas provide us with a kind of text of Act 14, *The Language of Zuyua* (Edmonson in press: Chs. 30, 31), the ritual riddles for examining the lords to be sure that they have received a proper education on the esoteric symbols of Mayan religion. The structure of this text makes it clear that the actual performance was extemporaneous, and we are simply being given examples of the kinds of riddles asked:

And so the second secret word
  That is to be asked of them
Is that they go get the brains of heaven,
  To be seen by the headman wherever he
  lives.
"I wish it to be seen:
  Let it be seen,"
Thus perhaps
  They will be told then;
For these brains of heaven,
  That is copal incense in Zuyua language.

(Edmonson in press: lines 3595–3604)

Zuyua is a place name directly associated with Tula, and hence with the Toltec Xiu. The *Chumayel* is a Xiu document. But the occurrence of a parallel text in the *Tusik* would appear to indicate that the Itza held closely similar ceremonials. Zuyua was also an Itza town near Motul.

5.3. THE EIGHTEENTH CENTURY. The literature of the eighteenth century includes chronicles, calendrics, theology, medicine, lyric poetry, and narrative. It is more fully documented than that of any other period.

5.3.1. CHRONICLES. Again the *Account of the Katuns* continued—now in Itza hands—from 8 Ahau to 2 Ahau (1697–1800). So did the *Chronicles* of Yaxkukul and Chac Xulub Chen, the *Titles of Ebtun* and the *Documents of Tabi*.

5.3.2. CALENDRICS. *Katun* 4 Ahau, which was to have run from 1737 to 1757, was an eventful time, marked by the final suppression of the tribute that was still being collected in the name of Chichen Itza, and by the adoption of a new calendar in 1752. This is related in *End of the Long Count* in the *Tizimin* (Edmonson 1982a: Ch. 38) and *Calendrical Notes* in the *Chumayel* (Edmonson in press: Ch. 39). The new calendar abandoned the *tun* (and hence the classic *katun*) as the basis of counting time, and substituted a new "*katun*" of twenty-four years (*haab*). *Katun* 4 Ahau was therefore reinaugurated at Valladolid, to run another twenty-four years (1752–1776). Valladolid claimed to seat the cycle (*may*) as well as the *katun*, thus ending the Itza tradition of honoring Mayapan as the City of the Cycle—a tradition that went back to 1204. All subsequent dating was in the Valladolid calendar, and some overeager copyists even fouled up the dating of passages on early Colonial history by applying it retroactively.

5.3.3. THEOLOGY. Valladolid also seated the following *katun*, 2 Ahau (A.D. 1776–1800). The syncretistic ideology of the Itza in the late eighteenth century is given in a mystical and numerologically brilliant text on *The Sevenfold Creation* (Edmonson in press: Ch. 41). Mixing garbled Spanish and Latin with esoteric Mayan, and elements of Ptolemaic, Christian, and Mayan cosmology, this work is important to understanding the religious background of the Caste War in the following century.

5.3.4. MEDICINE. *The Book of Chilam Balam of Ixil* took its present form in the eighteenth century. It is medical and calendrical in content. Another long medical work of the period has been published by Ralph L. Roys (1965) as the *Ritual of the Bacabs*. Five other medical works in Maya are known but undated: *Book of the Jew*, *Book of Maya Medicine*, *Book of Maya Medicine of Sotuta*, *Book of the Jew of Sotuta*, and *Notebook of Teabo*.

5.3.5. LYRIC POETRY. A unique eighteenth-century contribution to Mayan literature is the collection called the *Songs of Dzitbalche* (Barrera Vásquez 1965), containing fifteen lyric poems of great beauty, some of them

of considerable antiquity, and all of them of great literary value and interest. One of them, "Little Arrow," seemingly preconquest, comforts a sacrificial victim by stressing his role as a messenger to God:

Laugh then
  And rejoice your heart,
Because as for you there,
  As is being told you,
You are to report the word
  Of your fellow men
Before the face
  Of our blessed father,
According to the custom here
  On earth,
That came to pass long, long ago
  In written stone.
          (Edmonson 1982b: 204)

A "Flower Song" appears to be an excerpt from an orgiastic ritual performed by women:

We are here then in the heart of the forest
  At the edge of the stone pool
To await the appearance
  Of the beautiful smoking star over the forest.
Shed your clothes!
  Remove your hair stays!
Till you are
  As you arrived
Here
  On this earth,
O virgins,
  Maidens of the changing moon.
          (Edmonson 1982b: 183)

An interesting feature of these songs is that a number of them are divided into stanzas of from four to forty-two lines, the number of lines per stanza being irregular in any one song.

5.3.6. NARRATIVE. Probably eighteenth century in date is the atypical tale of *The Maiden Theodora* which is copied into the *Ixil*, *Kaua*, *Mani*, and *Chan Kan*. I quote from the last:

How a woman was carried
  By the merchant,
(Maiden Theodora
  Is her name)
Before the lord Al Manzur
  As he is called.

(Hires 1981: 275)

The tale goes on to describe a battle of wits between the beautiful maiden and the wise men of the kingdom, in which she shows herself their master in esoteric astronomical, medical, and theological lore, including the European zodiac. The tale must have had a European origin, but it was obviously popular with the Maya since it was copied into four of the *Books*.

6. MODERN LITERATURE. The Spanish empire and the long Mayan tradition of cumulative history came to an end in the early nineteenth century, after which there is an abrupt change in the content, style, and uses of Mayan writing. There are continuities with the past. In some places the *Books of Chilam Balam* still in native hands continue to be read and studied even today. Modern Mayan compositions continue to be cast in the rhetoric and poetry of former times. But increasingly it is to oral literature that we must turn for documenting the continuity of Mayan expression.

6.1. THE NINETEENTH CENTURY.

6.1.1. CHRONICLES. The final entries in the *Account of the Katuns* are for 13 Ahau (1800–1824) and 11 Ahau (1824–1848). The latter, in fact, may be more precisely datable (see section 6.1.2.).

6.1.2. DRAMA. The entry for 11 Ahau consists of the puzzling story of Antonio Martínez (Edmonson 1982a: Ch. 42; in press: Ch. 46; Craine and Reindorp 1979:65–70), versions of which occur in the *Chumayel, Tizimin,* and *Mani*. Because Juan Pío Pérez was copying it in *Mani* in 1837, this story and the *Books* that include it must have been written before that date. It dates itself to 11 Ahau, so should be post-1824. Antonio Martínez is unknown to history except that he appears in the *Chumayel* in 1 Ahau (1618–

1638) with a number of details confirming the identification (Edmonson in press: Ch. 34). He is thus an anachronism in the nineteenth century. The explanation appears to be that the "story" in 11 Ahau is not a story at all but a ritual, and the suggestion is strong that it is nothing less than the *Ceremonial of the May* for initiating a new *katun* cycle. The date (1824–1837) is right, and the story contains an identifiable eight of thirteen acts of that drama in the correct order. Antonio Martínez' life may have been selected for commemoration because it was the two hundredth anniversary of his involvement in a grass-roots Christian uprising in Merida. If this surmise is correct, the *Ceremonial* would have been performed, probably at Tizimin, in 1824, and was probably written at that time or shortly thereafter. This would date the *Chumayel, Tizimin,* and *Mani* to the same period. The *Kaua, Chan Kan, Nah,* and *Tekax* were possibly contemporary or somewhat later, and the *Tusik* could have been later still, though there is no clear evidence that it was. The lost *Books* remain undatable.

6.1.3. THEOLOGY. The effort to reinaugurate the *May* was a failure, and before the end of 11 Ahau the Caste War had broken out, in 1847. In 1850, the rebel Mayas founded a cult based on a Talking Cross, which was the source of religious proclamations and letters during the second half of the nineteenth century. An excerpt from a proclamation, dated 15 October 1850, documents the heavily syncretistic quality of that cult:

Because I it was who caused you to be created;
  I it was who redeemed you;
I it was who spilled
  My precious blood
On your behalf.
  Thus, then,
O ye my beloved people,
  Have ye perhaps seen
How my existence is:
  My feet nailed
With shackles?

Have ye perhaps seen
With how many coils of rope
    I am tied,
With which I am being punished
    By my Father's Perfect Beauty
On your behalf?
    Have ye perhaps seen
That I am supported by my Most Holy
Cross;
    That I am carried in a litter
By innumerable angels
    And seraphim?

(Bricker 1981:198–199)

The Talking Cross functioned as a head of
state, communicating by letter with the Governor of Yucatan, the Superintendent of British Honduras, and even Queen Victoria!
Letters from the Cross typically began with
an invocation, as in the opening lines of a
complaint to the Governor of Yucatan in
1851:

Jesus,
    Mary.
In the name of God the Father,
    And in the name of God the Son,
And in the name of God the Holy Spirit,
    Amen Jesus.
My beloved Governor,
    Don Miguel Barbachano,
Thou who art in the city of Merida:
    Today,
In the count
    Of the twentieth
Of the month
    Of August
While it is urgent
    That I send one of my commandments
To thee;
    To the end that
I might inform thee
    That a great many things
Were done to me
    By the troops

On the twenty-third
    Of March.

(Juan de la Cruz 1851; Bricker's
translation)

6.1.4. LYRIC POETRY. In 1864 Brasseur de
Bourbourg collected a *Prayer* from Xcancha-
kan and a *Love Song* from Izamal. The latter
has an unusual structure:

Strong is desire:
    Strong to enslave the strong.
I'm going to kiss your mouth
    Between the bars of your bird cage.

You are all my thought,
    You are all my good,
Even hunger has left me
    Except at your whim, beautiful Felipa.

Does this remind you of that day
    You were lying in the shade of an oak,
When you said only death
    Would make you leave off loving me?

I think I'll start at daybreak,
    I think I'll start off at dawn.
That way you, I think,
    May manage to leave me my life!

(Brasseur de Bourbourg 1872;
Edmonson's translation)

Stanzaic poetry is rare and late in Maya. This
is the first known instance of quatrains.

6.2. THE TWENTIETH CENTURY. Except
for a brief renaissance in the 1930's, Mayan
literature of the twentieth century has been
very much on the wane. Very little of what
we do have was actually written by the
Mayas themselves, though we have a number
of translations into Maya by others. Much of
the larger part of the corpus is oral literature,
largely recorded by scholars.

Some rare examples of twentieth-century
Mayan writing can be found in the post-
scripts to the copies of one of the proclamations of the Talking Cross (see section 6.1.3)
that are treated as sacred books in several villages in Quintana Roo. The following post-

script appears in the version of the proclamation of 1850 that is kept in a notebook in Tixcacal:

I am making known
  When I learned to believe in
The most holy commandments
  Of my Holy True Father,
Our Father,
  Sign of the Cross,
Papa,
  Lord Three Persons.
It was on a Holy Thursday,
  [The] nineteenth
Of December
  In the year,
1957
  [Years].
This
  Is the year.

(Bricker 1981:207n)

6.2.1. ORAL LITERATURE. Twentieth-century oral literature includes folk tales, historical narratives, proverbs, and poetry (prayers and songs). They will be discussed under these headings. These have been collected from various parts of Yucatan (Merida, Kom Chen, Chan Kom, Balankanche, Hocaba, and elsewhere) and from Quintana Roo (Xcacal, Felipe Carrillo Puerto), Belize (San Antonio, Sokotz), Guatemala (Flores) and Chiapas (Naha).

6.2.1.1. FOLK TALES. Many of the folk tales are animal stories, particularly favoring Rabbit, Squirrel, Coati, Rat, Monkey, Cockroach, and Turtle. They are mostly very brief and they are frequently cautionary. Many suggest European origin. A sampling is included here:

Cockroach and His Fiver (Kim de Bolles 1972)

Grandpa Squirrel (Kim de Bolles 1972)

Honey Fly and the Ant (Kim de Bolles 1972)

Horse of Seven Colors (Smailus 1975)

Little Girl Who Started to Ride a Little Horse (Kim de Bolles 1972)

Little Rabbit and the Squirrels (Kim de Bolles 1972)

Little Rabbit and the White Wax Person (Kim de Bolles 1972)

Little Rabbit in the Plaster (Kim de Bolles 1972)

Monkey (Andrade 1971b)

Monkey and Alligator (Smailus 1975)

Monkey and the Rain Lord (Smailus 1975)

Monkey's Haircut (McQuown 1979)

Mrs. Turtle and the White Birds (Kim de Bolles 1972)

Rabbit and Coyote (Andrade 1971b)

Rabbit and Mountain Lion (Baer 1970)

Rabbit and the Old Lady (Smailus 1975)

Rabbit, Firefly, Rat, and Frog (Andrade 1971b)

Rat Who Took Cockroach's Fiver (Kim de Bolles 1972)

Squirrel Fooled Me (Schumann 1971)

Tick and Coati (Kim de Bolles 1972)

Turtle and Deer (Romero Castillo 1965)

Turtle Man of Uxmal (Anon. 1939d)

Tz'intz'in Bug (Kim de Bolles 1972)

Why Coati Looks at Dog (Novelo Erosa 1941)

To illustrate the genre, we have selected a short but complete example: "Mrs. Possum Who Was Dying to Eat Papaya" (*Huntul Xnuc Och Hach Tac U Hantic Put*):

Once there was Mrs. Possum.
  She was really eager to eat a ripe papaya.
She went into the field
  And came to where there was a papaya tree.
It was just loaded with ripened fruit.
  She started to climb it.
But it was high then
  And she couldn't reach it.
So what she did
  Was to spend the whole night,
But she still couldn't reach
  Where the papaya was
To get it down
  And eat it.
She became angry

But she couldn't get it down.
When she saw that dawn had broken
Then she said this,
"Humph, I didn't want to eat that papaya in the first place.
It isn't ripe."

(Kim de Bolles 1972; Edmonson's translation)

The economy of this adaptation of Aesop's "Fox and the Grapes" is characteristically Maya. So is the poetry.

Another possible grouping of tales is the "John" (*Juan*) stories: "John Bear" (*Juan Oso*) (Poot Yah n.d.), "John of the Bush" (*Juan del Monte*) (Anon. 1953), and "John Lazybones" (*Juan Makol*) (Kim de Bolles 1972).

Yet another is pun stories: "Beefsteak" (*Bizcep*) and "Rat's Eye Beans" (*Ppichi Ichi Chho*) (Kim de Bolles 1972).

A quite different genre could be classified as legends, fragments of the older mythological tradition. These are relics of the myths of the ancient gods and goddesses:

Demon (*Xib Babaal*) (Kim de Bolles 1972)
Demons (*Los Aluxes*) (Smailus 1975)
Earth Man (Andrade 1971b)
Enchantress (*X'tabay*) (Cornyn 1932b)
Feathered Serpent (*Kukum Can*) (Poot Yah n.d.)
How the Xtabay Deceives (*Bix u Tabzah Xtabay*) (Anon. 1939c)
Rainbow Goddess (*Ixcit Cheel*) (Cornyn 1932a)
Seven Heads (Smailus 1975)
Xtabay and Xtabentun (*Xtabay iix Xtabentun*) (Anon. 1939b)

They tend to be quite fragmentary, but their evocation of preconquest tradition is unmistakable.

The remaining tales will have to be classified as miscellaneous. Their themes are correspondingly varied:

Chicle Workers (Smailus 1975)
Child Hunter (Andrade 1971b)
Child Who Didn't Want to Work (Andrade 1971b)
Deer Hunting (Smailus 1975)

Gachupín (Smailus 1975)
Hunchbacks (Burns 1983)
Hunter (Legters 1937; Romero Castillo 1965; Andrade 1971b)
Judge (Smailus 1975)
"Kid" the Hunter (Andrade 1971b)
King and the Bandit (Andrade 1971b)
King and the Three Brothers (Andrade 1971b)
Little Green Fruit (Cab Baz 1950)
Looking for Rubber (Smailus 1975)
Lost Brothers (Smailus 1975)
Lost Family (Smailus 1975)
Magic Table (Smailus 1975)
Magistrate Casserole (Andrade 1971b)
Man Who Finished Eight Quail (Kim de Bolles 1972)
Man with the Little Penis (Andrade 1971b)
Medicine for the King's Eyes (Smailus 1975)
Nazario (Andrade 1971b)
(Ni)colás (Burns 1983)
Owners of Rain (Burns 1983)
Palm Sprout (Souza Novelo 1947)
Poor Charcoal Maker (Andrade 1971b)
Poor Man (Andrade 1971b)
Rosary (Kim de Bolles 1972)
Seven Colors (Andrade 1971b)
Seven Rays of the Sun (Andrade 1971b)
She Didn't Grind My Posole (Kim de Bolles 1972)
Three Working Brothers (Andrade 1971b)
Two Jumps (Erosa y Sierra 1941)
What a Whiteskin Thought and How a Peasant Paid his Debt (Anon. 1939a)
Wife Who Sold Her Pig (Kim de Bolles 1972)
Work in the Fields (Andrade 1971b)

Additional tales are to be found in the works of Margaret Park Redfield (1935) and Allan F. Burns (1983), but without the native texts. The tales published by Alejandra Kim de Bolles (1972) are in Mayan text only.

6.2.1.2. HISTORICAL NARRATIVE. Quite separate from the folk tale tradition are the historical narratives. These include the *History of San Antonio* from Belize (Smailus 1975), *How the War of the Castes Began* and *The Talking Cross* from Quintana Roo (ibid.), and *The History of Chan Kom* (Andrade 1971b) and *The Defense of Huhi* (Bricker 1979c) from Yucatan. We have made only a bare beginning on the oral history of the Maya.

6.2.1.3. PROVERBS. There was a time when it was alleged that the Maya had no proverbs. They do. They are called *putzil t'an* 'measured words' (Barrera Vásquez 1980). Eleuterio Poot Yah (n.d.) has 244 of them, 58 of them original. The remainder appear to be traditional Maya, but of course reflect acculturation. A sampling will give the flavor:

Yan takine, tac zinic cu yokot.
If there is money, even the ant will dance.

Tac peke, yan u yum.
Even a dog has a father.

Le max ma tan u y ite, ma u baxal.
He who doesn't have the ass for it shouldn't gamble. [Don't gamble if you're not strong enough to lose.]

Pochile, ma tu cachic bac.
Insults don't break bones.

Chinu p' aane, ma tu y ocol xyaaxcachi.
En boca cerrada no entran moscas: Silence is golden.

Man hun tule, bey he u man u lake.
If one happens, another can happen the same way.

The couplet construction of Mayan riddles is indicated by commas; the author's orthography has been converted to the Colonial system. Additional riddles are quoted by Robert Redfield and Alfonso Villa Rojas (1934) and by Margaret Redfield (1935).

6.2.1.4. LYRIC POETRY. Twentieth-century lyric poetry includes prayers, songs, and non-musical poetic inventions, not only in Yucatec, but in the Mopan, Itza, and Lacandon dialects as well (see section 8.1). A list of these is given here. Some of them have been published, particularly in *Yikal Maya Than* (The Spirit of the Mayan Tongue), a journal published in Merida since 1939. A sample follows:

Bee (Kim de Bolles 1972)
Bull Song (Poot Yah n.d.)
Dream of Chichen (Rosado Vega 1929)
I Plead for Death (Poot Yah n.d.)
Little Bird (Poot Yah n.d.)
Mayan Tongue, You Are My Life (Poot Yah n.d.)
Night, Let Me Be (Poot Yah n.d.)
Prayer (Chimay 1925)
Prayer to the Bitter Wind (Pacheco Cruz 1938)
Song of the Mayab (Vivas 1925)
Spoiled Armadillo (Kim de Bolles 1972)
Sweet Is the Mayan Tongue to Me (Poot Yah n.d.)
To Isadora (Rejón García 1926)
Tulane (Poot Yah n.d.)

For additional prayers see Redfield and Villa Rojas (1934); Alfred M. Tozzer (1907); J. Eric S. Thompson (1930); and Ramón Arzápalo (1970).

6.2.1.5. DRAMA. Two texts have been preserved that give us a direct view of twentieth-century Mayan drama. This is in abrupt contrast to the situation in Quiche, which provides many more. The two are *Beautiful Skin* (*Hadzutz Othel Xoc*) (Pacheco Cruz n.d. [1938?]), a farce, and the *Rainmaking Ceremony* (*Ch'a Chaac* or *Tzikul T'an Ti Yuntzilob*) (Arzápalo 1970; includes disc recording). A number of others are known to exist, but have not been recorded. They include: *Breaking* (*X Pa' Pul*), *Burden* (*Cuch*), *Carnival*, *Field Feeding* (*Uhanli Col*), *First Fruits* (*Hol Che*), *Hammock* (*Kaan*), *Head Delivery* (*Kub P'ol*), *Housewarming* (*Ch'uyenil Na*), *Mead* (*Balche*), *Quenching Fire* (*Tup' Kak*), and *Seating Embrace* (*Hetz' Mek*). All of these are ceremonies, and they are certainly only a fraction of the ritual that has survived, much of it reflecting ancient tradition.

6.2.2. PROSPECTS. The establishment of *indigenismo* in the Mexico of the 1930's had a considerable impact on many of the native literatures, encouraging the composition, collection, and publication of works in the native languages. In Yucatan this is particularly associated with the founding of *Yikal Maya Than* (Spirit of the Mayan Tongue) in 1939. The effect, however, proved to be ephemeral, and there is neither a demand nor a vehicle for Mayan literary expression today.

Native literacy continues to the present time. In Tixcacal, Quintana Roo, the *Books of Chilam Balam* are still read aloud on ceremonial occasions, and they are read and studied in other towns of the region as well (Luxton 1978). Even in Merida there are considerable numbers of literate Mayas. In Mayan villages in the hinterland of Valladolid, in the center of the peninsula, schools supported by the state government of Yucatan teach basic literacy in Maya; commercials in Maya can be heard on the radio; and the itinerant Catholic priest delivers his sermons in Maya. Nevertheless, continued expansion of education in Spanish must inevitably erode the vitality of Maya, and its literary future is not bright.

7. GENRES OF YUCATECAN LITERATURE. There is no word for literature in general in Yucatecan Maya. Perhaps the nearest thing to it is *t'an* 'word, speech, language'. It may be differentiated into written and oral: *tz'ib* 'write, paint', *uooh* 'write, paint, letter, hieroglyphic', or *coh* 'write, letter', and *tah* 'speech, word'. The genre distinctions drawn below are all documentable from the dictionaries of the sixteenth century (Barrera Vásquez 1980).

7.1. WRITTEN LITERATURE. The inscribed monuments of the Classic period were apparently referred to as *natabal* 'memorials'. The codices were called *huun* 'book, paper'. These were further specified by form and content: *eteb huun* 'handbook', *pic huun* 'manuscript', *haklahil huun* 'memorial book', *tataah* 'scripture', *uuc tz'acab huun* 'seven step book'. The preconquest Maya did not have land titles but they may have had maps for a similar purpose. If so, none have survived, a surprising fact in comparison with the Aztecs.

After the conquest a number of things came to be written down which were largely oral in previous times, including letters and land documents, drama, poetry, narratives, and speeches. There may be some continuity with hieroglyphic tradition in the chronicles (*kahlay* 'memorial'), prophecy (*bobatil*), and works of divination (*tzol kin* 'count of days'), calendrics (*poop*), and astronomy (*u cambalil ekob*).

7.2. ORAL LITERATURE. There appears to be no general distinction in Maya between poetry and prose, nor between fiction and nonfiction. Perhaps the most general categories of literature are speeches (*chich*), dances (*okot*), stories (*can*), songs (*kay*), and accounts (*tzol* 'order').

The greatest emphasis in oratory is on sermons (*tzec, kaay*), which are usually prophetic and apocalyptic. Although it has been erroneously claimed that the American Indians generally lacked riddles (*naatal naat*) and proverbs (*putzil can, pizan t'an*), the Maya have both, and give riddles a prominent place in ritual.

The Maya do not appear to have a word for drama in general nor a distinction between comedy and tragedy. They do have dances (*okot*), both sacred and profane, though they don't make that distinction either. They do distinguish farce (*baltz'am, taach, taah*) from ritual drama (*tzol* 'order'), but since the former is part of the latter, the distinction is somewhat blurred.

There are various kinds of stories (*can*): tales (*ik*), legends (*uuch t'an*), origin stories (*can siyan*), and memorials (*kahlay*), the latter being both mythical and historical. Examples of all of these have been cited. Mayan written works rarely bear titles and even more rarely designate the class of literature to which a given work belongs. Classification of and titling of particular works or classes of works have been pretty much at the whim of the translators, with a great deal of consequent confusion.

Maya distinguishes vocal (*cal*) from instrumental (*pax*) music, but it is rarely clear whether a song (*kay*) was actually sung or merely recited. The word for poem (*ikat*) suggests that perhaps the distinction was made, but one never encounters a poem so labeled. Poems of praise (*tich'*) are also distinguished, as are prayers (*okotba*, *pay chi*).

The Maya word *tzol* 'order' may refer to a number of what appear initially to be disparate kinds of literature. It defines the divining calendar (*tzol kin*) and the works of divination based upon it. It defines ritual drama because that too is based upon the calendar. It also refers to a count or account of events, here too as an extrapolation of the Mayan concept of order and of the role of the calendar in it. The Mayan concept of history is a memorial (*kahlay*) that puts events in calendrical order, as in the *Kahlay Katunob*, the *Account of the Katuns*. They called Yucatan the "ordered country" (*tzolan peten*). Order is both the central feature and the central genre of Mayan literature.

7.2.1. LITERARY DEVICES. Maya makes considerable use of the rhetorical devices to be found in the Classical and even modern cultures of the Old World, certainly including alliteration, repetition, reversal of normal word order, antithesis, apostrophe, hyperbole, understatement, puns, personification, simile, satire, pars pro toto, rhetorical question, metonymy, euphemism, baby talk, chiasmus, and metaphor (cf. Fowler 1926: 597–627).

Its poetic devices are more restricted. Metric verse does not occur at all, nor does rhyme nor assonance nor regularity of stress or tone. Stanzaic poetry appears to have been a late diffusion from Spanish.

Mayan dramatic devices appear to have been extensive. Ritual dramas were divided into rigidly and numerologically defined acts, always recurring in the same order albeit varying in content to some degree. They were declaimed with elaborate costumes and masks to the accompaniment of vocal and instrumental music, feasting, drinking, games, and dancing. Although parts of the ceremony may have been chanted in unison, the use of choral narration as in Japanese or Greek drama does not appear. Farces and historical dramas were incorporated into these elaborate ceremonials, as well as sacrifices of incense, flowers, food, animals, and people, ceremonial parades, and the ceremonious seating of the lords and priests.

It will be obvious that a number of features of Mayan drama were unique to Middle America, if not to Yucatan itself. In the account that follows we shall concentrate on the literary devices that appear to be characteristic of Mayan, or perhaps Middle American literary expression.

7.2.2. POETRY. Perhaps the most distinctive quality of Mayan literature is that it is all poetry. If there is a distinction in Maya between poetry and prose, it would have to be made between formal and informal speech—a continuum on which Maya gives very short shrift to informality. Informal speech is almost never written, at least by Mayas. It has rarely been recorded even by outsiders.

Any degree of formalization of Mayan speech immediately indicates the use of at least rudimentary poetry. There is a continuum of formalization, but the basis of it is the semantic couplet, and virtually all of Mayan literature is cast in this form. In addition, there is increasing use of metaphor and kennings as the language becomes increasingly formal, and hence increasingly poetic.

7.2.2.1. COUPLET PARALLELISM. All of the quotations of Mayan literature cited above are given in parallelistic couplets; hence additional examples will not be cited here. The principle of this form is entirely semantic. Any two sequential lines should repeat the same idea in synonyms or antonyms. The more tightly they do so, the more formal the style. Sometimes the parallelism is syntactical, and occasionally therefore the same suffixes may terminate the lines, resulting in actual sound correspondence or identity, but that does not appear to be required or even necessarily desirable. It is the matching of meanings that matters.

Couplet parallelism is ubiquitous in the native literatures of Middle and South America. It is rare to nonexistent in native North America, though it also occurs elsewhere, in

Oceania and the ancient Near East, for example. It is the defining characteristic of formal style among the Maya (see Edmonson in press: Introduction).

Repetition by couplets produces a redundancy that often becomes reduced to the level of clichés, in which the original poetic force is lost. On the other hand, the very formal contexts in which they are employed may lend such expressions an additional and esoteric semantic force, endowing the coupled concepts with a third and dialectically derivative meaning. These may conveniently be called kennings.

7.2.2.2. KENNINGS. Kennings, or *difrasismos* 'disguise diphrases', are a specific feature of Nahuatl poetry and may in fact be a Nahua influence on Mayan poetry, Quiche and Tzotzil as well as Yucatecan. They differ from Norse kennings in being tied to couplets. They have not been documented in other Mayan literatures, but they may well occur. In Yucatec they are frequent, especially it would appear in very formal and very traditional texts. Most of them are culturally opaque and they are probably intentionally esoteric. As examples we offer: "rope and cord" means "war"; "throne and mat" means "power"; "cup and plate" means "food," and hence, derivatively, the fate of a time period; "sun and moon" means "beginning and end," and hence eternity, all time; "heaven and earth" is "up and down" and thus all space. Multiple additional examples are listed in Edmonson in press: Index.

7.2.2.3. METAPHOR. Mayan literature is richly decorated with metaphors independent of couplet repetition, many of them also esoteric. Contextually bound, they cannot easily be plumbed for their various levels of resonance. Many Mayan words have numerous homonyms, and sound alone may furnish the basis of extended meanings. But the Maya are very fond of puns, and the sound rules for their formation are not very strict, thus furnishing additional possible extensions. It is possible to demonstrate from specific contexts, for example, that red, east, strong, rain, god, first, birth, giant, direc-

tion, order, trample, cook, dawn, and appearance are associated meanings in Maya, even though a number of them are phonemically distinct. The long tradition of glyphic literacy could add still others, since ideas may resemble each other in logographic writing even when their pronunciation is totally different.

But Mayan metaphor is principally formed as elsewhere by contextual association dictated by Mayan cultural configurations. The central role of the calendar in Mayan culture provides a case, and calendrical metaphors are peculiarly broad, rich, and evocative. Time itself is a good example. Time is a man (with women), on a road, seated, or only temporarily resting, a trip with a burden, a simultaneous beginning and end, a sun, a day, heat, life, power, wounding, fate. Time, in fact, is the ultimate Mayan metaphor. Going and coming, life and death, ruling and obeying, duty and dishonor are all governed by time. The strong implication is that metaphorically time is life and vice versa, but a simple textual demonstration of this assertion is not available.

7.2.3. DRAMA. The primary context of Mayan drama is ceremonial. Fragments of the ancient dramas still survive in modern rituals, and in one case we have the text called *Tsikul T'an Ti' Yuntsiloob* (*Reverent Message to the Lords*) (Arzápalo 1970), which is a version of the widely performed *Ch'a Chaac* ceremony and corresponds to Act 7 of the *Ceremonial of the Baktun*. Mayan ceremonies were stately and carefully timed. It is likely that the *baktun* ceremonial took twenty days. The New Year ceremony took ten. The *Reverent Message to the Lords* at Balankanche cave in 1959 lasted from dawn on Saturday to dawn on Monday.

8. STYLE. Style is largely a matter of society and language. We shall take society first.

8.1. SOCIETY AND STYLE. Mayan society was and is strongly hierarchical. The subordination of younger to older, female to male, descendant to ancestor, uninitiated to initiated, poor to rich, governed to governors, lower to upper class verged on the absolute, and was projected in mythology, cosmology and calendrics, history, drama, and poetry. Mayan literature like Mayan life was governed by the numbers that govern time, and its predominant tone is formal, restrained, rigid, ceremonious, terse, esoteric, and fatalistic.

But there is certainly a variety of styles. There is no confusing the bleak opacity of the prophets, the scatological invective of the clowns, the sprightly humor of children's tales, the lyricism of lovers, the formulaic elegance of the priests. While it was primarily the latter who were responsible for the preservation of Mayan literary tradition, enough else has survived to legitimate the supposition that every institution of this complex society has contributed to stylistic variation— not only social, but ethnic, geographic, and temporal as well. Such variation is manifested in the language itself.

Perhaps the greatest variation within Yucatec relates to the differentiation of dialects, which is maximal in the cases of Itza, Mopan, and Lacandon. See, for example, Matthew and Rosemary Ulrich (1966) and J. E. S. Thompson (1930) on Mopan; Alfred M. Tozzer (1907), Roberto D. Bruce S. (1968; 1974; 1976), and Virginia Dale Davis (1978; 1979) on Lacandon; Otto Schumann G. (1971) on Itza.

Itza is only slightly differentiated from Yucatec. Here is the beginning of a Peten folk tale, "Once There Was a Child":

Yanaji jump'eel kin	Once upon a time there was
Juntuul mo'noc paal;	A small boy
Ma' yool u yubi t'ön u na'	Who wouldn't obey what his mother ordered.
Tu ya'la ti'i	She said to him:
Ma' a bel ti'	Don't go over
Yok a kuume;	And sit on that squash.

(Schumann 1971:57; Edmonson's translation and scansion)

Itza says *mo'noc* 'small' where Yucatec would say *chan*.

Mopan is more divergent. The following is the start of a tale about "The Man with Two Children":

Jun tu·l b'in winic	There was a man
Yan b'in u mejen ca' tu·l	Who had two children.
Pues ca' tu·lo·' u mejen yan.	So he had two children,
Pero c'u' b'etiqui a winiqui.	But what was he going to do?
Tz'i·c tu mejen,	He was angry at his children.
Jun tu·l ix ch'up	One was a girl
Y jun tu·l aj tz'i'	And one a boy,
Xidal u mejen.	His male child.
Pues te'i.	So it was.

(Ulrich and Ulrich 1966:379–380; Edmonson's translation and scansion)

Mopan has *xidal* 'male' where Yucatec, which has no *d*, says *xibal*.

Lacandon is more divergent still. Here is a fragment from a reportedly ancient Lacandon song celebrating the origin of the Rain People, the Ba'arkab (Yucatecan Ba Cab), who were generated by a typically Mayan pun: *ma¢* is 'semen, posole'.

Ma' na' in k'at
  Ten učeh wayǝh biren bentički'
Eh a'abih sur ma¢ in tar bentički'
  He sur ma¢eh bentički'
Eh ma' na' in k'at ne'
  Učeh ma' na' in k'at

I do not want a mother.
  Long ago I existed here as an orphan.
Eh, I came from a small gourd of posol.
  A small gourd of posol orphaned me.
Eh, I do not want a mother.
  Very long ago I did not want a mother.

(Davis 1979:24–26)

Many centuries of linguistic divergence separate Lacandon from Yucatec proper, but the two dialects remain by and large mutually intelligible, and their traditions are also clearly cognate. They are also differentiated. Lacandon Ba Cabs, for example, are not associated with the directions (Davis 1979:23–26).

Changes in Yucatecan tradition over time can be traced not only in vocabulary and the loss or addition of particular ideas, but in syntax as well.

8.2. SYNTAX AND STYLE. Several syntactic devices besides parallelism (see section 7.2.2.1 above) are common in Mayan literature. Normal, unmarked word order in Yucatec Maya is verb-object-subject (VOS) in transitive clauses and verb-subject (VS) in intransitive clauses. These word orders are frequently inverted in Mayan literature, through clefting. Temporal adverbs normally follow verbs in Yucatec Maya, but temporal focus constructions, a characteristic of hieroglyphic texts, were abundant in Colonial Yucatecan literature. They became less frequent after 1800, when the traditional calendar lost its importance.

8.2.1. CLEFTING. Two kinds of cleft sentences appear in Mayan literature. In subject-focus constructions (SVO or SV), the subject is moved to the beginning of the sentence, before the verb, as in the following example from the *Book of Chilam Balam of Chumayel* (Gordon 1913:17):

Ah Kin Caamal likul Campech
Ah Kin Caamal from Campeche

Subject

oces   ɔulob   vay ti peten   lae
admitted foreigners here in country this

Verb   Object

'It was Ah Kin Caamal from Campeche who admitted [the] foreigners here in this country.'

The normal word order of this sentence would have been:

t-uy-oces-ah   *ɔulob*
past-he-admit-past   foreigners

Verb   Object

Ah Kin Caamal   *likul*   *Campech*
Ah Kin Caamal   from   Campeche

Subject

vay ti peten   lae
here in country this

'Ah Kin Caamal from Campeche admitted [the] foreigners here in this country.'

These constructions differ not only in syntax, but also in morphology. The verb in the focused example (*oces*) appears without affixes, whereas it is accompanied by a pronominal prefix (*uy-*) and a tense/aspect prefix (*t-*) and suffix (*-ah*) in the "normal" example (*t-uy-oces-ah*).

In object-focus constructions (OVS or OV), the object precedes the verb. The following example comes from a petition by Diego Pox of Dzaan in 1587 (*Documents of Tabi*:fol. 33):

yan   ix   u-pax   in-yum
exists and his-debt my-father

Object

in-bot-ah   tin-hunal xan
I-pay-past   I-alone   also

Verb   Subject

'And there is my father's debt that only I paid also.'

The morphology of the verb in this example does not change, even when the object follows the verb. The Dzaan document contains a rephrasing of this statement with SVO order:

yokal   tin-hunal   in-bot-ah
because I-alone   I-pay-past

Subject   Verb

u-pax   in-yume
his-debt my-father

Object

'because it is only I who paid my father's debt'

The verb, in both cases, is *in-bot-ah*.

In general, verbs in subject-focus constructions lack pronominal prefixes. If, however, either the subject or the object is in the first or second person, as is the case in the second Dzaan example, then the deletion of the pronominal prefix is optional. The presence or absence of pronominal prefixes functions as a marking device for disambiguating subject-focus from object-focus constructions when both the subject and the object are in the third person.

8.2.2. TEMPORAL FOCUS. The syntax of dated constructions links Classical Yucatecan literature to the hieroglyphic inscriptions of the Classic period. Clauses in both types of texts were introduced by dates or distance numbers. The verb appeared next, followed by the object (if there was one) and the subject. This is not a "normal" word order in Yucatec Maya, and its unusual status is reflected in verb morphology.

Perfective intransitive verbs were marked by an *-i* suffix in Classical Yucatec. In dated constructions, however, they also took an *-ic* suffix (which was often represented as *-c* when followed by *-i*). The following example comes from the third chronicle of the *Book of Chilam Balam of Chumayel* (Gordon 1913:79):

Hoo ahau pax-c-i   u-cab
5   Ahau was-destroyed his-land

y-ahau ah-ytzamal
his-lord the-Izamal
'[In] 5 Ahau the land of the lord of the Izamals was destroyed.'

If the date were omitted, or moved to the end of the sentence, the verb would be *pax-i* instead of *pax-c-i*. The same chronicle contains an example of the same verb without a date (ibid.: 80):

ma pax-i   peten   tumenel-ob-i
not was-destroyed country by-them-enclitic
'[The] country was not destroyed by them.'

The intransitive perfective suffix (*-i*) was often omitted in texts of post-sixteenth-century date. Whenever that suffix was missing from intransitive verbs in dated constructions, the *-ic* suffix was represented fully:

Mil   quinientos   diez y Nuebe
one thousand five hundred nineteen
años kuch-ic
years arrived
'[In] 1519 he arrived.'

This example from the *Book of Chilam Balam of Chumayel* (Gordon 1913:17) is immediately followed by a distance number and an intransitive verb:

Vuc   kal   hab catac buluc pis
seven twenty year and   eleven measured
habi uch-c-i   consierto y   ɔulob
year occurred treaty   with foreigners
'[In] 140 years plus eleven years [the] treaty with [the] foreigners occurred.'

Sentences introduced by dates or distance numbers are focused constructions. Temporal expressions normally follow verbs in Yucatec Maya. The historical passages in the *Books of Chilam Balam* of *Chumayel*, *Tizimin*, and *Mani* contain numerous examples of temporal focusing.

9. CONCLUSION. Mayan literature is attracting increasing attention from a growing body of scholars. We have come a long way since John L. Stephens published the first translation from the Mayan *Chronicles* in 1843. Linguistics, archaeology, epigraphy, art history, ethnography, history and ethnohistory, musicology, and literature continue to broaden and deepen our grasp of the culture and traditions of this complex and sophisticated people who built and to a remarkable degree preserved in their literature the highest civilization of ancient America.

4. Tzotzil Literature

〓〓〓〓〓〓〓〓〓〓〓〓〓〓〓〓〓〓〓〓〓〓〓〓〓〓〓〓〓〓〓〓〓〓〓〓〓〓

GARY H. GOSSEN

1. FORETHOUGHTS. What is a literature? The term becomes feeble when one tries to apply it to nonliterate oral traditions. For literate traditions, the term carries some evaluative nuance; literature contains exemplary works of recognized genres: short story, poetry, essay, and so forth. For oral traditions, the task of considering them as literatures becomes enormously more difficult, for while there may be a native view of what counts as a native genre in the tradition, it is ultimately up to those of us who care to take them seriously as literatures to classify culturally significant genres and provide good examples of them. One cannot provide the woodsmoke and laughter or adequately transcribe the delight which listeners find in a well-turned sexual pun. Nor can one reproduce the complex cadence of spoken Tzotzil in the silent fog on a muddy mountain path as an old man tells you of his father's encounter with an earth lord. Much, therefore, is lost in sketching an oral tradition whose very life is ephemeral, highly variable, and always linked to a particular performance context which will never again be quite the same.

Given these limitations, what follows is a halting history and translation, several times removed, of a vital and complex oral tradition. It is a vital tradition because Tzotzil speakers number more than 200,000 at present. This places Tzotzil at sixth rank among the thirty Maya languages in terms of the number of native speakers. It also places it about seventh in rank among the surviving native languages of Mexico. Tzotzil is widely spoken in twenty-four semiautonomous communities, twenty of which have *municipio* (township) status. It is the principal language in thirteen *municipios*: El Bosque, Chalchihuitan, Chamula, Chenalho, Huistan, Huituipan, Jitotol, Larrainzar, Mitontic, Pantelho, Simojovel de Allende, Totolapa, and Zinacantan. In these towns, more than half of the population are monolingual speakers of Tzotzil, and civil and religious affairs are conducted primarily in Tzotzil. In the other seven *municipios*, Tzotzil speakers are a significant minority: Bochil, Iztapa, Pueblo Nuevo Solistahuacan, Soyalo, Teopisca, Venustiano Carranza (traditionally San Bartolome), and El Zapotal (traditionally San Lucas). In these towns, official public life is

64

mostly conducted in Spanish by the majority Ladino (Spanish-speaking) population; Tzotzil-speakers of course use their language in their own subculture, including domestic life, curing rituals, and other religious observances. In still another group of communities, which do not have *municipio* status, Tzotzil is widely spoken and is important in varying degrees in public life. These are San Felipe Ecatepec (now a *barrio* of San Cristobal de las Casas), Magdalenas and Santiago (pertaining administratively to Larrainzar), and Santa Marta (pertaining to Chenalho). In addition, small Tzotzil-speaking colonies are found in thirty other *municipios* of the state of Chiapas.

In all Tzotzil-speaking communities there is also some knowledge of Spanish. Knowledge of minimal Spanish is an ever-increasing economic necessity for thousands of Tzotzil men who work as laborers in lowland coffee plantations for several months a year. Spanish is also, of course, the required language of communication with state and national political authorities. The pragmatic reasons for learning some Spanish appear to be far more compelling to native Tzotzil speakers than the abstract goals of "national integration," which the Mexican government has pushed as its rationale for teaching Spanish in Indian primary schools. In some cases, such as those Tzotzil communities found in Bochil and Pueblo Nuevo Solistahuacan, there is widespread bilingualism in Spanish and Tzotzil. In others, such as Chalchihuitan, Pantelho, and Chamula, the vast majority of the population is monolingual in Tzotzil. In general, knowledge of Spanish is greatest among young and middle-aged men, least among middle-aged and older women. For women, a minimal market vocabulary is typical.

Tzotzil oral tradition can be called vital for still another reason: speaking well is highly regarded as a key trait of an accomplished adult; it may be the single most important qualification for leadership and public service. From formal prayer which clients must intone with shamans in household curing ceremonies, to formal orations delivered by the chief magistrate (*presidente municipal*) at fiestas before thousands of listeners, Tzotzil adults—particularly men, because they dominate public life and are formal heads of households—live in what might be called a verbally demanding environment. The primacy of language in the Tzotzil value system can be easily picked up in the vocabulary and narrative traditions. For example, *baȼ'i k'op*, the Tzotzil word for 'Tzotzil', means 'true, right, most representative, or genuine language'. Furthermore, the giving of *k'op* by the creator deity was the key event which turned clay and stick images into humans in Tzotzil accounts of the past. It was also because of failure to use language properly for communication with and homage to the deities that humanity was destroyed by the creator in Chamula accounts of the rise and fall of earlier periods of human history. Moreover, the teaching of new languages and creeds serves as a harbinger of political upheaval and war, as these events are remembered in Tzotzil oral history. Thus, it is fair to say that Tzotzil oral tradition is vital not only because of the very considerable numbers of monolingual Tzotzil speakers, but also because they themselves view their 'true language' and accomplished use of it as central to the human condition.

I have also said that Tzotzil literature is complex. The first reason for this is that twenty-four different semiautonomous communities reckon the past, pass on knowledge, and conduct their domestic, civic, and religious affairs in as many different dialects and subdialects of the language. Some larger Tzotzil communities, such as Chamula, have at least two different subdialects complete with characteristic differences in phonology, vocabulary, and syntax. The second reason for the complexity of Tzotzil literature is that it has a tendency to split into a staggering array of subtypes, whether these are called genres or characteristic styles of speech. Charles Frake has observed that native classification schemes tend to split into semantic domains most vigorously in areas which have a broad array of different use contexts (Frake

1961). About the only sphere of Tzotzil life which would compete with language in this regard is corn and corn farming. Thus, it is a sobering task to try to summarize a part of Tzotzil life which Tzotzils themselves regard as so important and which nevertheless exhibits such complexity and variation.

The premodern history of Tzotzil literature is not a long one; its key works are few. Furthermore, the major collections of contemporary Tzotzil oral tradition date from around 1960 and come from only two communities, San Lorenzo Zinacantan and San Juan Chamula. Good but scattered data are also available from San Andres Larrainzar, San Pedro Chenalho, San Pablo Chalchihuitan, Huixtan, and San Bartolome. Finally, my own experience has been in only one of these communities, San Juan Chamula. These facts dictate the structure, content, and limits of this essay.

1.1. NOTE ON ORTHOGRAPHY. Tzotzil orthography has not been standardized. There are two common modern notations: (1) is closer to the conventions of the International Phonetic Alphabet; (2) acquiesces to the realities of available typeface and broader intelligibility, and is also closer to the orthography used in older Tzotzil/Spanish–Spanish/Tzotzil manuscripts. Equivalences of potentially ambiguous letters and sounds are generally as follows. Some manuscripts and published texts use a combination of parts of both orthographies.

(1)	(2)
ʔ (glottal stop) as in ʔon 'avocado'	= 7 or ' as in 7on or 'on
h as in hmeʔ 'my mother'	= j as in jme7
š (sh) as in ši 'he or she said'	= x as in xi
č as in čiʔ 'sweet'	= ch as in chi7
č' as in ʔič' 'chile'	= ch' as in 7ich'
¢ as in ¢eb 'girl'	= tz or ts as in tseb or tzeb
¢' as in ¢'iʔ 'dog'	= tz' or ts' as in tz'i7 or ts'i7
k as in k'an 'to want'	= c as in c'an

b (glottalized) as in   = m as in nam
nab 'sea'

2. HISTORY.

2.1. BEFORE 1940. Research in the history of the Maya family of languages traces the roots of Tzotzil to the beginning of diversification of Proto-Mayan at around 2200 B.C. The center of this divergence was probably the northwestern highlands of Guatemala. Several major out-migrations, yielding first the Huastecs, then the Yucatecs, seem to have preceded that of 1000–500 B.C., the period at which the Western Mayas moved north into the jungles of Chiapas. This Western Maya exodus included the Cholans and probably the Tzotzilans. The Tzotzilans split off from the Cholans at around 100 B.C. By around A.D. 700 the Chiapas highland groups were split into the Tzotzils and Tzeltals, who to this day share this mountainous habitat (Laughlin 1975:2; Kaufman 1970).

No Precolumbian Tzotzil document has been discovered, nor is there any evidence that Tzotzil was a written language before the conquest. There were apparently some Colonial documents giving native accounts in Tzotzil of the conquest and its aftermath as well as some letters sent by Tzotzils to the Spanish Crown. None of these survives. The earliest major document written in Tzotzil was a dictionary, *Diccionario en lengua sotzil*, compiled by an anonymous lexicographer in the sixteenth century. This is also known as the *Diccionario grande*. The original manuscript survived until the early twentieth century, at which time it was copied under the direction of the great scholar Francisco Orozco y Jiménez, Bishop of Chiapas from 1902 to 1912. The copy was dispatched from San Cristobal shortly before the revolutionary troops reached the town; the original was not seen thereafter. It was apparently destroyed when Carranza's cavalry stabled their horses in the bishop's library in 1915. Orozco y Jiménez' copy of this important document found its way to the Rare Book Collection at the Princeton University Library. This dictionary represents a massive undertaking, containing over 350 pages of Spanish-Tzotzil.

66

It will surely be of great value to future scholars who wish to explore the modern history of Tzotzil language and literature. It is of particular importance as a tool for exploring the structure of Tzotzil formal couplets, for these poetic formulas show the tendency to juxtapose archaic and modern words as synonyms in consecutive lines of couplets. Modern Tzotzil speakers sometimes have difficulty explaining or translating the archaic members of these word pairs. A sense of earlier usage of course also clarifies ritual language.

Another major sixteenth-century document was Francisco de Zepeda's *Artes de los idiomas chiapaneco, zoque, tzendal y chinanteco* (1560); it too has disappeared. Somewhat later appeared the *Arte de la lengua tzotzlem o zinacanteca* (1688), compiled by Juan de Rodaz. This work is still extant, and consists of a thorough grammar and description of the calendar. In 1732 Dionycio Pereyra built upon this work, adding material on kin terms, body parts, and conversational examples, the latter of interest for purposes of understanding the development of Tzotzil spoken style.

The major work of the eighteenth century was originally compiled by a cleric, Manuel Hidalgo. His manuscript (which apparently bore no title) consisted of a Spanish-Tzotzil vocabulary and a collection of sermons, prayers, and catechisms. The original has disappeared but apparently served as the basis of two subsequent anonymous publications, *Gramática del tzotzil* (1818) and *Libro en que se trata de la lengua tzotzil* (1832). Several other works seem to derive from Hidalgo's work (Charencey 1866; 1885; 1889; 1910; 1912; Sánchez 1895; Schuller 1925). Robert M. Laughlin (1975:2) and Antonio García de León (1971:13) believe that Hidalgo's work and its derivatives are based on Chamula material.

Following is a fragment from one of the sermons which appeared in the 1832 anonymous manuscript (*Libro en que se trata de la lengua tzotzil*) which draws on Hidalgo's work. Although this text was written by a cleric who was probably not a native Tzotzil speaker, it may nevertheless be the earliest extant text in the language. It deals with the difficult concept of the Christian soul.

(1)

ghalal nichnab
Dear children,

toghmelel zcotol viunic oy ztacupal
it is utterly certain that all men have their bodies

zchiuc yanima
and their souls.

ate tacupalzcham li ta balumil
The body dies here on the earth.

ate anima muxu slagh
The soul cannot die;

cuxul xcom tazbatel ozilcuxel
it remains alive through eternal life.

ate tacupal zetagh ta lum ta smuquenal
The body is committed to the earth, to the grave.

ate anima cuzi chalibil teyeh xbat
The soul detaches itself and departs.

muxu xil xloc calal xcham xlaghel vuinic
One cannot see it leave (the body) when a man dies and perishes.

muxlagh anima
The soul does not die.

> (García de León 1971:98–99; my translation)

Perhaps the major premodern document of direct relevance to the history of Tzotzil literature is the *Proclama del duque infantado presidente* (1812). This was copied under the auspices of Bishop Orozco y Jiménez in the early twentieth century and the original is now in the Princeton University Rare Book Collection. Laughlin describes its significance as follows:

In eloquent couplets the Tzotzil are exhorted to remain faithful to the King of

Spain and to spurn the advances of the "Whirlwind," the "horned serpent," the "jaguar," Napoleon! A small number of lapses suggest that the author was not a native speaker of Tzotzil, but rather a Spanish churchman. To this proclamation is appended explanatory notes of great sensitivity, as relevant to modern Tzotzil as to its colonial ancestor.

(Laughlin 1975:2)

Particularly noteworthy for comparison with modern Tzotzil texts is the formal rhetorical style, which has not changed significantly in nearly two centuries. The following excerpt (further exhortations against the threat of Napoleon) is from the original (1812):

(2)

Bu xtal cux leg cuuɲtic
Where is our happiness to come from

te me ja noox ta spu qu'ih
if he [Napoleon] does nothing more than to spread

chamebal
sickness,

hilbajinel
torment,

icti
anxiety,

huocol
difficulty,

malchun huaneg
bearers of false beliefs,

mean al
poverty,

huinal
hunger,

pogh vaneg
usurpers,

mil huaneg
murderers,

schiuc yantic pojou xulun chon
and other snake venoms

mu ilbiluc ta hom cuuntic
never seen before in our midst?

(*Proclama* 1812:36; my translation; from the Robert Garrett Collection of Manuscripts in the Indigenous Languages of Middle America, the Princeton University Library)

2.2. 1940 TO 1981. Although the Colonial and early Modern history of Tzotzil language and literature is scant, recent research has transformed Tzotzil into one of the better-known native languages and literatures of the hemisphere. The very recent character of research in Tzotzil literature can be readily observed in E. Michael Mendelson's and Munro S. Edmonson's 1967 summaries of Mesoamerican mythology and narrative folklore that appeared in the *Social Anthropology* volume of the *Handbook of Middle American Indians* (vol. 6). Together, they cite only three sources on Tzotzil folklore and mythology. J. Eric S. Thompson (1970:346−347) cites only two sources (Holland 1963 and Guiteras-Holmes 1961) in his survey of contemporary Maya mythology. Reasons for this relatively late development of interest in Tzotzil are several.

The Tzotzil-speaking area of the Chiapas Highlands was marginal to both Colonial and nineteenth-century economic development, a fact which encouraged the development of a distinctive insular cultural style with a great deal of intraregional community variation. The nineteenth-century development of commercial agriculture in Chiapas ironically encouraged both conservatism and worldliness in the highland Indian towns. A mosaic of semiautonomous conservative Indian *municipios* arose and survived into the mid-twentieth century. At about that time the Mexican government became actively interested in programs of national integration aiming at incorporating the isolated Indian populations into the mainstream of Mexican culture. The conservative Chiapas Highlands were an early focus for this policy. In 1950 the Instituto Nacional Indigenista founded the Centro Coordinador Tzotzil-Tzeltal in San Cristobal de las Casas. This center encouraged scientific study of the culture and language of the Indian communities, with an eye to initiating programs of planned cultural change, the teaching of Spanish, and the extension of Mexican government services to Indians. This climate of Mexican policy encouraged anthropological and linguistic research by Mexicans and foreigners. Research in the area was further facilitated by the construction of the Pan-American Highway through the highlands to the Guatemalan border in 1950. The area had previously been accessible only by an ox-road.

2.2.1. EARLY WORK. The first modern anthropological research in the area was Ruth Bunzel's work in Chamula in the 1930s (Bunzel 1940; 1959; 1960), followed by Sol Tax's (1944) research in Zinacantan, begun in 1942. This early work was fragmentary and did not contain detailed information on language and literature. However, two young Mexican scholars, Calixta Guiteras-Holmes and Ricardo Pozas Arciniegas, became major contributors to our knowledge of Chenalho (Guiteras-Holmes 1961) and Chamula (Pozas 1959). Guiteras-Holmes' *Perils of the Soul* (1961) became the first major monograph to describe (in admirable detail) the outlines of Tzotzil myth and religion. Although it contains texts only in translation and in composite form, it remains a classic source on Tzotzil thought and world view. Pozas' work (1959) is strong on Chamula economics and social organization, but considerably weaker on language, religion, mythology, and world view. William Holland's major monograph on Larrainzar (1963) and shorter papers (1961a; 1961b; 1965) contain detailed information on religion and cosmology with particular reference to comparisons with analogous concepts among the ancient Maya. He gives composite reports, but few full texts.

2.2.2. THE CHICAGO PROJECT. Several waves of international interest in the Tzotzil took the form of major long-term projects. The first of these was Norman A. McQuown's "Man-in-Nature" Tzotzil-Tzeltal Project, sponsored by the University of Chicago. This project produced a large quantity of anthropological and linguistic data, most of which remain unpublished. It is particularly strong on data from San Bartolome de los Llanos (Venustiano Carranza) and Chalchihuitan. Most of the manuscript material is now available on microfilm. This work and the overall goals of the Chicago project are discussed in McQuown 1959. Items of particular interest to Tzotzil language and literature in the Chicago project corpus are as follows: on San Bartolome de los Llanos (Venustiano Carranza), Bartolomé Hidalgo Sabanilla (1977a; 1977b), McQuown et al. (1977), Mariano Gómez Takiwah (1977); on Chalchihuitan, Nicholas A. Hopkins (1967; 1977b); on Zinacantan, Antonio López (Pérez) Tzintan (1976), Hopkins (1977a); on Chamula, *Textos de Chamula* (n.d.); on Iztapa, *Vocabulario tzotzil de Istapa* (n.d.).

2.2.3. THE SUMMER INSTITUTE OF LINGUISTICS. In 1939 the American Summer Institute of Linguistics (S.I.L.) began a major effort, supported by the Mexican government, to develop Tzotzil vocabulary lists, grammars, and some pedagogical materials. While the major goal of the S.I.L., a Protestant evangelical organization, was to translate the New Testament into several Tzotzil dialects, trained linguists with the Institute also began to collect Tzotzil narrative texts. The following is a list of their published work and Tzotzil manuscripts as of 1980: on Chamula, Marion M. Cowan (1975), Cowan and Kenneth Jacobs (1975), Jacobs (1960), Jacobs and Robert E. Longacre (1967); on Chenalho, Kenneth and Nadine Weathers (1949a), N. Weathers (1947b; 1950); on Huixtan, Cowan (1958b; 1960; 1961; 1967; 1968a; 1968b; 1969; 1970; 1972a; 1972b), Cowan and William R. Merrifield (1968; 1971), Pedro Pérez M. (1973); on Larrainzar, Cowan (1956; 1958a), Alfa Delgaty (1961), Colin C. Delgaty

(1953; 1956; 1961; 1964), Weathers and Weathers (1949c; 1951); on Zinacantan, Ethel E. Wallis (n.d.), Weathers and Weathers (1949b; 1951), N. Weathers (1947a; 1949; n.d.a; n.d.b).

A major Spanish-Tzotzil dictionary, with primary emphasis on Larrainzar dialect and secondary attention to Chamula, emerged from nearly thirty years of S.I.L. research in the area (A. Delgaty and Augustín Ruiz Sánchez 1978). S.I.L. work with Tzotzil texts has generally been of high technical linguistic quality; textual transcriptions are accurate, with proper attention to dialect variation, but the published texts contain virtually no background ethnographic information. Thus, S.I.L. materials are of limited value for understanding the role of language and literature in everyday life.

2.2.4. THE HARVARD PROJECT. In 1957 Evon Z. Vogt launched a long-term field program known as the Harvard Chiapas Project, with general emphasis on cultural change in the Tzotzil-speaking zone of Chiapas and with particular concentration on Zinacantan and, somewhat later, Chamula. This project, although funded from the beginning by U.S. granting agencies, also had from its inception the support of Mexican government agencies, in particular the Instituto Nacional Indigenista. It is fair to say that the Harvard project is primarily responsible for thrusting Tzotzil culture, language, and literature from relative obscurity to considerable prominence in the anthropological and linguistic record of Mesoamerican Indian communities. See Vogt's brief history and bibliography of the Chiapas project (Vogt 1978) for background on the design of the project and its methods, goals, publications, and unpublished papers. Because of the size of the project bibliography, I have selected items in it which are directly pertinent to Tzotzil language and literature.

One of the guiding principles of the Harvard project since its inception has been a firm commitment to use of Tzotzil rather than Spanish as the field language. This ideal was pursued with relative success, usually involving Tzotzil language training in Cam-

bridge before students went to conduct field work in Chiapas. In addition, several members of the project came to focus on the Tzotzil language itself, its technical character, art forms, and use in social context. This has led to the collection and publication of a large corpus of materials dealing with the language and literature.

The project has been fortunate in having an early and continuing interest in anthropological linguistics. Lore M. Colby's lexical (1960), phonological (1964), and morphological (1966) work paved the way for a series of works by others on the Tzotzil dialects of San Lorenzo Zinacantan and Chamula. Colby was followed in this area by Robert M. Laughlin, who began in 1958 to amass data for a series of major publications on Zinacanteco language and literature. Laughlin's pursuit of a comprehensive Tzotzil word list led to the publication in 1975 of his monumental *Great Tzotzil Dictionary of San Lorenzo Zinacantán*. Consisting of over 25,000 entries, this Tzotzil-English/English-Tzotzil dictionary must be reckoned among a handful of truly comprehensive dictionaries of native American languages. Its landmark significance lies not only in its exhaustive coverage, including place names and animal and plant names (together with Linnaean classification), but also in its sensitive incorporation of thousands of ethnographic notes on the use of the language in context. These notes range from performance data on obscure archaic words used only in ritual formulas to the particular use of wild plants in native technology. This dictionary, in its various stages of evolution from word slips to massive tome, has been the backbone of the Harvard project's field endeavors and will surely prove to be the foundation for future decades of research in Tzotzil ethnography, language, and literature.

Laughlin collected hundreds of texts of many genres during his research. These, too, are an invaluable resource, as they constitute one of the major corpora of published Mesoamerican native texts now available for comparative purposes. Nearly two hundred myths, tales, and legends in Tzotzil with lively English translation appear in Laughlin's *Of Cabbages and Kings* (1977). This volume includes major collections from six key informants (whose biographies are included), together with comparative commentary and notes linking the Zinacanteco corpus to other Tzotzil, Mesoamerican, and Hispanic sources. There is also a good introduction to the social context of Tzotzil story-telling. It should also be noted that one of the narrators was a woman, making this one of the truly rare Mesoamerican collections to provide a large sample of texts from a virtuoso female raconteur. *Of Wonders Wild and New* (Laughlin 1976) is a major collection (in English translation) of Zinacanteco "reports" of dreams from more than a dozen men and women. The tone of the dream texts is like narrative; indeed, talk about dreams is a significant Tzotzil speech form. Zinacantecos and other Tzotzils regard dreams as an important source of knowledge about the present and future. Laughlin provides an ethnographic background on the significance of dreams in general as well as a set of standard motifs with cultural interpretations; e.g., to dream of receiving a wasp sting means one will be bothered by earth lords (Laughlin 1976:7). The collection contains little interpretation beyond the ethnographic report and texts. *Of Shoes and Ships and Sealing Wax* (Laughlin 1980) deals with sundries, as its subtitle promises. Of particular interest is a remarkable series of reflections and journal-type narratives in Tzotzil with English translation about two Zinacantecos' trips to the United States. The narratives are a wonderful resource for Tzotzil perceptions of cultural "otherness." This volume also contains a splendid sampling of the oral tradition as used in everyday and ritual life, including magnificent prayer and ritual language texts, as well as contextual transcriptions of formal speech use in daily life, and several song texts together with ethnographic context of performance (but without musical transcription). Like all of Laughlin's work, it is characterized by translations and notes with extraordinary sensitivity to the nuances of Tzotzil language and poetics. Examples of his poet-ethnographer's sensitivity may be found in his discussions of flower symbolism in Zinacanteco ritual language and religion (Laughlin 1962) and in his interpretation of Zinacanteco dream texts (1966).

Some sense of the complexity of moving from Tzotzil text to English translation may be found in a more technical report (Laughlin 1979) in which a literal translation of several dream texts is given in addition to the final, figurative translation. Laughlin has also collaborated with the distinguished poet W. S. Merwin (Laughlin and Merwin 1972) to render two Zinacanteco poems in an even more subjective medium.

Following closely in the chronology of the Harvard project work in language and literature is the work of Victoria R. Bricker, a gifted ethnographer and an able linguist who has produced a major series of publications on Zinacanteco ritual humor, joking behavior, oral history, ethnosemantics, and technical linguistics. She has also been the chief pioneer in an area which might be called Tzotzil comparative literature. Her work in ritual humor began with Zinacantan (1968) and came to include Chenalho and Chamula as well in a full-length monograph (1973b), which is a pioneering work in controlled comparison of humor, ritual drama, and clowns as these themes occur with variations in three closely related, contiguous Tzotzil communities. The work is richly documented with humorous texts and carefully transcribed sequences of language in ritual drama. The analytical focus is upon stylized humor as social control and native commentary about ethnicity. A brief summary of her findings on this topic, with emphasis on Zinacantan, appears in Bricker 1980. She has extended this analysis to a broader comparative perspective on humor in a paper (1979a) which compares and contrasts Mayan and Aztec ritual humor.

Another series of papers deals specifically with native classification and social dynamics of Tzotzil humor and joking behavior (Bricker 1973d; 1974a; 1974b; 1976; 1979d). All of these contain texts in Tzotzil with translations. One (1979d) is a technical translation of a verbal dueling text. Another (1974b) is particularly important as a critical commentary on informant variability in eliciting native categories of Zinacanteco speaking. Bricker, with George A. Collier, has also contributed important work on nicknaming and social structure (G. Collier and Bricker 1970). This study incorporates baptismal lists from the Colonial period as a longitudinal perspective on how nicknames evolve into surnames. Bricker has also contributed significantly to Tzotzil ethnosemantics in her exploration (1973c) of the pervasive junior/senior ranking principle in what she calls Tzotzil "ethical" language. This study, too, is comparative in scope, incorporating material from Zinacantan, Chamula, and Chenalho. The paper documents underlying assumptions, linguistically coded, about order in the universe, varying from greater (*bankilal*) to lesser (*ʔiȼʔinal*) worth, power, and status. Since these evaluative dimensions apply to phenomena as diverse as kin terms, rank of deities, and power of sacred places, they are clearly of relevance to an understanding of the Tzotzil world as reflected in ritual language, prayers, and sacred narratives. Bricker has also used modern Chamula Tzotzil texts to explore ways in which contemporary ritual language of festivals may be used to illuminate the issue of rank and social stratification among the ancient Maya (1978). Finally, she has recently published on Tzotzil ethnohistory and oral history, including a comparative study of historical dramas in Chiapas using contemporary ritual, oral historical data, and written history to assess the nature of historical "memory" in nonliterate communities (Bricker 1977). She also applies contemporary Tzotzil oral historical and ethnohistoric materials to her interpretation of nativistic movements in Chiapas (1973a; 1979b). Her 1981 book, *The Indian Christ, the Indian King*, extends her general findings on the structure of the Tzotzil-Tzeltal revitalization movements to the Maya area as a whole, using both comparative synchronic

and diachronic perspectives. This book contains four Tzotzil texts, and thus constitutes an example of an emergent Tzotzil "comparative history and literature."

John B. Haviland has more recently added another Harvard project voice to the extensive published coverage of Zincanteco Tzotzil literature. Haviland is a gifted anthropological linguist whose mastery of spoken Tzotzil is matched among non-native speakers only by Laughlin's. His research focus in Zinacantan has been on "ordinary language," with less emphasis on texts per se and more emphasis on the creativity, style, and knowledge embodied in everyday speech. His work on Zinacanteco gossip (1971; 1977a; 1977b) is a *tour de force*, offering an interpretation of Tzotzil gossip which is essentially a theory of knowledge, communication, and information networks in a nonliterate society. The line which separates gossip, anecdote, and traditional narrative from oral history is of course a fuzzy one, so Haviland's work is critically important as a source on speaker idiosyncracy and vested interest as factors which operate in sustaining the vital Tzotzil oral tradition. Haviland has also assembled a pedagogical grammar of Tzotzil (1976) which will be published in Mexico.

Another Harvard project–sponsored corpus of work on Tzotzil oral tradition has been compiled since 1965 by the present author. The focus of my work has been to consider the whole Chamula oral tradition as a stylistic and generic continuum, beginning with everyday language and continuing through more complex and fixed genres. I have attempted to show how the oral literature shares structural information with other domains of Chamula life. This work adds many Tzotzil texts from San Juan Chamula to the corpus available from Zinacantan. Since Chamula is contiguous with Zinacantan, the two Tzotzil-speaking communities offer a good opportunity for comparison of the oral traditions in two closely related communities which nevertheless have distinct dialects and dress, and separate civil and religious organizations.

A series of papers (Gossen 1972a; 1974c; 1976a) and a monograph (1974b) give the general ethnographic background, Chamula classification scheme, stylistic characteristics, and textual examples of the many genres of verbal behavior that Chamulas recognize. Another set of papers draws from narrative texts to present the Chamula Tzotzil concepts of cosmos, world view, and time reckoning as symbolic constructions that anchor the reality of their everyday lives (Gossen 1972b; 1974a; 1979). More specific genre descriptions with ethnographic performance context and analysis are as follows; proverbs (Gossen 1973), punning humor and verbal dueling (1976b), oral history (1977), ritual language (1976a), dreams and shamanism (1975). The last of these also considers language as a key to understanding Chamula philosophy of individual being. The ancient Maya solar calendar as it survives in Chamula is discussed in an article (Gossen 1974a) based on a Chamula calendar-board and a long almanac-type Tzotzil narration about native reckoning of traditional times for agricultural activities according to the ancient calendar. Other links of the Chamula narrative tradition with that of the ancient Maya, specifically the *Popol Vuh*, are discussed in two articles (Gossen 1978; 1984). Links of Chamula narrative tradition with the *Chilam Balam of Chumayel*, the *Popol Vuh*, and the *Annals of the Cakchiquels*, as well as with other Mesoamerican, European, and Latin American narrative traditions, appear in annotations to 184 text abstracts that make up an appendix to *Chamulas in the World of the Sun* (Gossen 1974b:253–346; Spanish ed. [1979]: 319–428). Two other Chamula creation texts appear with full Tzotzil text, English translations, notes, and ethnographic context (Gossen 1980). A forthcoming book (Gossen and Gossen n.d.) presents one hundred full Chamula narrative texts beginning with the primeval chaos and moving forward through four great temporal epochs into the present era. This book will also contain a discussion of Tzotzil poetics and a Tzotzil "theory of history." Finally, I

have collaborated in two efforts to present native narrative texts in teaching materials intended for supplementary use in Chiapas Indian grammar schools (Gossen and López Méndez 1979; Modiano, Dileanis, Gossen, and Wasserstrom 1977).

Evon Z. Vogt, founder and coordinator of the Harvard project, has also contributed significantly to our understanding of Tzotzil language and literature, in particular the role of Zinacanteco ritual language in social context. Vogt's general ethnography, *Zinacantan* (1969), contains many texts of ritual formulas and prayers as they are embedded in civic, religious, and shamanistic events. These texts are of particular value, for they are not given in isolation as "texts," but as parts of ongoing social transactions which also involve economic, social, and ritual events of remarkable complexity. This monograph also contains more than a dozen myth texts, some of which are given with the original Tzotzil text; most of the texts were collected and translated by Laughlin (1977). The small myth corpus given by Vogt is useful because it presents a selection of tales which are truly "popular" in that they are the ones most likely to be known by a broad cross-section of Zinacantecos. Vogt's *Tortillas for the Gods* (1976) is an analysis of ritual symbolism in Zinacantan. In this book he uses ritual language and prayer in English translation as key sources of native exegesis in the interpretation of what is "getting said" in ritual action. The strength of these texts is Vogt's explicit reporting of their role in the whole flow of Zinacanteco religious and ceremonial observance. Shamanistic prayers and ritual language also appear as key ethnographic documents in his joint paper with Catherine C. Vogt (1970) on the logic and structural pattern of a Zinacanteco curing ritual.

Sarah C. Blaffer's *The Black-Man of Zinacantan* (1972) is an exhaustive description and analysis of variants of texts, anecdotes, and dramas about a central spook/bogeyman figure in Zinacanteco narrative folklore. This is one of the few intensive comparative studies in Tzotzil literature. Beginning with many

Zinacanteco narrative texts (mostly collected and translated by Laughlin), the scope goes far afield into other contemporary Tzotzil- and Maya-speaking traditions, as well as into Nahuatl and Maya antiquity. The orientation is not only comparative—identifying the black-man as a relative of a well-known Pre-columbian Maya bat demon—but also structural. The black-man emerges as a clarifying anomaly between man and animal.

Other studies of Zinacanteco Tzotzil narrative tradition have been done by John N. Burstein (1975), Vivian Lewis (1969), Jessie E. Pinkham (1970), and Milbry C. Polk (1973); these are all unpublished but available in the Harvard Chiapas Project archives.

There are several excellent published studies in which ritual language and prayer texts figure in description and analysis: Jane F. Collier (1968; 1973) on courtship and marriage and on law; Frank Cancian (1965) and Renato I. Rosaldo (1968) on formal language used in the civic and religious cargo ceremonies; and Horacio Fabrega and Daniel B. Silver (1973) on shamanism. Among the unpublished studies on this subject, Priscilla Rachun Linn's doctoral dissertation (1977) is of particular value in that many texts of formal language are presented in the context of ritual sequences. Thor R. Anderson (1975) deals with ritual language in household rituals of dedication and renewal; Carolyn C. Pope (1969) is concerned with prayer and ritual language in funeral ceremonies; Daniel B. Silver (1966) with the language, substance, and logic of shamanism; and Robert F. Wasserstrom (1970) with the ritual language associated with saints' cults and ritual exchanges of saints.

There are also studies on the structure of ritual language: Denise Z. Field (1975) and Nancy A. Zweng (1973) on prayer and Elizabeth A. Werby (1971) on couplet pair formation. All of the above are available at the Harvard University libraries or in the archives of the Harvard Chiapas Project.

Several other valuable studies pertinent to the Tzotzil oral tradition include: William N. Binderman (1960) on Zinacanteco Tzotzil oral

history of the Mexican Revolution; Eliot M. Gelwan (1972) on starlore and ethnoastronomy; and Marta Turok's brilliant published study (1976), based in part on narrative stories, of motifs in a traditional weaving design from Magdalenas.

Carter Wilson, an able fieldworker and speaker of Tzotzil, has written two anthropological novels which are fictional recreations of events that might also live in the Chamula oral tradition. *Crazy February* (1966) is a novel of patricide which occurs in the context of Chamula Carnival, a great festival of ritual reversal. Dialogue and ritual language, although all in English translation, nevertheless give a vivid portrait of language use in a native Tzotzil setting. *A Green Tree and a Dry Tree* (1972) recreates the life history of one of the most celebrated figures in Chamula oral history, Pedro Díaz Cuscat. Cuscat was the Chamula leader of a major nativistic movement of 1867–1870. He lost, but this novel recreates vividly his dismal and wandering youth and his extraordinary career as a cult leader and religious militant. The novel is based on both written and oral history and (thanks to Wilson's first-hand knowledge of the community, of the language, and of how Tzotzils think) it is more than a historical novel. It is actually an approximation to Tzotzil story-telling in translation.

John N. Burstein has contributed an innovative effort in editing an inexpensive Tzotzil-language pamphlet series for recreational and pedagogical use in Tzotzil communities. This publishing effort is supported by a small private foundation, Instituto de Asesoría Antropológica para le Región Maya, Asociación Civil, and has achieved some visibility in the Tzotzil communities near San Cristobal de las Casas. Topics of the pamphlets are festivals (Burstein 1977b; 1978b), Tzotzil oral history of the Mexican Revolution in Chiapas (Burstein 1977a), oral history of the "old days" (Gossen and López Méndez 1979), and a biography of a Chamula political leader (Burstein 1978a). They are excellently illustrated by a Chamula artist, Mariano López Méndez, and provide, as of this writing, the only casual reading material other than formal school texts and Protestant missionary tracts available in the Tzotzil language. All five of these pamphlets derive from texts of the Tzotzil oral tradition. Two of them (Burstein 1977a; 1978b) contain brief abstracts in Spanish.

Tzotzil music has not been thoroughly researched by the Harvard Chiapas Project or by any other institution or individual. The few published sources include a brief ethnographic sketch of Zinacanteco music, including the drum and flute group and the string ensembles (Vogt 1969:399–402); a discussion of percussion in Zinacanteco ritual (Vogt 1977); an ethnographic discussion of music, song, and song texts (Tzotzil with English translation) from Chamula (Gossen 1974b:216–229); and a set of beautiful Zinacanteco song texts in Tzotzil with English translation (Laughlin 1980:272–284). Details on instruments and the ethnography of musical ensembles and their role in festivals and other ritual proceedings may be found in Georges S. Arbuz (1963) and Haviland (1966), both unpublished but available in the Harvard Chiapas Project archive.

2.2.5. INDEPENDENT SCHOLARS. In addition to the Tzotzil research carried out by the major projects, several independent efforts have contributed to our knowledge of Tzotzil oral tradition. Ethnomusicological discussion and transcription of representative Tzotzil (Chamula and Zinacanteco) drum and flute music and string ensemble music are provided by Frank Harrison and Joan Harrison (1968). Ulrich Köhler has carried out extensive ethnographic research in San Pablo Chalchihuitan, with some emphasis on religion and cosmology. Religion, cosmology, and mythology are considered in Köhler (1974a). A prayer text (Köhler 1974b) and a shamanistic incantation for curing snakebite (1975), both with Tzotzil text and German translation, add material in the San Pablo dialect to the reservoir of comparative data.

Several works of fiction, all based on the authors' first-hand knowledge of the Chiapas Highlands, contribute indirectly to an understanding of the Tzotzil language in everyday discourse and ritual transactions. Although none is written by an accomplished Tzotzil speaker, all reflect some sensitivity to the "other" world inhabited by Tzotzil Indians. Ricardo Pozas Arciniega's *Juan Pérez Jolote* (1952) is a vivid "autobiographical" recreation of a Chamula who fought in the Mexican Revolution and then went home again, changed. This was made into a less-than-successful Mexican commercial film of the same title and has also been translated into English (1962). The hero, Juan Pérez Jolote, really lived, and his grave is marked in the San Sebastián Cemetery near the Chamula town center. Rosario Castellanos is a distinguished Mexican novelist who wrote most of her works about her native Chiapas. Her short stories and novels (1957; 1960; 1962) deal extensively with the caste circumstances of Indian–Ladino (Mexican Spanish-speaking) relations in Chiapas. Her protagonists are often Tzotzil Indians, and her re-creation of their speech in dialogue, although in Spanish translation, is surprisingly faithful to reality. Another major literary figure who knew and wrote with great sympathy for the Tzotzil Indians is B. Traven. Although he is better known for other novels, his *March to the Montería* (1971) is about a Chamula Tzotzil who leaves home and family to seek some cash to improve his life, only to become involved in debt slavery as a mahogany logger in the jungle lowlands. It is a hair-raising polemical tale which re-creates accurately the type of experience which Chamulas themselves relate in their oral tradition about their past and present as labor pawns of Mexicans and foreigners. Finally, there is a highly biased novel of Protestant evangelism called *They Dared to Be Different* (Steven 1976). This novel is ethnographically flawed and evangelically motivated, but nevertheless reflects some research into Tzotzil custom and speech. It is the tale, from the Protestant point of view, of the rise and persecution of the evangelical movement in Chamula since 1965. Although a routine missionary novel about the evils of witchcraft, drinking, paganism, etc., it is nevertheless useful as a quasi-historical guide to understanding recent political upheavals centering on the challenge of Protestantism to traditionalism in Tzotzil communities, a topic of great current interest in the native oral traditions of the area as well.

Another work of historical interest to Tzotzil literature is Prudencio Moscoso Pastraña's *Jacinto Pérez "Pajarito"* (1972). This is a reconstructed account of a revitalization movement in Chamula in 1910–1911. It contains useful biographical material on the heroic Tzotzil figure, Pajarito, who led this movement. For the most part a conventional history, based on conventional sources (published documents, letters, and manuscripts), it also draws to some extent upon oral historical accounts from surviving eyewitnesses. Although heavily· biased against what Pajarito's side stood for in this conflict, it is useful for comparative purposes, for Tzotzil oral tradition· remembers Pajarito well.

There is also an important source on Tzotzil education, socialization, and language-learning by Nancy Modiano (1973). This work considers informal socialization in the home as well as government-sponsored efforts to teach Tzotzil and Spanish in Indian grammar schools.

It is fitting as a final note in this survey of the rather extensive sources on modern Tzotzil literature to recognize a native Tzotzil politician and scholar who may very well prove to be among the first in a contemporary tradition of native Tzotzil intellectuals. Jacinto Arias, a native of Chenalho and past principal officeholder, is currently a doctoral candidate in the Department of Anthropology at Princeton University. His thesis will consider the role of mediator in Chenalho social and public life. To my knowledge, this will be the first formal work of scholarship by a Tzotzil. It will contain an appendix of Tzotzil texts with English translation. Furthermore, Arias has published a Tzotzil translation of *Where There Is No Doctor*, by David Werner (1980). This publication is worth noting, for it is to my knowledge the

first modern book-length work to appear entirely in the Tzotzil language which does not have a hidden agenda, e.g., religious conversion or programmed teaching of Spanish. Comprising over three hundred pages, it is a practical health-care handbook for those who live far away from Western medical facilities, doctors, and pharmacies. Aside from its potential practical value, it is also noteworthy in its assumption of literacy *in Tzotzil*. Such an assumption may be viewed as subversive in the political climate of Mexico, which views literacy in Spanish as one of the ultimate goals of national Indian policy. Teaching of Tzotzil, in this view of Mexican Indian education, should be a stepping stone to the universal learning of Spanish, the national language. Arias has sidestepped this goal by taking his own language seriously as a medium of written communication. This may prove to be a vital step in establishing Tzotzil as a written language.

3. SOCIAL CONTEXT. Whether you look or whether you listen, you cannot spend time even as a casual visitor in a Tzotzil community without coming away impressed by the intensity and vitality of public ritual life. There are no scripts or notes, of course; only knowledge, precedent, and advisors. All that is done—the processions, the songs, the seemingly endless prayers and exchanges or ritual language—is carried in the oral tradition. In similar fashion, the daily round of domestic life in Tzotzil households typically begins with prayers to the Sun/Christ and other deities at the household shrine, and ends with tortillas, beans, gossip, and joking around the fire.

Although most households now have transistor radios, most of the programming is in Spanish, creating an effect rather like background noise. As of 1979, one hour of programming daily was available in Tzotzil, on a government-sponsored station called "Radio Comunidad Indígena." Some households have phonographs and tape recorders. Yet the tone of Tzotzil life remains overwhelmingly that of a traditional oral culture. As noted above, men typically speak some Spanish, although fewer than 10 percent read or write it. Most women speak little more than a market repertoire of Spanish. Since women remain at home while men work in the fields, in town, or on the lowland coffee plantations, women are the principal socializers of children, and the language of the Indian household is Tzotzil (Modiano 1973). Although the Mexican government endeavors to teach Spanish to Tzotzil-speakers in hundreds of grammar schools in the Chiapas Highlands, the domestic situation which sustains nearly monolingual Tzotzil-speaking communities is powerful. Consequently the Tzotzil language and its oral traditions are not moribund or vestigial. They are omnipresent in the highlands, as much so as corn and bean agriculture.

Most native narrative accounts of Tzotzil history emphasize the learning of *baȼ'i k'op* ('the true language' or Tzotzil) and its specialized forms—such as prayer, ritual speech, and song—as the threshold of humanness in man's progress through the ages. As it was in human progress as a species, so it is with Tzotzils as they move through the life cycle. Infants are classified as monkeys (*maš*)—precultural beings without language—until they are named and baptized, usually in the first two years of life. According to Tzotzil theories of self and individual being, a human life is a cycle of heat, beginning as a cold fetus and acquiring ever-increasing measures of spiritual heat as the individual moves through the life cycle. Language-learning and increasing sophistication in language use, particularly in punning and joking behavior, are signs of increasing social maturity. Skillful use of language, like sexual maturity and wealth, is likened to powerful heat, the desired and the desirable (Gossen 1975). Those men and women who achieve rank and status in shamanistic careers and public ritual life do so in part through their linguistic competence. So complex are the specialized linguistic requirements of civil and religious officeholders and shamans that formal and informal apprenticeship is the norm. Major civil and religious offices carry as a requirement

the engagement of ritual advisers (*yahvotik*), typically past holders of the office, whose task is to accompany the officials and to teach them proper ritual behavior, prayers, songs, and ritual formulas. Aspiring shamans must not only dream to receive their calling, but also find (and sometimes pay) a mentor from whom to learn prayers and other specialized knowledge. Musicians (those of string ensembles) occupy a culturally important role as ritual accompanists and as informal ritual advisers. A prestigious musician not only knows song sequences involving hundreds of formal couplets but also is able to prompt ritual officials and assistants about matters of etiquette, protocol, and specialized language use (see Gossen 1974c; 1976a).

If specialized language use is crucial to the success of a "public service" career, it is also laced into the fabric of countless everyday social transactions. To borrow money, to ask a favor, to ask for help, to share a drink of rum (*poš*), to enlist a ritual kinsman (*compadre*) for the baptism of one's child, even to pay a visit to one's neighbor's house, all require the use of formal language, a style of speech which is formulaic and fixed rather than spontaneous and free-form.

The importance of stylized speech in everyday transactions is surely related to the ranked structure of Tzotzil societies (see Bricker 1973c). To a Tzotzil, the social, spiritual, and inanimate worlds are structured in a non-egalitarian way. Some mountains are *bankilal* ('senior' or 'larger'); others are *ʔiȼ'inal* ('junior' or 'smaller'). One is *bankilal* to one's younger siblings; one is *ʔiȼ'inal* to one's older siblings. A man is *bankilal* to a woman; a boy is *bankilal* to a girl. A past officeholder is *bankilal* to an incoming officeholder. The Sun/Christ deity is *bankilal* to other deities. A person whose animal soul is a jaguar is *bankilal* to a person whose animal soul is a rabbit. Any child is *ʔiȼ'inal* to any adult. This ranked universe is usually clear to speakers; sometimes it is not (as in relation to the unmentionable topic of animal soul companions). In either case, careful attention to deferential behavior, respect, and self-

77

deprecation assure one of not offending, of putting one's best and safest image forward, for, as Laughlin observes of Zinacantan, "life is not to be taken on trust" (1975:17). Language is a power broker. To use it to one's advantage, to hedge one's bets, it is usually best to underestimate one's rank and power. This minimizes one's vulnerability, and will guard against the possibility of offense to one's fellows, to the structure of society, and to the spiritual order. Acknowledging one's humility puts one in a better position to receive favors from those who can grant them. As Marcel Mauss (1954) observed, to grant a favor enhances the giver and thus reaffirms, for that transaction, the unequal status of the participants; yet the transaction also delivers something to the petitioner. This applies to the social world and also to the pattern of reciprocity between humans and gods. It is thus to a ranked world of finite resources (e.g., money, life, health, prestige, supernatural favor, help, corn, human labor) with a frank acknowledgement as to who controls them, that the genius of the Tzotzil language, and indeed much of the energy of Tzotzil social life, is directed.

Here is part of a transcription of a casual visit of two *compadres*, as recorded in Zinacantan by Laughlin. There has apparently been a misunderstanding. The visitor seeks to assuage bad feelings by offering rum, talk, and camaraderie.

(3)

MARYAN	Are you there, young lady?
MATAL	I'm here, sir.
MARYAN	Is your husband there?
MATAL	He's here, sir.
MARYAN	Are you there, Romin?
ROMIN	I'm here, sir.
MARYAN	Are you still at home?
ROMIN	I still seem to be at home for awhile, sir.

MARYAN	Ah, God, I've come here, son. I wonder if I can visit you for a minute?
ROMIN	Ah, what do you want, sir?
MARYAN	I don't want anything, son. I just [want] to visit you for a minute. Can I come in?
ROMIN	Come on in, sir. What do you want?
MARYAN	All right son. I'm paying you a visit for a minute, then, son.
ROMIN	Fine sir, Come on in, sir. Sir! (bowing)
MARYAN	Come here, at ease!
MATAL	Sir!
MARYAN	Come here, at ease!
ROMIN	Sit down, sir! There's a little chair.
MARYAN	All right son. Are you still at home, son?
ROMIN	I'm still at home, sir. I'm still at home. We haven't been able to go very often, it seems. It seems I'm still here for a day or so.

If the talk and perhaps the cane liquor flows, formal discourse subsides and is replaced by a rapid exchange of pleasantries interspersed with verbal pyrotechnics, duels, and taunts lightly testing who is master, and then the sober insistence of ritual phrases demanding that individual differences be forgotten so that the proper way, the traditional way continue unabated.

MARYAN	I am paying you a visit here. Grant a little pardon for our tiny bit of cold water, since you suffered the pain and the hardship. You sustained the lowly soul, the lowly spirit of God's humble angel.

78

ROMIN   God, are your lordly heads
         still anxious, your lordly
         hearts, My Father, My Lord?
         That should have been all, I
         wish nothing, My Father, I
         wish nothing, My Lord. I wish
         nothing, my holy companion,
         my holy compadre. Thank you
         so much. May God repay you
         a little. It isn't that I have said
         a thing, it seems.

MARYAN   This way it has always been
         from the beginning, from the
         start, grant a very little par-
         don. God, compadre, grant
         the holy pardon, a little, a bit.
         I have brought, I come holding
         in my possession, the sun-
         beams, the shade of Our Lord.
         Thanks for suffering the lordly
         pains, enduring the lordly
         hardship, you sustained the
         lowly soul, the lowly spirit of
         God's humble angel, the way
         you, too, are measured as a
         lordly man, as a lordly person.

ROMIN   God, thanks, then, thanks.
         They say there is still a little, a
         bit.
            Well, see here, compadre, it
         seems that now you offered me
         the little, the bit, it seems.
         I partook of the lordly liquor
         of your table. Let's share the
         little, the bit, it seems of what
         you offered me, too. It's not as
         if I am fine, by myself, proper
         by myself. It won't happen that
         I will go by myself to drink
         next to the house, of course.

MARYAN   Think it over, if you [want] to
         go out now that we have
         finished drinking, too.

ROMIN   Lord, no! Let's share a little,
         let's share a bit, otherwise,
         then you'd certainly mock me!

MARYAN   Why would I mock you if you
         know how to toss down a
         whole liter?

                          (Laughlin 1975:17)

It is easy therefore to recognize among
the Tzotzil, as Edmonson observed of the
Quiche, that "words matter, and formal
discourse matters even more" (Edmonson
1971:xii).

4. GENRES. All literatures have typical,
representative genres. I have attempted in
my research on the oral tradition of Chamula
(Gossen 1974b) to work within a genre taxonomy that includes types of speech that the
Chamula Tzotzil recognize. It is here offered
in summary form (from Gossen 1974c:394–
398) as a means of organizing in coherent
fashion a part of Tzotzil life that is at once
important and complex.

4.1. LANGUAGE. A bewildering number of
processes, abstractions, and things can be
glossed as *k'op*, which refers to nearly all
forms of verbal behavior, including oral tradition. The term *k'op* can mean word, language, argument, war, subject, topic, problem, dispute, court case, or traditional verbal
lore.

Chamulas recognize that correct use of
language (that is, their dialect) distinguishes
them not only from nonhumans, but also
from their distant ancestors and from other
contemporary Indian- and Spanish-speaking
groups. According to Chamula narrative accounts, no one could speak, sing, or dance in
the distant past. These were among the reasons why the sun creator destroyed the ex-
perimental people of the First and Second
creations. The more recent people learned to
speak Spanish and then everyone understood
one another. Later, the nations and *municipios* were divided because they began quar-
reling. The sun deity changed languages so
that people would learn to live together
peacefully in small groups. Chamulas came
out well in the long run, for their language
was the best of them all.

The taxonomy of *k'op*, which appears in

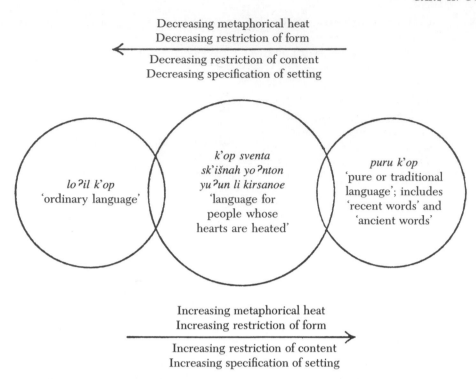

Decreasing metaphorical heat
Decreasing restriction of form

Decreasing restriction of content
Decreasing specification of setting

lo ʔil kʼop
'ordinary language'

*kʼop sventa
skʼišnah yo ʔnton
yu ʔun li kirsanoe*
'language for
people whose
hearts are heated'

puru kʼop
'pure or traditional
language'; includes
'recent words' and
'ancient words'

Increasing metaphorical heat
Increasing restriction of form

Increasing restriction of content
Increasing specification of setting

FIGURE 4-1. A brief scheme of a Chamula folk taxonomy of verbal behavior. Adapted from Gossen 1974c ("To Speak with a Heated Heart: Chamula Canons of Style and Good Performance," in *Explorations in the Ethnography of Speaking*, edited by Richard Bauman and Joel Sherzer, published by Cambridge University Press).

Figures 4-1 and 4-2, was elicited several separate times from six male informants ranging in age from eighteen to sixty-five over the period of one year. The two figures should be more or less self-explanatory. The reader will probably note that I have not made an effort to describe the taxonomy in Figure 4-2 as a grid of uniform or symmetrical criteria and distinctive features. Such a scheme would be a distortion of the way in which Chamulas view the taxonomy. For example: time is a relevant criterial attribute for distinguishing level-3 categories of 'new words' and 'ancient words'; for other categories at the same level (3) of the taxonomy, place of performance is a defining feature ('court speech'); for still others at the same level (3), performer of the words is the relevant feature ('children's im-

provised games'). Similarly, heat appears as a stated defining attribute in the name of only one level-2 category ('speech for people whose hearts are heated'). We know, however, that genres of 'pure speech' have greater metaphorical heat value than the intermediate category which bears its name. Therefore, although I use the term "level" in referring to the scheme, I do not attach any uniform "deep structure" information to it. Levels are used only as descriptive conventions.

4.1.1. ORDINARY LANGUAGE. 'Ordinary language' (*lo ʔil kʼop*) is restricted in use only by the dictates of the social situation and the grammaticality or intelligibility of the utterance. It is believed to be totally idiosyncratic and without noteworthiness in style, form, or content; it is everyday speech. As one moves

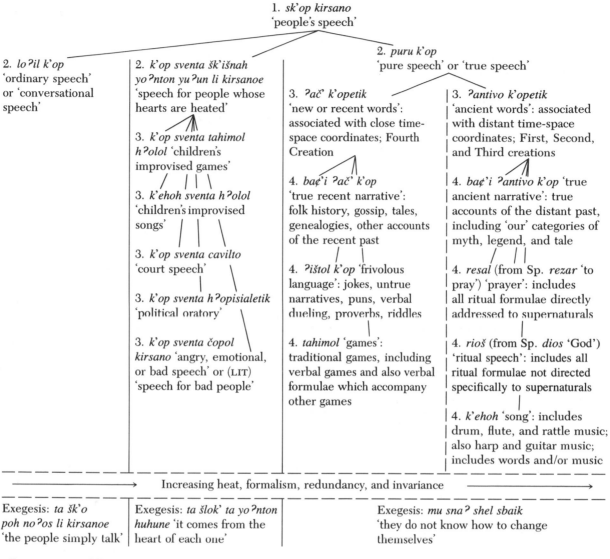

1. *sk'op kirsano*
'people's speech'

2. *lo ʔil k'op*
'ordinary speech'
or 'conversational
speech'

2. *k'op sventa šk'išnah
yo ʔnton yu ʔun li kirsanoe*
'speech for people whose
hearts are heated'

3. *k'op sventa tahimol
h ʔolol* 'children's
improvised games'

3. *k'ehoh sventa h ʔolol*
'children's improvised
songs'

3. *k'op sventa cavilto*
'court speech'

3. *k'op sventa h ʔopisialetik*
'political oratory'

3. *k'op sventa čopol
kirsano* 'angry, emotional,
or bad speech' or (LIT)
'speech for bad people'

2. *puru k'op*
'pure speech' or 'true speech'

3. *ʔač' k'opetik*
'new or recent words':
associated with close time-
space coordinates; Fourth
Creation

4. *baǰ'i ʔač' k'op*
'true recent narrative':
folk history, gossip, tales,
genealogies, other accounts
of the recent past

4. *ʔištol k'op* 'frivolous
language': jokes, untrue
narratives, puns, verbal
dueling, proverbs, riddles

4. *tahimol* 'games':
traditional games, including
verbal games and also verbal
formulae which accompany
other games

3. *ʔantivo k'opetik*
'ancient words': associated
with distant time-space
coordinates; First, Second,
and Third creations

4. *baȼ'i ʔantivo k'op* 'true
ancient narrative': true
accounts of the distant past,
including 'our' categories of
myth, legend, and tale

4. *resal* (from Sp. *rezar* 'to
pray') 'prayer': includes
all ritual formulae directly
addressed to supernaturals

4. *rioš* (from Sp. *dios* 'God')
'ritual speech': includes all
ritual formulae not directed
specifically to supernaturals

4. *k'ehoh* 'song': includes
drum, flute, and rattle music;
also harp and guitar music;
includes words and/or music

Increasing heat, formalism, redundancy, and invariance

Exegesis: *ta šk'o
poh no ʔos li kirsanoe*
'the people simply talk'

Exegesis: *ta šlok' ta yo ʔnton
huhune* 'it comes from the
heart of each one'

Exegesis: *mu sna ʔ shel sbaik*
'they do not know how to change
themselves'

FIGURE 4-2. A folk taxonomy of Chamula verbal behavior. Adapted from Gossen 1974c (see Fig. 4-1).

from left to right in Figures 4-1 and 4-2, progressively more constraints of various sorts apply to what one says (content) and how one says it (form).

4.1.2. INTERMEDIATE LANGUAGE. The intermediate category ('language for people whose hearts are heated') contains kinds of verbal behavior that are neither 'ordinary language' nor 'pure words'. They are restricted with regard to form (that is, how people will speak), but they are unpredictable as far as content is concerned. A common Chamula explanation for this kind of emotional speech emphasizes the individual, idiosyncratic qualities of the performance: "It comes from the heart of each person." The term referring to all of these intermediate forms, 'language for people whose hearts are heated', implies an elevated, excited, but not necessarily religious attitude on the part of the speaker. The state of excitement produces a style of verbal behavior that also occurs in the genres of 'pure words'. Yet, because content in the intermediate forms depends on the individual whim of the speaker, these forms are not included by Chamulas as part of 'pure words'. It is only with the joint presence of prescribed content and form in genres to which all people ideally have equal access that we reach 'pure words', on the right-hand side of the continuum shown in Figures 4-1 and 4-2. As Chamulas told me, "'Pure words' do not know how to change." The heat metaphor (see section 4.2.2) implies a transition into a more stylized form of speech, and continues from the intermediate category into the domain of 'pure words', which contains the 'genuine' Chamula genres of oral tradition. The implication is an obvious, but, I believe, important one: Chamula oral tradition ('pure words') is only a part of a continuum of styles of verbal behavior occurring in other, less standardized contexts. The transitional classes of verbal behavior carry vital information for making sense of 'pure words'. Furthermore, Chamula children begin to learn some of the transitional forms (particularly improvised games, songs, and emotional

speech) long before they begin to experiment with 'pure words'. It therefore seems crucial to consider the whole of verbal behavior rather than just those genres having constant form and content.

4.1.3. PURE WORDS. Within 'pure words', the criterion of time association is the most important one in distinguishing the secular forms ('recent words,' associated with the present Fourth Creation) from those having greater ritual and etiological significance ('ancient words', associated with the First, Second, and Third creations). 'Recent words' are colder, for they do not refer to the full four-cycle creation period. 'Ancient words' are hotter, for they were given in and refer to events from the very beginning of order (see section 4.2.2).

Several apparent discrepancies in the scheme strike the non-Chamula observer. For example, certain stylistic features of 'ancient words' may also be found in verbal aspects of 'children's improvised games', which are thought to be idiosyncratic expressions of individual whims in the present. This does not constitute an internal inconsistency in the taxonomy, but rather illustrates an important aspect of Chamula language-learning: children are prepared to recognize, understand, or learn the formal genres of 'ancient words' through experimentation with the content, styles, rhythms, and syntax in their informal play behavior.

Surprisingly, in Chamula, gossip is considered 'pure words' most of the time. Gossip, as the Chamulas see it, is not idiosyncratic or original in the way that intermediate types of verbal behavior are. It is part of 'true recent narrative' because it is a statement of fact, a segment of information known by several people in a single form, which ideally will be passed on as a whole. The gossip among women at a waterhole about the chief magistrate's oration to the Chamulas at a past festival is 'true recent narrative', whereas the oration itself is not. The oration ('political oratory') belongs to the transitional category of 'speech for people whose hearts are heated' because no one knew what he was going to say, only how he would say it. Another illustration may help to clarify the taxonomic criteria. Emotional speech ('speech for bad people') uses devices of cadence, repetition, syntax, and metaphor that are also found in 'pure words', but the content varies with the occasion; however, if a murder or some other noteworthy event followed a quarrel, an account of the entire event, including the language used in the quarrel, would probably be worthy of retelling as 'true recent narrative'.

4.2. COSMOLOGY. Two key evaluative notions, those dealing with time and heat, emerge as important taxonomic and exegetical criteria. The following discussion (from Gossen 1977 and 1974c) describes the Tzotzil view of these categories.

4.2.1. TIME. As heirs to their own Maya past and to Colonial missionization, Chamulas and other Tzotzils subscribe to the principle that the Sun deity, who is the same as Jesus Christ, began the temporal scheme of things when he first ascended into the sky to fix in place all of the temporal cycles: days, years, and seasons. He did this after being killed by the monkeys, demons, and Jews, only to be resurrected as the Sun on the fourth day after his death. The Sun/Christ established all order on earth. He did this in various stages. His first three consecutive creations were failures because the human beings he made did not get along well among themselves and simply could not cope with life in many ways. For these reasons he destroyed them. The creation in which we live, the fourth, was the only one which pleased the Sun/Christ. Even it continues precariously, ever in threat of destruction if people behave in a manner disapproved by the Sun/Christ.

Some form of the cyclical creation cycle is found in nearly all Maya communities (J. E. S. Thompson 1970:330–348; Villa Rojas 1968). The four-part scheme dates at least from the sixteenth century, as recorded in ethnohistoric sources such as the *Popol Vuh* (Edmonson 1971:xiv). There is every reason to believe that the fundamental cyclical view

of time dates from ancient Mayan antiquity (León-Portilla 1968). In the Tzotzil area, Chamula tends to a four-cycle scheme. Chenalho and Larrainzar seem to have a more truncated, three-part scheme (Guiteras-Holmes 1961:156–157, 176, 182, 186–187, 194, 253–254, 282, 287; Holland 1963:71–72). Zinacantan has a more ambiguous view; the two- or three-part scheme seems to be predominant (Laughlin 1977:76–77).

The four-creation scheme comprises the largest temporal entity that Chamulas recognize. Although it is a cyclical scheme, it is important to keep in mind that the more recent stages are not mere repetitions of earlier ones. Rather, these stages have a pattern of cumulative development; each consecutive creation has turned out somewhat better than its predecessor. In this sense, Chamulas view historical development with some optimism, not unlike nineteenth-century positivists in our own tradition, who were committed to the idea that things were getting better and better through reason and science. In the Chamula view, things are getting better and better only because people know better how to do the bidding of the Sun/Christ. Both improved knowledge about proper human behavior and genuine fear of destruction if people misbehave keep the Fourth Creation on an even keel. Yet people are aware that this creation is full of evil and that they must do what they can to defend it from the perverse and evil ones who would do it in.

Chamulas do not assign specific durations to the successive creations. For example, people's opinions about the time of the beginning of the First Creation vary from 80,000 to 120 years (five or six generations) ago. Views of the age of the Second and Third creations vary similarly.

The following sketch of Tzotzil cosmology is summarized from Gossen 1974b. The First Creation had its origins in a sad primitive darkness. The Moon (known as "Our Mother" or the Virgin Mary) walked about in the primeval darkness and somehow conceived a child. She was pursued in the darkness by demons, monkeys, and Jews, who suspected that the child in her womb would ultimately threaten them. The Sun/Christ child (known as "Our Father") was born and in nine days grew to manhood. At all times in his brief childhood and youth he was pursued by his enemies. They eventually crucified him, after which he was buried. He rose from the dead as the mature Sun God/Jesus Christ and traveled to the western horizon on the first day and then spent the second day in the underworld. On the third day he rose on the eastern horizon and proceeded to the center of the sky on the fourth day. The monkeys, demons, and Jews perished under the heat and light of the Sun/Christ on the fourth day, and so order was established: the first true day, the first light, the first heat. Afterward the Sun/Christ gave the earth its landforms and bodies of water and began to experiment with creating forms of life. The Sun/Christ fashioned the first people out of clay (or, in some accounts, sticks). These people failed for many reasons. Some accounts say that their most notable sin was boiling and eating their own children. Other explanations focus on linguistic and religious incompetence. For these reasons and others, they and the whole First Creation were destroyed. In most versions destruction comes in the form of a rain of boiling water.

The Second and Third creations form a kind of "heroic age" in Chamula history. Twice again the Sun/Christ created the earth and all that it contained. The people of these periods dealt informally with the saints (who are younger relatives of the Sun/Christ) and with the Sun/Christ himself and with the Virgin Mary/Moon. These people were able to deal directly with supernatural beings and anthropomorphic animals. The deities basically had a fairly good time of it, committing some errors and enjoying adventures whose results contributed to the reservoir of custom which is Chamula life today. In these two creations domestic plants and animals were created. For example, milk from the Virgin Mary/Moon's breasts formed potatoes. Chiles

came from the bloody heel of the Sun/Christ. Most important, the Sun/Christ created maize from a piece of his own groin. In this age Spanish was the only language, but at the end of the Third Creation people began to fight and argue too much, so the Sun/Christ sent all the groups in different directions so that they might live peacefully in their own territories with their own languages and customs. This plan did not work out, however, for people continued to do much evil, so the Sun/Christ destroyed the Third Creation by sending a great earthquake.

The Sun/Christ gave humanity one last try. This was the Fourth Creation, the world as we know it. The most common way of referring to events in the Fourth Creation is not by years or dates, but by reference to major temporal landmarks whose relative order most adult Chamulas know precisely. Generally, these temporal landmarks do not go back much beyond 120 to 150 years. People are able to discuss the recent past with considerable precision, placing events before, during, or after one of the following landmark events:

The Time of Father Miguel Hidalgo (1812–1815), the Wars of Independence.
The Time of the War of Pedro Díaz Cuscat or the War of Galindo (1865–1870), a nativistic movement centering in Chamula; a Chiapas extension of the Yucatecan Caste Wars.
The Time of the Ash (1903), the eruption and widespread ashfall of a volcano near Tapachula.
The Time of the War of Pajarito (1910–1911), a Chamula rebellion and civil conflict that occurred when Chamulas were pitted against state authorities by the Bishop of Chiapas, who resided in San Cristobal de las Casas.
The Time of the War of Carranza (1912–1920), the Mexican Revolution.
The Time of the Fever (1918), the influenza epidemic of 1918.
The Time of the Closed Church (1934–1936), the religious persecution and anticlerical policy that occurred under the administration of President Lázaro Cárdenas. During

this time the Chamula religious organization operated in secrecy.

The Time When Elders No Longer Had High Positions in Municipal Government (1937–1941), the events following an order given by the San Cristobal Office of Indian Affairs requiring youth, literacy, knowledge of Spanish, and an attitude of "cooperation" as qualifications for Indians to hold municipal offices.

The Time When They Built the Road to Tuxtla (1946–1950), construction of the section of the Pan-American Highway between San Cristobal and Tuxtla Gutierrez, the state capital. Many Chamulas were employed in this project.

Events more recent than 1950 have not been sifted by tradition for consistent use as temporal landmarks. A serious drought in the early 1960's will probably become a point of reference in the future, but it is still too early to know with certainty. Also likely as temporal landmarks are the exploration for oil in Chamula in the early 1970's and the purge of Protestants, which began in 1965.

4.2.2. HEAT. As the temporal backdrop is crucial to Tzotzils in distinguishing recent narratives and other secular genres associated with the present era from "ancient" narratives and ritual genres referring to events of earlier creations, so also the metaphor of heat is central to an understanding of the Tzotzil view of language.

Heat is divine and primordial; its primary referent is the Sun creator, giver of temporal, spatial, and social order. Second, heat, like its primary Sun referent, is cyclical. Each day finished is both a cycle of heat completed and an affirmation of the holy integrity of the Sun deity. The same can be said of each year, each agricultural season, each festival, each human life, and the cycle of creation. In all of these, cycles of heat express and confirm the most basic principles of patrifocal order. Male religious officials constantly partake of the heat metaphor in properly carrying out their duties. They are said to be "helping the Sun (or the saints, the Sun's kin) to bear the bur-

den of the year," by conducting ceremonies using ritual substances such as rum, tobacco, tropical flowers, incense, fireworks, candles, which express actual and metaphorical heat. Furthermore, the counterclockwise direction which religious officials invariably follow through ritual circuits is, according to Chamula premises, the horizontal equivalent of the Sun deity's vertical orbit. Officials thus move as the Sun moves in their microcosm of ritual space (see Gossen 1972b). Another critically important aspect of ritual action which relates to the Sun is of course the language used to conduct it. Ritual language, prayer, and song are all laced with metaphors for heat, as expressing homage, praise, and petition to the Sun deity and his kin. The highly redundant style of the ritual genres expresses the sacred and cyclical heat of religious transactions.

Heat expresses order in everyday life as well. The daily round of domestic life centers on the hearth, which lies near the center of the dirt floor of nearly every Chamula house. The working day usually begins and ends around the fire, men and boys sitting and eating to the right of the hearth (from the point of view of one who faces the interior from the front door), women and girls to the left of the hearth. Furthermore, men in this patrifocal society always sit on tiny chairs and wear sandals, which separate them from the ground and complement their masculine heat. Women, on the other hand, customarily sit on the ground and always go barefoot, symbolically maintaining direct contact with the cold, feminine earth. Coldness, femininity, and lowness are logically prior to heat, masculinity, and height. This follows from the mythological account of the coming of order. The male Sun was born from the womb of the female Moon and was then killed by the forces of evil and darkness. This in turn allowed him to ascend into the sky to create the cosmos, cyclical time, and patrifocal order.

The individual life cycle is also conceived as a cycle of increasing heat from a cold beginning. A baby has a dangerously cold aspect. The individual acquires steadily increasing heat with baptism and sexual maturity. The heat of the life cycle reaches a fairly high level with social maturity, expressed by marriage and reproduction. The acquisition of heat may be carried further through a cargo or shamanistic career. Death plunges one into the cold from whence one came. Thus, life and death are also elementary expressions of the hot-cold cycle. Life-crisis rituals and cargo initiations include symbols of life (hot and integrative) and death (cold and disjunctive). Hot and cold are also fundamental categories in Chamula theories of illness. In sum, in nearly all aspects of Chamula life, mundane and sacred, increasing heat expresses the divine and order-giving will of the Sun himself. Language is no exception to this rule.

5. STYLE AND POETICS.

5.1. INFORMAL AND FORMAL SPEECH. All who have dealt with modern Tzotzil language and literature generally agree that there is a clear distinction between formal and informal styles. Chamula and Zinacanteco genre taxonomies agree on this fundamental distinction, and it is apparent from scattered texts available from other Tzotzil communities (Larrainzar, Chenalho, and Chalchihuitan) that the distinction is pervasive there as well. At the most fundamental level, we are talking about the contrast between the following two types of phrases.

(4) Informal speech (*loʔil kʼop* 'ordinary language'):

a li špaškue batem ša ta jobel pere ta sut talel ta ʔora 'Pascuala has already gone to San Cristobal, but she will soon be back.'

(My fieldnotes)

(5) Formal speech (*resal* 'prayer'):

Chʼul totiletik
Holy fathers,

   Chʼul meʔiletik
   Holy mothers!

Tzauk ʔune, htot
Take heed, my Father,

86

Tzauk ʔune, kahval
Take heed, my Lord!

(After Laughlin 1980:260)

Example 4 is ordinary, secular, cold, and idiosyncratic and could be said anywhere, anytime. Example 5 is exalted, ritually significant, hot, and fixed; it can be said only in a formal context. Between these two types of language, however, there is a continuum of different types of redundancy. The various genres of Tzotzil literature are built stylistically upon variants of these elementary structures.

5.2. EMOTIONAL SPEECH AS KEY. Emotional speech (see section 4.1.2) is a key to understanding what happens to language when the "heart is heated." In a word, it multiplies; the same information is repeated. To get a dog out of the house in Chamula, you might say:

(6)

lokʼ an ¢ʼi ʔ
Get out, dog.

   lokʼan kabron
   Get out, he-goat.

(My fieldnotes)

Once is not enough. A swift kick in the ribs might be added as a nonlinguistic emphatic.

This elementary and simple technique of information redundancy lies at the root of all Tzotzil specialized linguistic forms, from court speech and political oratory and children's games to the most exalted forms of narration, ritual speech, and song.

5.3. COUPLETS. A second technique for intensifying messages—which must be described as a tendency, not as a rule—is to speak in pairs. In Tzotzil, as in many languages, repetition is not random. It tends to couplet structures. This has been described by Edmonson for the classic Quiche of the *Popol Vuh* as follows: "A close rendering of the Quiche inevitably gives rise to semantic couplets, whether they are printed as poetry or as prose. In no case, so far as I can determine, does the Quiche text embellish this relatively primitive poetic device with rhyme, syllabification or meter, not even when it is quoting songs. The form itself, however, tends to produce a kind of 'keying', in which two successive lines may be quite diverse but must share key words which are closely linked in meaning" (1971:xii).

The importance of this semantic coupling technique in formal discourse has been generally recognized in many Maya and other Mesoamerican traditions (Bricker 1974a), but the significance of the semantic couplet in Maya narrative traditions has been a subject of debate. Laughlin believes that Zinacanteco narratives proceed in language which is an exact replica of that of everyday life (Laughlin 1977:5). He also, however, notes the pervasiveness of repetition and frequent occurrence of couplets in the narrative tradition (ibid.:6). One infers that everyday language sometimes exhibits this tendency. Regarding the Quiche, Edmonson's argument for the omnipresence of the couplet in Quiche literature has been challenged by James L. Mondloch (1984) and Dennis Tedlock (1984), who note that parts of the *Popol Vuh* text do not scan neatly into couplets; other polysegmentary forms and simple prose are also present. Their argument seems to be somewhat overstated, because the couplet—however imperfect and expandable—remains the dominant form whenever formal discourse occurs. Whatever variants there are on the theme, pairing of ideas and phrases—semantic and syntactic couplets—is as common to Tzotzil language use as corn is to their diet.

5.3.1. SEMANTIC DUALISM. Couplet structure has at least two basic forms. The first is characterized by repeating ideas without necessarily repeating exact syntax. I have elsewhere called this pattern "nonparallel repetition" (Gossen 1974c:408). It is analogous to Edmonson's Quiche semantic couplets, as discussed above, and occurs frequently in narrative and in conversation. An example comes from Zinacantan:

(7)

¢o¢ ša ?ip ?un
He was very sick now.

mu ša bu lek ?un
He wasn't at all well now.

(After Laughlin 1977:6–7)

5.3.2. PARALLEL SYNTAX. The second basic form of the couplet follows parallel syntax, or "parallel repetition" (Gossen 1974c:407–409).

(8)

k'usi la ti hmule, tottik
What do they say is my crime, sir?

k'usi la ti hkolo?e, tottik
What do they say is my evil, sir?

(After Laughlin 1977:7)

The couplet based on parallel syntax may be freely constructed or idiosyncratic (example 8) or may behave as a fixed formula (Lord 1960) that enters as a whole two-part unit into the composition of prayers, ritual speech, and song. An extremely common fixed couplet formula is the following, which introduces many Tzotzil prayers:

(9)

lital ta yolon ?avok
I have come before your feet,

lital ta yolon ?ak'ob
I have come before your hands.

(After Gossen 1974b:194; reprinted by permission)

Such fixed formulas exist by the hundreds in Tzotzil, and the eloquent formal utterances which can be generated with them must surely be infinite. Mastery of these couplets, their permissible combinations, and their place in ritual action characterizes an accomplished civil or religious official or a shaman. More than mere language, these couplets, chanted and sung in seemingly endless redundancy, are themselves ritual symbols which convey the heat of the ritual mood in which one seeks an affinity for the primordial order of the Sun/Christ and other deities (Gossen 1976a).

While fixed formal couplets are neatly marked by parallel syntax, nonparallel semantic couplets which occur in narrative discourse are sometimes not so clearly marked. Although I am convinced that nonparallel couplets (example 7) are the fundamental elements of narrative discourse, it is nevertheless necessary to show systematically how they work. This is an issue of some importance because it has to do with translation. Is Tzotzil narrative literature to be transcribed and translated as prose (as in example 4) or as semantic couplets (as in example 7)? In either or both cases, what constitutes a narrative phrase matters if we are to deal with Tzotzil literature according·to its own phrase structure and performance conventions.

5.4. THE ENCLITIC *e*. A promising key to this problem lies, I think, in a final phrase marker which, in the Chamula and other dialects of Tzotzil, takes the form of an enclitic *e*. It can be suffixed to any final consonant or vowel, including another *e*. Some examples follow (enclitic *e*'s are romanized):

(10)

*bat ša k'alal ta hobel*e
He went to San Cristobal

    or

*la ša sta li be ʔ*e
He found the path.

(My fieldnotes)

It seems that these *e*'s have no grammatical function. They occur alike in the narrative present and past tenses. Native speakers repeatedly say that their effect on the meaning is nil; one simply uses them because it "sounds right" to do so. These *e*'s, however, do seem to carry information about the reality status of the event, that it has happened and that someone said it was true. Furthermore, the enclitic *e* invariably precedes a slight

pause in the flow of narration. This *e* and the related pause have several characteristics:

(a) They create a breath marker of indefinite length, rather like ⌢ in music.

(b) They usually signal the narrative mode of discourse.

(c) They indicate an accomplished event.

(d) They serve as an emphatic or truth marker: "It is certain that the event happened."

(e) They provide a cue to listeners for appropriate moments in which to offer supportive or participatory statements. Examples of these audience response phrases are: *ha ʔ heč* 'That is so'; *ha ʔ melel* 'That is true'; *mi melel* 'Is that true?'; *mi ha ʔ* 'Is that so?'; *ha ʔ* 'Yes'; *melel ʔun bi* 'That is indeed so'; *mo ʔoh ʔun bi* 'That can't be'; *ta na* 'Of course'; *ta na li un e* 'To be certain'.

The Tzotzils, like so many native Americans, view narrative performance as a group event; thus, the enclitic *e* appears to cue listeners with great frequency that the moment is right for participation. Furthermore, the enclitic *e* diminishes in regularity of use in those genres that have rigid, bound couplet structure and are more formal than narratives: ritual speech, prayers, and songs. For example—

(11) Prayer:

muk'ul san huan
Great San Juan,

    muk'ul patron
    Great Patron.

k'u yepal čital ta yolon ʔavok
How much I come before your feet,

    k'u yepal čital ta yolon ʔak'ob
    How much I come before your hands.

(Gossen 1974b:203,
reprinted by permission)

Another curiosity follows: the enclitic *e* also appears with relative infrequency in everyday social transactions.

(12) Everyday speech, request for favor:

(Visitor [speaker *b*] arrives.)

a. k'usi mantal kiȼ'in
What do you want, my younger brother?

b. č'abal hbankil
Nothing, my elder brother.

a. mi heč čaval
Is that true?

b. heč škal baȼ'i č'abal melel
That's right, absolutely nothing; it's true.

Ha ʔ no ʔoš mu hna ʔ mi šak'an čavič'
*ʔavuni moton*e
Only that I wonder if you might want to
receive your small gift.

pere baȼ'i hutuk no ʔoš
It is really but a little bit.

(Visitor produces a gift of liquor preceding
the request for a loan.)

(My fieldnotes)

Note that the enclitic *e* appears only in the
last speech of example 12, almost by way of
an emphatic, saying, 'This is really what I
came for." In example 11 (prayer), there is no
enclitic *e* at all, although it may occasionally
appear in formal genres. In comparative
quantitative counts based on relatively small
four-hundred-line samples, enclitic *e*'s appear
in everyday speech about 25 percent of the
time; in formal genres the average is less,
about 15 percent. In the narrative mode,
however, the frequency averages over 60
percent.

In summary, the enclitic *e* is far more
likely to appear in the narrative mode of
speaking than in everyday or formal speech.

Several reasons for the enclitic *e* distribution may be inferred:

(a) The *e* marker is unnecessary in the
shorter phrases of everyday speech. It appears in these contexts only as a kind of optional emphatic, as in the following:

(13)

bat ša ʔe
It is certain that he already left.

(b) In formal speech, the obligatory parallel syntax (which implies a more rigid truth
value, invariable content, and greater metaphoric heat) already explicitly marks binary
units. Indeed, most of the functions performed by the enclitic final *e*, in narrative,
including the related pause, are accomplished in formal speech by parallel syntax
alone (example 11). Further marking of formal speech phrases is not necessary except as
an emphatic at certain intervals. Sometimes
both parts of the formal couplet receive the
final *e*. These are usually key or "topic"
couplets or litany or chorus couplets. Thus,
the enclitic *e* becomes a kind of verse marker
in the formal speech genres.

(14) Prayer:

misirikočyo kahval,
Have pity on me, my Lord,

misirikočyo, hesus,
Have pity on me, Jesus,

toȼan, salvarol,
Rise up, Savior,

toȼan, manvel,
Rise up, Emmanuel.

*hoybih talel ta ʔaničim ba*e,
Turn your flowery countenance toward me,

*hoybih talel ta ʔaničim sat*e
Turn your flowery face toward me.

(Gossen 1974b:198,
reprinted by permission)

(c) Another possible reason for the relative
infrequency of the enclitic final *e* in everyday
and formal speech is that neither requires audience support phrases in the form described
above. Everyday speech is by its nature
keyed to immediate response from conversation partners; formal speech has as its logical

response the good (or ill) will of supernaturals, who do not by their nature respond verbally. Thus, the narrative mode seems to have a phrase structure of its own, marked primarily by the enclitic *e*.

How, then, does the couplet enter into narrative discourse? The elementary forms of the couplet may occur as emphatics in the redundancy of everyday speech; for example,

(15)

lok'an
Get out!

   lok'an
   Get out!

(My fieldnotes)

The formal couplet uses the same principle of parallel syntax in its fixed formulas; for example,

(16)

muk'ul san huan
Great San Juan

   muk'ul patron
   Great patron.

(My fieldnotes)

In narratives the "couplet situation" is far more ambiguous, much more variable, and much, much harder to hear. There is nevertheless a distinct tendency for narratives to follow a pattern of semantic coupling, as in this ordinary example:

(17)

ʔi k'alal lik'ot ta hobel muk bu la hta hci ʔile
And when I got to San Cristobal I did not find my friend,

   pere č'abal le ʔe
   he simply wasn't there.

la hsa ʔ ta huhot lum
I looked for him everywhere,

   pere muk bu la hta ta sa ʔele
   but my search came to nothing.

(My fieldnotes)

It is as though the narrative mode "leans toward" formal couplet style, but most often does so through semantic keying of related phrases, not through exactly parallel syntax. It is precisely in these narrative situations—without parallel syntax—that the enclitic *e* appears with greatest frequency. In example 17, three of the four lines have the final *e*. This is about average for the many thousands of narrative lines with which I have worked.

In other words, the narrative mode of speaking tends to semantic dualism. This is of course not a clean rule. For example, semantic linking of three or more lines occurs with some frequency. It could even be argued that example 17 should properly be scanned as a four-part structure, rather than as two semantic couplets. Whatever the variation, some general patterns seem to apply to couplet structure in narrative discourse:

(a) One must say the thing at least twice, either by simply repeating the same information in slightly different words (example 17) or by adding new information. For example—

(18) Narrative in twos:

ba¢'i toyol sik ša ʔi tahmek
He truly felt very, very cold,

   yu ʔun č'abal sk'ok'e
   For he had no fire.

(My fieldnotes)

(19) Narrative in threes:

puru la stenleh ʔoy la ta huhot banamile
There was nothing but flat land in all directions

   mu ʔyuk la ton
   There were no stones.

   mu ʔyuk la vi¢e
   There were no mountains.

(My fieldnotes)

(b) One may use parallel syntax to emphasize the greater thematic importance of some couplets over others; for example—

(20) Narrative:

šinulan ʔanȼ
A mestizo woman,

    šinulan ȼeb
    A mestizo girl.

                    (My fieldnotes)

In this case (as in example 19), the need for the *e* seems to diminish as parallel syntax appears.

(c) One may use question-and-answer frames; for example—

(21) Narrative:

k'u yepal ʔoy sči ʔuk li ʔanȼ
How many were there with the woman?

    ha ʔ no ʔoš li ȼ'i ʔe
    There was only the dog.

                    (My fieldnotes)

(d) The greater the use of formal stylistic structures (parallel syntax and question-and-answer frames), the less the need for the enclitic *e* phrase marker *within* the structure. If it appears at all, it tends to be at the end of the couplet.

5.5. STACKING. The more important and fundamental the narrative information, the more likely it is that the narrator will "stack" couplets for emphasis. (The highly redundant couplet structures of prayers, ritual speech, and song used in formal situations and to address deities are obvious extensions of this rule.)

"Semantic stacking" simply amounts to the addition of consecutive semantic couplets about the same event or circumstance when the narrator wants to emphasize a point. It means, simply, patterned redundancy of metaphor and semantic elements for emphasis (Gossen 1974c; 1976a). Redundancy of message in speech is related to the primary

Sun/heat symbolism in Chamula cosmology. This is a way to indicate that one is excited or "up," that one is talking about something that matters and that the audience should listen carefully. Thus, to build a sequence of couplets which generally carry the same message is a way of building climaxes and revealing the narrator's evaluation of the saliency and importance of narrative information. As the importance of the theme increases, there is even a tendency for semantic stacking to move from the mode of semantic coupling to semantic coupling *with* parallel syntax. Example 22 speaks better than paraphrase. It is a narrative fragment which reports the creation of woman from clay in the Second Creation. Our Father Sun has just presented her to the first man.

(22)

veno li ʔ ne ha ʔ me ʔači ʔil une, ši la ti htotike ta vinahel
"Very well, here is your companion," said Our Father Sun in Heaven.

    li ʔ ne ha ʔ me spas vah ʔave ʔ ʔun
    "Here you have the one who will make tortillas for you to eat,

    li ʔ ne ha ʔ me škom ta ʔana ʔun
    Here you have the one who will dwell in your house,

    li ʔ ne ha ʔ me spas ʔak'u ʔ ʔun
    Here you have the one who will make your clothing,

    li ʔ ne ha ʔ me spas ʔave ʔel ʔun
    Here you have the one who will prepare your food,

    li ʔ ne ha ʔ me ʔači ʔil ta vayel ʔun
    Here you have the one who will sleep with you,

    li ʔ ne ha ʔ me ʔači ʔil ta ʔave ʔel ʔun
    Here you have the one who will share your food with you,

li ʔ ne, ši la ti htotike
Here you have her," said Our Father Sun.

veno, ši la ti vinike
"Very well," said the (first) man.

(My fieldnotes)

6. SELECTED TEXT EXTRACTS. Several speech styles lie between the everyday and the formal, but space does not allow examples of all the genres which Tzotzils recognize. Those chosen for inclusion here can do no more than provide a glimpse of a rich and diverse literature. Since this survey is intended to cover the whole Tzotzil area, it would be inappropriate to follow the Chamula genre taxonomy too closely, so I shall use more conventional labels.

6.1. LEGAL LANGUAGE. Emotional speech occurs in countless contexts of everyday and ritual life. It invariably leans toward the redundant and formal, for such are the qualities of the heated heart of a Tzotzil speaker. A good example of this style from Zinacantan appears above (3). Another example which shows these qualities vividly is Chamula legal language. The chief magistrate addresses an accused sheep thief and his mother.

(23) *Magistrate:*

k'u ča ʔal ʔeč šapas šavelk'an ti čihe
Why did you do such a thing as steal sheep?

k'u ča ʔal mu ša ʔabteh
Why don't you work?

vinikot mu yu ʔunuk ʔan¢ukot
You're a man and not a woman.

k'u ča ʔal mu šasa ʔ ʔabtel
Why don't you get a job?

keremot to
You're young yet.

mu yu ʔunuk molukot ša
It's not as if you were an old man already.

buč'u la hyalbot čavelk'an čih
Who told you to steal the sheep?

mi ʔame ʔ
Was it your mother?

ʔo mi ʔahol la hyal
Or did you decide to do it yourself?

Thief:

č'abal
No.

č'abal
No.

(The magistrate questions him further, but he does not say who suggested it.)

Magistrate (to the thief's mother):

mi Ho ʔot lavalbe mantal la ʔavol ta šbat čih ta ʔak'obaltike
Was it you who ordered your son to go thieving sheep at night?

Mother:

Ho ʔon nan
Yes, it was probably I.

hna ʔun bi
I admit it.

Ho ʔon la hkalbe, batikik ta ʔelek' čih ba hčontikik ta hobel
I told him, "Let's go steal sheep and sell them in San Cristobal.

hk'eltikik mi šč'am, škut li kole
Let's see if they'll lend them," I said to my son.

mu hna ʔ k'usi tal ta hol
I don't know what came into my head.

ʔa ʔ li čubahun
I must be crazy.

ʔo no ʔoš.
That's the only reason.

(The magistrate extracts more confessions and then speaks to the mother again.)

Magistrate:

ʔeč štok mu ʔa ʔuk to sba velta čavelk'anik čihe
This is not the first time you have stolen sheep

> ʔoy ša shayibuk velta ʔelk'anik
> Many times already you have stolen.

šavelk'an ti cihe
You steal sheep,

šavelk'an ti ʔalak'e
You steal chickens.

šavelk'an ti ʔisak'
You steal potatoes.

šavelk'an ti ma ʔile
You steal squash.

šavelk'an ti k'u ʔile
You steal clothing.

šavelk'an ti ʔitahe
You steal cabbages.

šavelk'an ti tuluk'e
You steal turkeys.

> *skotol k'usi šavelk'an*
> You steal anything.

ʔa ʔ ša no ʔoš muyuk bu šavelk'anbe li sbek' yat li kirsano ʔetik
The only thing you don't steal from people is their testicles;

> ʔa ʔ no ʔoš čalo ʔe
> And those you only eat.

(The woman, terribly shamed, looks down, as does her son. They are sentenced to a week in jail with hard labor—he, carrying stones; she, sweeping up rubbish—at the end of which time they must pay a fine of three hundred pesos.)

(After Gossen 1974b : 71–73)

Note that legal language is not only formal and emotional, with much redundancy, but is also structured to shame the offenders publicly. Many Chamulas believe that the most important aspect of the punishment dealt out by officials consists of public shame. Shame is the more bitter if it is brought to public attention repeatedly. The court style facilitates such repetition:

šavelk'an ti čihe
You steal sheep.

šavelk'an ti ʔalak'e
You steal chickens.

šavelk'an ti ʔisak'e . . .
You steal potatoes . . .

The repeated syntax, with one-word substitutions, is related to the formal couplet. It serves as an intensifier of the message, ultimately accusing the woman of oral-genital contact, which is disapproved of by Chamulas as animal-like. The words are a metaphoric culmination of the animal-like qualities of her habitual thievery, which have been stated in parallel syntax seven times.

Other examples of emotional language can be found in Gossen 1974b:56–77. Laughlin (1980:149–204) presents a series of excellent dialogues involving many contexts of formal language use. Haviland also discusses patterns of repetition and occasional formalism in gossip (1977b:48–67).

6.2. HUMOR. Victoria R. Bricker's many publications on humor (1973b; 1973d; 1974a; 1976; 1979a; 1980), as well as my own (Gossen 1973; 1974b:91–122; 1976b), make available a fairly extensive comparative corpus. Many Western genre labels, such as jokes, proverbs, puns, verbal dueling, riddles, and ritual humor, are subsumed in Tzotzil by some variant of the term ʔištol lo ʔil 'play talk' or ʔištol k'op 'play language'. The main attribute they share is that they elicit laughter from participants and audience. The themes addressed are most typically sexual and scatological items and derisive commentary on odd personal habits and public appearance (mussed hair, dirty clothing), deviant social behavior (drunkenness, arrogance), improper sex role and public service behavior, and the absurdity and amoral qualities of other ethnic groups: Ladinos, other Indians, and foreigners. Also treated with great frequency is the human tendency to lapse occasionally into animal-like behavior (mindless promiscuity, nakedness, bestiality). Humor in Tzotzil communities is to be enjoyed, but also taken seriously because it is an informal technique of socialization and social control, as well as ritualized social criticism. Without exception, Tzotzil laughter addresses that which is askew from the normative order; through laughter, moral order is restored or at least acknowledged.

The following example of ritual humor occurs as a part of the change-of-office rituals that take place in January at the festival of San Sebastián in Zinacantan. The six actors are actually past officeholders who masquerade as pre-social beings, Blackmen. They are dressed in leather breeches and jackets. Five actors have their faces and hands blackened with soot. The sixth is dressed as a Ladino woman who carries a white doll in her arms and wears a blue mask with white rings around the mouth and eyes. They carry stuffed animals (squirrels and a spider monkey) and sharply pointed sticks. They go about poking the animals with the sticks as if simulating sexual intercourse with them, making the animal sound *ves—ves—ves*. These costumed entertainers make ritual visits in the early morning to the homes of incoming officeholders.

(24)

At 3:45 A.M. on January 20, 1966, the first group of "visitors" arrived at the house of the Second Regidor. After reciting the prayers of greeting at the entrance to the *regidor*'s house, the junior entertainers entered and began their performance:

FIRST BLACKMAN: Look, ladies and gentlemen! See how long the neck ribbons of Lol ʔUč's wife are. They just buy for themselves, but they don't pay for his *cargo*.

SECOND BLACKMAN: Look also at Marian Peres from Masan! He does nothing but fuck all the time at the foot of a mango tree.

FIRST BLACKMAN: Look, my mother; look, my lady, at what Lol ʔUč is doing with Maruč [his wife]! How shameless they are, always fucking each other, even when not in their own home. [To squirrel] Now don't *you* kneel and fuck here! Ha, ha, ha. Is this your house here? Yes, you may join the musicians, but don't fuck each other by the fire.

ANOTHER BLACKMAN: *Huh-huh*, tricky jaguar, licentious jaguar. *Hurr-hurr-ves-ves-ves*. Look! Maruč is above and Lol ʔUč is below! Look, mother; look, my lady! See what Lol ʔUč is doing! Look at Lol caught in his wife's embrace! Look at Lol lying above his wife! He is hanging his head over there where you keep your pots [in the corner of the room].

The implications of the words of the Blackmen are clear. Both Lol ʔUč and Marian Peres are men who served as policemen during the year 1965 but did not appear to finish their terms of office during the fiesta of San Sebastián. The accusation against Marian Peres is particularly pointed:

Labal kobvaneh ta spas ta h-mek to yolon manko.

He does nothing but fuck all the time at the foot of a mango tree.

This resembles in form, but contrasts in meaning with the ritual statement of a Zincanteco's duty to the saints:

. . . *spas ʔabtel ta yolon yok ti kahvaltike.*
He does his duty at the feet of Our Lord.

"At the foot of a mango tree" refers to the settlement of Masan, the home of Marian Peres, which specializes in growing mangoes. The gist of the Blackman's attack on Marian Peres is that Marian ought to be carrying out his ritual obligation "at the feet of Our Lord" in Zinacantan Center, instead of indulging in carnal pleasures "at the foot of a mango tree" in his hamlet.

In their attacks on Lol ʔUč, the Blackmen point out some moral and psychological flaws in his character. His wife is the center of his universe. That is why he spends all his money on elaborate neck ribbons for her and nothing on ceremonies in honor of the saints. That is also why he succumbs to sexual temptation at a time when *cargo* holders are required to abstain, thereby defiling himself and his office. And what is more, Lol is apparently not master in his own home: "Maruč is above and Lol ʔUč is below!" implies that Lol is dominated by his wife—that she is the more aggressive partner.

(Bricker 1973b:57–59)

The message is clear. The new office-holder—the Second Regidor or Second Policeman—is reminded humorously of infractions committed by former occupants of the position. Most Tzotzil festivals involve such humorous ritual personages—varying in form from monkeys to clowns to male transvestites to Mexican soldiers. In all cases, the message is moral education via the inverse, which is always funny.

6.2.1. PROVERBS. The stage for humor even more often appears in the nonritual set-

tings of everyday life. Proverbs (*k'ehel k'op* 'obscure words') typically function in such an informal context.

(25)

li vinike likel ta šk'elvan, pere ta šnihi
The man takes a quick look, but bows his head.

This proverb concerns problems of male-female relationships in Chamula. This being a delicate subject (for a man can go to jail and/or pay a fine for no more than speaking to an unmarried girl on the road), the language used to talk about it is ambiguous. To bow one's head in Chamula refers to a gesture that is expected of both men and women when they meet or greet individuals of either sex whose age or rank requires a respect relationship. Among males, the inferior bows his head and removes his hat; the superior releases him, touching the top of his bowed head, after which the inferior replaces his hat and states his business or greeting. This bowing and releasing procedure is sometimes used also in ritual drinking sessions. One drinks in order of seniority and offers a verbal toast to all present, bowing to one's superiors in rank order, shaking hands with one's equals, and simply toasting one's inferiors. The rank order is: all males first, in descending order of seniority, then all females in descending order of seniority. Thus, bowing and releasing are gestures which emphasize rank and the respect of it in many settings of Chamula social interaction. An understanding of these gestures is necessary for an understanding of the various levels of meaning in this proverb.

The proverb is said to and about men, particularly eligible bachelors, who are watching women at fiestas or along the road. Premarital chastity and avoidance and marital fidelity are the norms for male-female relationships in Chamula, and one of the most frequent minor charges brought against young men in court is "talking to young women in the road." Any kind of greeting or passing remark may be interpreted by a young woman

95

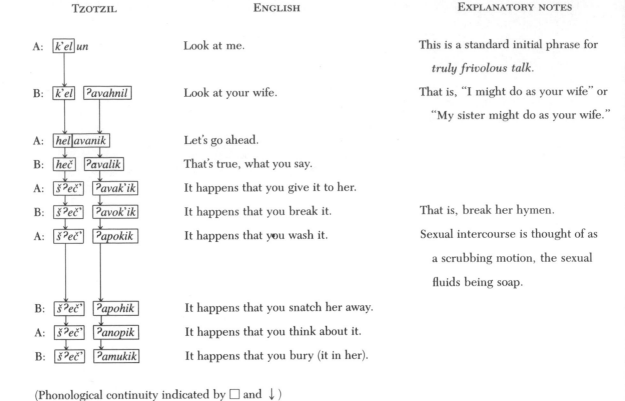

TZOTZIL	ENGLISH	EXPLANATORY NOTES
A: k'el un	Look at me.	This is a standard initial phrase for *truly frivolous talk*.
B: k'el ʔavahnil	Look at your wife.	That is, "I might do as your wife" or "My sister might do as your wife."
A: hel avanik	Let's go ahead.	
B: heč ʔavalik	That's true, what you say.	
A: š ʔeč' ʔavak'ik	It happens that you give it to her.	
B: š ʔeč' ʔavok'ik	It happens that you break it.	That is, break her hymen.
A: š ʔeč' ʔapokik	It happens that you wash it.	Sexual intercourse is thought of as a scrubbing motion, the sexual fluids being soap.
B: š ʔeč' ʔapohik	It happens that you snatch her away.	
A: š ʔeč' ʔanopik	It happens that you think about it.	
B: š ʔeč' ʔamukik	It happens that you bury (it in her).	

(Phonological continuity indicated by □ and ↓)

FIGURE 4-3. A verbal duel from Chamula. After Gossen 1976b:131.

as a proposition. If the girl chooses to tell her father, he can bring formal charges against the boy or man involved, who will have to plead his case in court and possibly spend a few days in jail and/or pay a fine. Young bachelors and married men are very careful about what they say to young women. The proverb is a word of caution. It says, quite literally, that the man goes out to look but keeps respect ("bows his head").

Another level of meaning makes the point more graphically. The "man" in the proverb refers to the penis. The phrase "takes a quick look" refers to an erection. "He bows his head" means, of course, that the head of the penis bows or becomes flaccid, for no women are available to satisfy it. In other words, the man or the erect penis is forced to express humility by bowing or becoming flaccid; one

may not do as one pleases but must submit to the rules of society and show respect. The impetus for performance of proverbs is one of threatened deviance. The performance reinforces the norm through humor (Gossen 1973:223).

6.2.2. DUELING. Proverbs, with their penchant for sexual pun, introduce still another type of Tzotzil humor, verbal punning games. These games, called ʔištol loʔil ('play talk'), account for a great deal of Tzotzil leisure activity. They generate occasions for laughter among all male and, reportedly, female age groups. Verbal dueling may involve a single exchange or as many as two hundred exchanges between two partners. The goal is to put down one's opponent through virtuosity in the use of the derisive pun. Bricker has described this form and its variants in

Zinacantan (1973d; 1976); Chamula descriptions appear in Gossen 1974b:97–106 and 1976b. Figure 4-3 shows a typical exchange from Chamula.

Note that sound shift with each exchange is minimal, but that the participants manage with each step to escalate an imaginary sexual encounter toward penetration. However, the participants in this exchange are both unmarried men, and the ambiguous range of imaginary partners might be (1) opponent and girlfriend, (2) opponent and speaker's sister, or (3) each other! All three are improbable: the first because neither can afford marriage; the second because it would be illicit without petition, bride price payment, and marriage; the third because homosexual contact is incessantly joked about but seldom practiced and vaguely disapproved of. The exchange is therefore uproariously funny, for it explores the realm of the possible but improbable. In this exchange (which eventually involved 210 responses), player B eventually lost. Thus, for that moment, player A became the victor and player B the vanquished. Ranking in play of course is but an anticipation or echo of the game of ranking which is the stuff of real life in Tzotzil society. Verbal dueling "plays" with normative order and virtuosity in speaking. Real life ranks real people according to normative issues and competence in public speaking. Tzotzil punning is not to be taken lightly.

6.3. NARRATIVE. The most comprehensive discussion of Tzotzil narrative tradition is Laughlin's *Of Cabbage and Kings* (1977), which includes nearly two hundred full texts in Tzotzil with English translations. This volume is significantly supplemented by his volume of dream texts (1976) and his *Sundries* volume (1980), which includes a long narrative journal of Zinacanteco experience abroad. My book *Chamulas in the World of the Sun* (Gossen 1974b:78–90, 140–158, 253–346) also discusses the Chamula narrative tradition at length and includes some full texts and a collection of nearly two hundred text abstracts in English. A forthcoming work (Gossen and Gossen n.d.) presents about one hundred full texts with ethnographic notes. The Laughlin and Gossen collections are cross-referenced and annotated with comparative Mesoamerican and European sources. These collections provide a rich source of Zinacanteco and Chamula data. The narrative traditions of Larrainzar (Holland 1963) and Chenalho (Guiteras-Holmes 1961) are also documented, but neither collection is extensive and neither contains full Tzotzil texts.

Tzotzils are not fond of formal tale-telling sessions. They tell stories nearly anywhere—at home, at work, on the road, and at fiestas. The only constant which can be established about context of performance is that there is a reason for telling stories: they are told when circumstances make the information useful, illuminating, or amusing.

The recent political purges of the Protestant converts in Chamula elicited great enthusiasm among my Chamula friends and acquaintances for telling me why it was necessary to get rid of these subversive elements in the community. Narrators recited tales of previous wars and conflicts which resembled current events. "Bearers of new words" always seek confrontation and produce trouble, I was told. One had to eliminate the troublemakers before they got out of hand. Examples were given in the form of narratives about the Mexican Revolution and other previous wars in which Chamulas had been involved. In other words, narratives were cited as precedent, as legitimation, as "charters" in Malinowski's sense, for events in time present (Malinowski 1926).

Similar circumstances—usually threats and dangers to the present order—elicit story-telling in everyday Tzotzil life. A long rainy spell may bring speculation about another deluge, like the floods of primeval antiquity. A drought may elicit tales of famine. An illness such as *mahbenal* ('punishment sickness') may elicit tales of an acquaintance who suffered the same fate at the hands of a witch some years ago. Dense weeds encountered in a cornfield during hoeing may elicit an account of Our Father Sun's treaty with the grass long ago, which established that grass, too, should have a right to exist. Sighting an armadillo during a work party in the lowlands may prompt someone to tell of how, long ago, Our Father Sun used an armadillo as a stool. A mother may warn a child not to go to a distant Ladino town, for Ladinos, like the ancients, cook children to render lard from them. In summary, story-telling for amusement alone is not to my knowledge the Tzotzil way. Something must happen to prompt a performance, to make the information relevant.

There are no sex and age restrictions on tale-telling. However, adults are more likely than children to have the cumulative reservoir of experience and knowledge to pass on as narrative. Tale-telling always involves audience participation. I have noted above that narrative style is keyed with pauses which invite audience support, affirmation, exclamation, doubt, or delight.

Narrative style is formally described above (see also Laughlin 1977:6–7). Here I want to point out the substantial difficulty one encounters in trying to render a Tzotzil text in translation. Repetition is rampant, making for slow-moving plot development. In contrast, startling discontinuity can occur, sometimes leading one from the Second to the Fourth Creation with a mere *veno* ('well, then'). Tzotzil narrative dialogue is frequently embedded in a "quote-unquote" sandwich structure, with 'he (she or it) said' (*ši*) at the beginning and end of a dialogue phrase. This creates a translation dilemma of considerable proportions because of its "unrelieved frequency" (Laughlin 1977:6) and also because of lack of specificity about whether *ši* means 'said', 'asked', 'cried', 'exclaimed', 'demanded', or something else. Tzotzil narrative style is "telegraphically terse," to use Edmonson's term for describing the Quiche (1971:xii), in that subject-verb agreement in number is not at all compulsory. Once it is established that several actors are present, the plural number may be dropped altogether from both nouns and verbs for the duration of the episode. Another trying trait

of Tzotzil narrative style for a translator is double subjects, e.g., *a li ¢'i? sut tal ta sna li ¢'i?e* ('The dog came home the dog'). There is no way to render this in English without producing a stilted construction such as: 'The dog came home. Yes, he did.' The greatest challenge to the translator is whether to translate Tzotzil narrative as semantic couplets and variants thereof, or as prose with occasional moments of formalism. I opt for the former, for reasons discussed above. Laughlin (1977:5) opts for the latter, since narrative language is so close to that of everyday life.

6.3.1. PLOT. The content of Tzotzil narrative literature is vast. Laughlin (1977:7) has suggested a typology of five basic Zincanteco plot types:

(a) Events are presented in episodic series. (This form appears to be of Spanish origin.)

(b) A problem is gradually introduced and wrestled with (possibly producing new problems) until the final climax is reached.

(c) Similar to (b), except that the initial problem is stated at the very outset.

(d) Like any of the above, but followed by an anticlimactic relaxation of tension.

(e) Similar to (b), (c), or (d), but flashbacks are inserted within the progressive temporal development. (This does not include the common insertion of afterthoughts.)

I have noted in section 4.2. the general development of content of Chamula narratives of the four creations. Here I would like to sketch briefly the types of narrative likely to appear in the repertoire of a good Chamula story-teller, noting however that it is unlikely that he or she will ever tell a story the same way twice.

Stories from the early epochs include the following:

(a) One or several narratives of the cyclical creations of Our Father Sun, assisted by Our Mother Moon (the Sun's mother). These are grand etiological chronicles, involving creation of life forms, landforms, cosmos, and customs. These chronicles usually end in destruction, typically a flood, earthquake, or rain of boiling water.

(b) Etiological narratives of Our Father Sun's interaction with the saints (his kin), demons, and other supernaturals, leading to founding of churches, shrines, etc.

(c) Legends of saints, usually giving their particular niche in the supernatural division of labor, e.g., St. Michael as the lord of music and earthquake; St. Peter, the judge; St. Jerome, the patron of animal souls.

(d) Animal trickster tales, typically involving Rabbit as hero and Coyote or Deer as dupe; human trickster tales of the picaresque type, probably of European origin.

(e) Human encounters (usually disastrous) with supernaturals, spooks, demons, bogeymen, jaguars, headless women, earth lords, and so forth.

(f) Human descent into the underworld, and related adventures.

(g) Long tales of heroes—kings, whirlwinds, wasps—who save Indian communities from threat and destruction.

(h) Abduction tales in which bears, demons, and men take innocent women on wild sexual adventures. The women often deceive their captors and escape.

(i) Localized origin stories of place names and landforms.

(j) Tales of European origin (*Märchen*).

More modern stories may include the following types:

(a) Chronicles of encounters with supernaturals (similar to e above).

(b) Chronicles of natural disasters, e.g., volcanic eruptions, floods, famines, epidemics.

(c) Chronicles of wars and political conflict.

(d) Chronicles of travel, supernatural (e.g., dreams of narrator's soul wanderings) and natural (e.g., work experience on the coffee plantations).

(e) Miscellaneous historical notes (e.g., construction of the Pan American Highway).

(f) Personal anecdotes about times past; content is highly variable.

(g) Localized gossip about the narrator's hamlet and community (witchcraft accusations, current court cases, thefts, misfortunes, so forth).

As examples, I shall present two tales, a typical Chamula text of an early epoch and a Zinacanteco tale of a time closer to the present. I have deliberately chosen to include texts which are not only representative of two different time periods, but also of two different Tzotzil communities and two styles of scansion and translation.

6.3.2. AN EARLY TALE. The first tale is a brief but typical account of major events which occurred at the time of the great flood in antiquity. Manuel López Calixto, of Peteh hamlet, Chamula, told me this story. He was around thirty years old in 1968 and had never been to school. He and a group of Chamulas were resting by a river bank in the lowlands, where they had gone to work on a coffee plantation. The river was rising to flood stage, and so the tale began. The text tells clearly the original setting in which he had heard the tale.

(26) The Flood

A story about long ago . . .
    There was an old man who was talking.
When the old man started to talk,
    It was because there was a large river
    near his house.
Thus he started to tell his tale,
    For the river was rising to flood stage.
It seems that the old man was scared when he saw the river rising.
    That is the reason the old man started to
    tell his story.
"Ay, if the river rises, we'll all drown in the river in no time," he said.
    "That is just how it still was long ago,"
    said the old man when he was talking in
    Hot Country.
    "That is just what my late grandfather told
    me," said the old man.
"Long ago there were still no pathways for the rivers.
    The rivers were just spread out over the
    earth.
The people were just drowning in the great lake,
    Those who lived long ago.

99

Then Our Holy Father Sun in Heaven
thought about things,
  For he saw that the earth was nothing but
  a great lake.
'Ay, but what shall I do with this great lake?'
asked Our Holy Father.
  Then he consulted with the Earth Lords.
'But do you want us to make pathways for
the rivers?'
  So he discussed it with the Earth Lords.
'That's fine,' said the Earth Lords.
  Together they came to an agreement
  about where to put the pathways of the
  rivers.
  So it was that Our Father Sun in Heaven
  and the Earth Lords were of one mind.
'Do you want to open the way at the foot of
your houses [in the valleys]?' asked Our
Father Sun in Heaven.
  Thus the Earth Lords quickly obeyed the
  order of Our Father Sun in Heaven.
Quickly they scooped out the pathways of
the rivers.
  When the riverbeds were set in order the
  great lake quickly began to shrink.
Then Our Father Sun in Heaven arrived on
the following day.
  'Is your part all ready?' asked Our Father
  in Heaven when he arrived.
He came to talk to the Earth Lords.
  'Well, now it's fine,' they said to each
  other.
'Well, now we shall leave the riverbeds just
like this,'
  So ordered Our Father Sun in Heaven.
'All right,' said the Earth Lords.
  'That's fine with us too.'
'I am also going to evaporate the sea,' said
Our Father Sun in Heaven.
  'When I rise, I shall cause the [eastern]
  sea to evaporate,' he said.
'When I set, I shall cause the Sea of the
Setting Sun to evaporate,' said Our Holy
Father.

'Then the earth will no longer be covered
  by the sea.
It is better that we are thinking along these
lines.'
  So they discussed it, Our Father Sun in
  Heaven and the Earth Lords.
  So it was that the riverbeds were left that
  way long ago," said the old man.
"That's why there are sinkholes.
  They, too, are the [underground]
  pathways of the rivers," he said.
"That is why the earth is not covered with
water," said the old man.
  "That is why the sea does not flood.
It is because the sea evaporates every day,"
said the old man.
  "When Our Father Sun rises, he
  evaporates the sea.
  When Our Father Sun sets, he evaporates
  [the water] when he goes down.
For there is a Sea of the Rising Sun.
  There is also a Sea of the Setting Sun,"
  said the old man.
"But who knows how many years ago all of
this happened," said the old man.
  "But this is the reason why the rivers
  have their pathways,
  For they evaporate at their destination,"
  said the old man.
"Our Father planned this with the Earth
Lords.
  Thus, although the rivers become full,
  they evaporate where they go," said the
  old man.
"So, also, although the seas fill up, they do
not flood.
  Don't you see that is because water
  evaporates when it reaches the great sea?
So, thus there is a sea where Our Father
Sun in Heaven disappears.
  But it's very far away," said the old man.
  "We don't really know where it is," he
  said,
"But I think it is at the foot of the sky," said
the old man.

"It is there where Our Father Sun goes down.

That is why the sea evaporates.

I think it might even be at the end of the earth," said the old man.

(After Gossen 1980:139–145,
by permission of *Tlalocan*)

6.3.3. A MODERN TALE. The second tale is from Zinacantan. I selected it from hundreds of possible texts because it is relatively brief and also because it introduces a spook of whom the Tzotzil are especially fond or, better said, afraid. Variants of this story appear in all the major Tzotzil collections and also in the greater Mesoamerican context (see Laughlin 1977:305).

(27) The Charcoal Cruncher

There was a man sleeping with his wife.
She was a Charcoal Cruncher.

The man touched his wife in the dark. She wasn't there, just the stump of her was there. She had no head.

He looked. He lit a match. "Where did my wife go?" he said. "How could it be? Where did her head go? Could someone have cut her head off?" said her husband. "Eh, who knows. There must be a reason. Maybe she's bad. Maybe she took a walk," said her husband. "No, I guess we'll see what happens to her, if she's a devil." He put salt on her. On the place where the cut was, he put salt.

When [her head] arrived it couldn't stick on anymore. Her head was just flopping about like a chicken. It just bounced and bounced now. "Why are you doing this to me? Why are you doing this?" the woman asked her husband when she arrived.

"But why do you go out wandering then? Are you a devil? You are a devil!" he told his wife. She crie—d now.

"Well, why is it? But where can I go now that my flesh doesn't fasten on anymore?" said the woman.

"Oh, I don't know. See for yourself! I don't want to be with you any longer. What you

are doing is too awful," said her husband. "You're a devil. You're not good," said her husband.

[Her head] bounced. It landed and perched on his shoulder. It landed there. Now he had two heads. The man had two heads. "Eh, but this is no good at all," he said. He prayed to Our Lord. "My Lord, but why is this? This is terrible. If the other one sticks on I'll have two faces!" said the man. "One a woman's, the other a man's, it seems. That is too awful," he said. "What can I do about this? What?" he said. "If Our Lord would only do [me] a favor. If there were something, if there were something, if only there were someone who would take it away, make it go, have it thrown away," he said.

He tricked it. "All right, it's nothing much, come down a minute, stay on the ground! I'll climb the pine tree. I'm going to get pine seeds. So you'll eat them. So we'll eat them," he said. "So you'll chew them," he said.

"Go on then, climb up, then!" He climbed up the pine tree.

When he climbed the tree, the—n the woman's head bounced and bounced at the foot of the pine. It bounced, but it didn't get up. It tried to climb the tree. "God, my Lord, but what can I do about this? If there were something, if there were something that would come and take it away," said th man. "All right, please eat," he told her. He dropped the pine seeds down [to her].

A deer came along.

[Her head] landed and stuck on the deer's back. [The deer] was terribly sca—red. It ran very fast. Then the woman's head was lost. That's the way it ended.

(Laughlin 1977:333–334)

6.4. RITUAL. The pervasiveness and stylistic characteristics of ritual genres have been discussed above. They are known to all Tzotzil speakers, for they must be present as a key ritual substance at festivals, curing ceremonies, morning prayers, formal petitions, and so forth. Two typical texts are included to give a sense of the heights of which Tzotzil formal language is capable.

6.4.1. PRAYER. Zinacanteco ritual language is chanted by assistants at a house dedication ceremony to those who remain at home while the assistants depart for the mountaintop shrines to pay homage to the ancestral deities:

(28)

God, see here, My Father,
  See here, My Lord.
May I pass before Thy glorious faces,
  May I pass before Thy glorious eyes,
My Father,
  My Lord.
We go stepping,
  We go walking
To the thresholds,
  To the altars
Of the holy fathers,
  The holy mothers.
You shall await our lowly earth,
  You shall await our lowly mud [flesh],
Whatever the hour,
  Whatever the day,
We turn back,
  We return,
My Father,
  My Lord.

(Laughlin 1980:215–216)

6.4.2. SONG. A fragment follows from a Chamula song (accompanied by harp, guitar, and gourd rattle) sung as ritual officials supervise the cooking of sweet maize gruel in great ceramic pots for the induction ceremony of the Mayordomo Santo. The gruel symbolizes the "heavenly rain" of San Juan (patron saint of Chamula) and of Our Father Sun which comes down to earth as the warm rays of heat from the sky.

(29)

ta ša me šyal ta Hoʔ
Now it is surely descending as rain,

la ʔačʼul šohobale bi
Your blessed radiance.

ta ša me šyal ta Hoʔ
Now it is surely descending as rain,

  la ʔačʼul nakʼobale bi, mukʼul patron
  Your blessed shadow, Great Patron.

la la li la lai la ʔo
  la la li la lai la a
la li la la lai la ʔo
  la la li la lai la a

ta ša me šyal ta Hoʔ
Now it is surely descending as rain,

  la ʔačʼul kompirale bi
  Your blessed ritual meal.

ta ša me šyal ta Hoʔ
Now it is surely descending as rain,

  la ʔačʼul korason bi, mukʼul patron
  Your blessed heart, Great patron.

la la li la lai la ʔo
  la la li la lai la a
la la li la lai la ʔo
  la la li la lai la a

(Gossen 1974b:228–229;
reprinted by permission)

The sweet gruel is expressed metaphorically in five different ways: as rain, radiance, shadow, ritual meal, and heart—all of San Juan, who is the sun's kinsman. This is a good example of metaphoric stacking for emphasis upon a key ritual symbol. The incoming Mayordomo gives the gruel as a sacrifice and sacrament which expresses his willingness to assist San Juan in the maintenance of moral order, heat, and the life force in Our Father Sun's universe.

7. THE FUTURE. I conclude with an assortment of thoughts about the future of Tzotzil literature as a field of scholarship, as a living phenomenon, and as an art form.

7.1. PROVENIENCE. As a result of the relative abundance of Tzotzil material, there exists an opportunity for comparative work on a fairly grand scale. Laughlin (1977), Bricker (1973b; 1977; 1978; 1979a; 1981), and I (Gossen 1974b; 1977; 1978) have begun exploring the roots and variants of the Tzotzil oral tradition in both the diachronic dimensions (comparison with written historical accounts as well as with ancient Maya and ancient Nahuatl ethnohistoric texts) and the synchronic dimension (comparisons with other Tzotzil, other Maya, other Mesoamerican, and European traditions). However, the question of the degree to which Tzotzil traditions are autochthonous and the degree to which they are borrowed, derivative, and shared has not yet been systematically explored. Laughlin estimates that no more than 20 percent of the motifs and tale types of his narrative collection are of European origin (1977:4). I would concur with similar estimates for the Chamula tradition. It is easy to find whole texts which are obviously international tale types (for example, Aarne-Thompson Tale Types 34, 175, 313, 565, 1168, and 1373 [S. Thompson 1961]). Biblical stories, homilies, and saints' legends also abound. It is just as easy to locate whole passages which vary in only the slightest degree from the Maya Quiche traditions of the sixteenth century as recorded in the *Popol Vuh* (Gossen 1978). Systematic analysis of Hispanic, Precolumbian, and syncretic aspects of the Tzotzil oral tradition is only now being launched. A seminal work on this subject is Eva Hunt's *The Transformation of the Hummingbird* (1977), which begins with a contemporary Zinacanteco poem (from Laughlin) and proceeds through exhaustive consideration of cognate ideas and texts, ancient and modern, from elsewhere in Mesoamerica to locate its origins. She concludes that there is an ancient Mesoamerican cosmological template (she calls it an "armature") which undergoes a series of transformations to yield modern expressions such as the Zinacanteco hummingbird text. Blaffer's examination of the Zinacanteco "Black-man" myth (1972) is a similar, though somewhat

less ambitious, quest for the historical antecedents of a contemporary Tzotzil tale type. Bricker's *The Indian Christ, the Indian King* (1981) provides a pan-Mayan comparative view of a major Tzotzil tale-type which is associated with revitalization movements.

7.2. ACCULTURATION. A second subject which I have neglected to consider systematically is the impact of literacy and acculturation on the Tzotzil oral tradition. At present, demographic data indicate that the Tzotzil-speaking community, at around 200,000 and increasing annually, is in no danger of disappearing in the next few generations. However, it would be naïve to think that Tzotzil language and literature will be immune to the massive presence of Spanish language and Mexican popular culture, as these are accessible on tens of thousands of radios and hundreds of phonographs in Tzotzil homes. The language and oral tradition have been changing since time immemorial, and there is every reason to believe that such change will be accelerated in the present and future. The unknown factor of course is whether, in the absence of actual speaking and listening knowledge of Spanish, this saturation of the air waves will be absorbed as more than background noise. To the extent that the state and national government-sponsored *castellanización* programs succeed in the Indian schools, it will be increasingly easy for Tzotzil speakers to incorporate Ladino language and culture into their life styles. There is a problem here, however, in that the price of *castellanización* in the schools is the lack of serious attention to the teaching of literacy in Tzotzil and the merits of Indian culture. This makes many parents reluctant to send their children to school, for success in school is likely to remove them forever from the Indian home, the community, and the domestic labor force. It seems, then, that in spite of increasing exposure to Ladino culture, at least some of the communities, notably Chamula and Chenalho, are more determined to edit carefully those parts of Mexican national culture which they wish to encourage. Since language ranks as a key factor of Indian identity, it is unlikely that they will be willing to accept its being programmatically undermined in the schools. They can easily intervene by not sending their children. While there is considerable support among Indian leaders for teaching Spanish as a desirable second language, there is also a desire for acknowledgment of their own language as worthy in its own right. The solution is teaching literacy in Tzotzil. Since this is politically unacceptable to Mexican leaders, progress is not too likely on this front as far as the federal schools are concerned.

7.3. LITERACY. Several recent events, though modest in proportion, give some reason to believe that literacy in Tzotzil, together with some motive for achieving it, is not an impossible prospect. First, the Protestant evangelical movement, through the Summer Institute of Linguistics, has been active in the Tzotzil area for the last thirty years. The New Testament has been translated into several dialects of Tzotzil, among them those of Huixtan, Larrainzar, Zinacantan, and Chamula. Several broadside hymnals have also appeared, giving Tzotzil texts to standard American fundamentalist hymns. Thus, Protestants at least have something to read if they read Tzotzil. Perhaps this has something to do with Protestant success in the Tzotzil area. Second, a privately funded foundation, Instituto de Asesoría Antropológica para la Región Maya, Asociación Civil, whose headquarters are in San Cristobal, has published several Tzotzil pamphlets (Burstein 1977a; 1977b; 1978b; Gossen and López Méndez 1979) which provide light reading material with no political or religious agenda. These publications are available at fiestas and regional markets at nominal cost, and some have proved quite successful. Burstein's *Ja' slo'il jun vinik Chamula k'uxi ch'i tal* (1978a) is worth citing as a great hit in Chamula in 1979. It deals in comic book format with the biography of a popular Chamula political leader and past *presidente municipal*. The two final illustrated episodes in the pamphlet are shown in Figure 4-4. Another

Tzotzil language publication, a comprehensive three-hundred-page local health care handbook (Werner 1980), promises to have some impact as an incentive for encouraging literacy in Tzotzil, for the information it contains is practical and specific, providing a guide to such diverse topics as hygiene, setting a broken leg, and what medicine to purchase in the pharmacy for skin infections. It is of course impossible to predict the future of Tzotzil as a written language and literature, but the potential for a successful turn of events exists.

To conclude, I should like to return to my first rhetorical question: What is a literature? While it has been possible to sketch for Tzotzil some of the things we talk about as literature, it nevertheless remains true that living oral traditions do not conform to the formal, critical, and interpretive canons of written traditions. Even the notion of "the text" to be addressed is illusory, for as Lévi-Strauss has said of myth, a text consists of all of its variants (Lévi-Strauss 1963:217). Even if we had all of the variants, they would of course change tomorrow in the act of re-creation as performance. As the great Spanish ballad scholar Ramón Menéndez-Pidal wrote of his subject, traditional oral poetry "lives in variants" (Menéndez-Pidal 1953:40), so we must accept that any consideration of an oral tradition can be no more than a snapshot in words of what is actually an ephemeral, ever-changing scene.

Therefore, why does it matter at all to take Tzotzil oral tradition seriously? It matters because it is an expressive form which matters to Tzotzils. The vitality of their language carries the very essence of their culture; bearer of its past, medium of its present, and bulwark and teacher for the future. If there is a future for Tzotzil identity in pluralistic Mexico, language will be an important vehicle for its continuance. The Tzotzils for the time being can no doubt take care of themselves on this front.

However, there is the wider world which, ironically, whether left or right in political stance, views minority cultures as nuisances,

FIGURE 4-4. Two episodes from Burstein 1978a, reprinted by permission.

EPISODE 1:

Left: Ruling *presidente* (to hero, Tumin): 'Well, now, you will succeed me one year from now, Tumin Lunes.'

Right: Tumin (replying): 'Well, I don't know if I would do in the Presidency.'

Below: 'But Tumin Lunes is obliged to assume the Presidency.'

EPISODE 2 (*one year later*):

Left: Ruling *presidente* (to hero, Tumin): 'Now, then, we will work in the House of Our Father (Sun).'

Center: Tumin (replying, just after he has received the staff of the Presidency): 'Very well, then, *Presidente.* I will assume your task.'

Right: 'The End.'

Below: 'Tumin Lunes finally assumed the Presidency. He entered office in 1958.'

obstacles to national integration. One way for pluralism to work in Mexico or any nation is for the majority culture to realize that its minorities are an integral part of its national heritage. The potential exists for the Tzotzil to become a major source of communication on this issue, for Mexico's official and popular ideology acknowledges and, in a peculiar way, respects its Indian past. To document the Tzotzil heritage in literature in accessible popular and scholarly works is surely one way that such an educational process can proceed. The foundation for such an enterprise, whether for scholarly or popular ends, exists now. Here are some thoughts for what might be done to enhance the visibility and scholarly significance of Tzotzil literature.

(a) More extensive narrative and other genre collections are needed, beyond Chamula and Zinacantan. There are more than twenty Tzotzil communities for which comprehensive comparative data are not yet available in published form.

(b) Old Tzotzil manuscripts may exist, though very few have surfaced. Persistence and luck may locate them.

(c) Comparative studies of both diachronic and synchronic nature, along the lines laid out by Hunt, Bricker, and Blaffer, can easily be made with data that are available now.

(d) The rich Tzotzil musical heritage, consisting of hundreds of song texts, awaits recording and careful transcription. This has barely been touched by present scholarship.

(e) Oral historical research of a systematic sort· has barely begun in the Tzotzil area, which offers abundant opportunities for such research.

(f) Tzotzil formal couplets and related semantic couplets as they exist in a full and vital Tzotzil tradition offer opportunities to replicate some of Milman Parry and Albert Lord's work on the oral composition of Yugoslav epic songs (Lord 1960). This is, in my opinion, a particularly important line of research to pursue, for Parry and Lord's work led to new understanding of the essentially oral structure of ancient Greek texts, particularly those of the Homeric period. Perhaps the oral formulaic structure of modern Tzotzil poetry, prayer, song, and narrative may provide clues to the interpretation and decipherment of ancient Maya texts, glyphs, codices, and iconography.

(g) If there were a way to facilitate things with government agencies, pedagogical materials for teaching literacy in Tzotzil could easily be prepared. This, of course, is problematical, for any such action would require both community and government backing. Who will bell the cat?

(h) Finally, the Tzotzil area offers immense resources for the hand and mind that can synthesize an epic history of the Tzotzil-speaking peoples. It is pertinent to recall that the great founding epics of modern nations, such as Finland's *Kalevala* (Lönnrot 1963) and Spain's *El Cid* (Menéndez-Pidal 1944–1946), did not flow in a direct way from the bosom of the people. They were synthesized by scholars and artists, Elias Lönnrot and Ramón Menéndez-Pidal, who saw the potential and had the artistic vision and perhaps the ethnic or nationalistic motives to use the people's wisdom and art to synthesize works of grander, more universal scope. The potential for such an undertaking exists in the Tzotzil area. A contemporary *Popol Vuh* awaits its master.

5. Quiche Literature

MUNRO S. EDMONSON

1. INTRODUCTION. The history of Quiche literature, oral and written, like that of other Middle American literatures, can only be described as fragmentary. It may be, however, that we possess more of the relevant fragments than ordinary, and can place them in better historical sequence than is the case for any other aboriginal literature of the Americas. Yucatecan Mayan literature certainly goes back farther, could we but read it literarily. Tzotzil oral literature is vastly better documented. Nahuatl literature is more voluminous. But the literature of the Quiche Maya, seemingly for accidental reasons, is more continuous, or perhaps more continuously documentable, than others.

This fact is largely owing to the preservation of the *Popol Vuh*, the *Book of Counsel*, often called the "New World Bible," and to the lively and still surviving tradition of Quiche drama, traceable from long before the Spanish conquest to the present day. In this chapter I shall delineate the Classic, Postclassic, Colonial, and Modern history of Quiche literature. The previous summary treatments are by Adrián Recinos (1959), Edmonson (1964; 1967), and Robert M. Carmack (1973).

The Maya of Guatemala conceived of time in cycles, and the sixteenth-century *Popol Vuh* (Edmonson 1971) depicts four separate creations, somewhat confused by historical accretions to the text. The Fourth Creation obviously deals in large part with relatively recent history, but the first three could relate to earlier periods. I believe that, at least in part, they do.

Like the Bible itself, the *Popol Vuh* must be regarded as a synthetic literary work. Various elements, motifs, characters, and themes have been added at different dates. The text of the *Popol Vuh* gives us a clue to the antiquity of these additions: it sometimes uses Nahuat.

2. CLASSIC PERIOD. There have been at least five waves of major Mexican contact with Guatemala, to judge from archaeological remains: (1) Olmec, (2) Teotihuacano, (3) Toltec, (4) Nahuat, and (5) Aztec. I believe that the third and fourth of these can be linguistically recognized in the text of the *Popol Vuh*. The fifth was postconquest. It is clear that the Utoaztecan influences are potentially separable into: (a) a segment of the text in which the Nahua has been Mayanized to

an almost unrecognizable degree, and (b) a segment in which the Nahuat (Pipil) words are clearly intelligible in Nahuatl. An example of the first is Xmucane, the name of a goddess, which I reconstruct as *yex-(pa)-omoccan-e* (Nah. 'three things taken two at a time [voc.]': hence three generations on two sides of the family: 'great grandmother'). An example of the second is *tinamit* (Nah. *tina-mitl* 'town'). (See Edmonson 1971: notes to lines 3, 30.)

2.1. MYTH. In its description of the first three creations (Edmonson 1971: lines 1–4708), the *Popol Vuh* has five lengthy passages devoid of Nahuatl words. I conclude that these passages are plausibly the oldest segments of the work and may reasonably be supposed to go back in substantially their extant form to the period of Classic Mayan culture. Taken together, they present a coherent and characteristically Mayan version of the four creations.

2.1.1. THE CREATION OF ANIMALS. The Mother and Father, Former and Shaper, created the animals and gave them their assignments, but found them incapable of speech and hence of worship, so they were killed (Edmonson 1971: lines 261–324).

2.1.2. THE MUD PEOPLE. Since dawn was approaching, Former and Shaper tried again, and made beings of mud, but they dissolved in water (Edmonson 1971: lines 325–484).

2.1.3. THE DOLLS MADE OF WOOD. Former and Shaper then carved wooden dolls, but they had no hearts and minds and were incapable of worship, so they were destroyed in a great rain of glue and were attacked by fierce bats and jaguars and by the rebellion of their domestic animals and household utensils, and were finally transformed into monkeys (Edmonson 1971: lines 667–820).

2.1.4. THE HERO TWINS. The story of the Twins begins with their father and his brother who descended to Hell and were tricked and defeated by the Lords of Hell. A virgin maiden was then impregnated by the spirit, the Word (the skull spittle of the Twins' fa-ther), and they grew miraculously and overthrew their older brothers, the monkeys. By sheer cleverness they overcame the relevant obstacles, recovering their father's ball game equipment with the assistance of the Rat that still crawls along Mayan ridgepoles (mythologically speaking: Wauchope 1938), descending to Hell, successfully surviving its houses of torment, and defeating the Lords of Hell in a memorable ball game (as the preceding generation had failed to do). They arranged for their own ritual death and revival and were invited back to Hell, where they defeated the Lords of Hell for a second time by legerdemain and avenged their ancestors by denying Hell any future tribute (Edmonson 1971: lines 1675–1686, 1979–3218, 3349–4705).

Something of the feel of the classic myth (and drama) of *The Hero Twins* may be illustrated in the following passage.

And the lord (of Hell) spoke to them:
"Let this dog of mine be sacrificed
And let his face be revived by you,"
They were told.
"All right," they said.
Then they sacrificed the dog,
Reviving his face again.
And truly the dog was happy
When his face was revived.
He wagged his tail delightedly
When his face was revived.
(Edmonson 1971: lines 4395–4404)

This scene, in which the Twins amuse the Lords of Hell with their dances, appears to have been a favorite of the Classic vase painters.

The question arises as to whose myths these are. Brief as they are, the first three creations are occasionally and variously represented in other recorded Mayan mythologies, and the version in the *Popol Vuh*, while laconic, is visual enough to justify the speculation that it might find identifiable expression in the iconography of the Classic Maya. So far as I am aware, no such identification has been proposed. On the other hand, a number of Mayan scholars are persuaded that scenes from *The Hero Twins* are depicted on Classic Mayan polychrome vases. I am sympathetic to this point of view, but until recently the evidence has been flawed by the fact that none of the relevant vases, dozens of them in private hands, had a known provenience. Recently four such vases have been recovered in situ (Chase n.d.), and provisionally dated to the Middle Classic or even earlier.

It seems clear that the myth was not restricted to the "ancestral Quiche," whatever may have been the language spoken by the linguistic antecedents of the Quiche in, say, the eighth century. Presumably this would have been what Lyle Campbell (1978 : 36) calls Core Quichean. Jaguar Deer (Exbalanque) appears in Kekchi myth, but I know of no cognate expression in Yucatec.

2.2. POETRY. The *Popol Vuh* also contains evidence of Classic period drama, poetry, and oratory. The American Indians generally place great emphasis on the formality and elegance of public discourse, and those of Middle America are no exceptions. This is underlined in the *Popol Vuh* in a number of references to the importance of the Word. Indeed, the act of creation is repeatedly depicted as an act of speech:

The Mother said this,
    And the Father:
"Should it only be still,
    Or should it not be silent
Under the trees
    And shrubs?
Indeed it would be good if there were
    Guardians for them," they said.
And when they thought
    And spoke,
At a stroke there came to be
    And were created
Deer
    And birds.

(Edmonson 1971: lines 273–286)

Creation began with a rhetorical question, not to be satisfactorily answered until discourse became reciprocal between gods and humans.

As is true of other Middle American languages, Quiche formal discourse is intrinsically poetic, being composed of semantic couplets linked to each other by the synonymy or antonymy of one or more pairs of words, as in the passage just cited (see also Neuenswander and Arnold 1977; Norman 1976a). The tightness of the parallelism varies with the formality of the discourse and becomes strongest in lyric poems and prayers. Unfortunately none of these are quoted in the sections of the text that appear to belong to the Classic period, though there is a reference to the *Spider Monkey Hunter* song (Edmonson 1971: line 2790). There is also one near-prayer—perhaps more accurately interpretable as an incantation (Edmonson 1971: lines 2525ff).

There is extensive use of humor in *The Hero Twins*, as in the mad chase of the Lords of Hell after a rabbit masquerading as a bouncing ball, or the reaction of the Twins' father and uncle when they were tricked into sitting on a hot rock. There is also occasional use of punning, as in line 4209 (Edmonson 1971), which produces a triple pun on *ch'ohih* 'straighten out', *ch'ooh* 'fight', and *choh* 'oven'.

2.3. RHETORIC. Formalism is also represented in the Classic texts by the use of formulas of address. Thus in lines 3595ff (Edmonson 1971) the Hero Twins greet the Lords of Hell politely with the formula *q'ala* 'may it brighten', perhaps the eighth-century equivalent of the modern *zaqarik* 'it has whitened'. Quiche also uses polite address, though the antiquity of the forms employed may be questioned. Polite address does occur in the Classical section of the text (Edmonson 1971: note to line 1003). When the mother of the Twins addresses her mother-in-law for the first time, she uses both formalisms:

"I have come, (formula)
    Oh (*lal*) mother-in-law." (polite address)

(Edmonson 1971: lines 2437–2438)

Her mother-in-law replies in the familiar and with a comic inversion of the formula:

"If you see that you (*at*) have come then, (familiar)

Go on back." (antiformula)
(Edmonson 1971: lines 2451–2452)

2.4. DRAMA. The saga of *The Hero Twins* is more than a myth: as it is presented in the *Popol Vuh* it is also a drama. The narrative is spun out in lengthy direct discourse—almost a script for the ritual drama. Most of the chapters could serve equally well as scenes. Brasseur notes that the *Spider Monkey Hunter* dance (*Hun Ah Pu Q'oy*) was still performed under that name in the mid-nineteenth century (see Edmonson 1971: note to line 2790), and other dances are also referred to in the Classic section of the text: the *Weasel Dance* (*Xah Kux*), the *Screech Owl Dance* (*Xah Puhuy*), and the *Armadillo Dance* (*Xah Iboy*). (The Quiche still refer to their dramas as dances—Sp. *baile*, Qui. *xahoh*.) These four "dances" were probably scenes from the larger ritual drama of *The Hero Twins*. The cast of characters (in order of appearance) was as follows:

One Hunter, the Twins' father
Seven Hunter, his brother
The four Roads
One Death, first Lord of Hell
Seven Death, second Lord of Hell
Blood Girl, the Twins' mother, daughter of Blood Chief
Blood Chief, her father, fourth Lord of Hell
The four Owls, messengers of Hell
Grandmother, mother of One Hunter and Seven Hunter, possibly Coyote
One Monkey, older brother of One Howler and half-brother of the Twins
One Howler, younger brother of One Monkey and half-brother of the Twins
Hunter, older son of One Hunter, the elder Twin
Jaguar Deer, younger son of One Hunter, the younger Twin
The Helpful Animals (Dove, Panther, Jaguar, Deer, Rabbit, Wildcat, Coyote, Pig, Coati, Rat)

Hawk, ninth Lord of Hell
Mosquito, a Helpful Animal
The remaining eight Lords of Hell (Flying Noose, third; Pus Maker, fifth; Bile Maker, sixth; Bone Staff, seventh; Skull Staff, eighth; Snare, tenth; Bloody Teeth, eleventh; Bloody Claws, twelfth)
Ants, the twelfth Helpful Animal
Grandfather; Possum, the thirteenth Helpful Animal
Poor
Rich

The numerology of the cast is of interest. There are nine members of the Twins' family, thirteen Helpful Animals, thirteen Lords of Hell, four Roads, four Messenger Owls, five Demons (One Death; Seven Death, Blood Chief, Blood Girl, and Hawk), and two Clowns (Poor and Rich). There is a measure of overlap in this classification, as the Twins' mother has been included both as a member of their family and among the Lords of Hell (as the daughter of one); and the Twins' Grandmother and Grandfather may be equated with two of the Helpful Animals (Coyote and Possum). The permutation of these numbers provides a redundant reference to all of the basic cycles of the Mayan calendar: 2, 4, 5, 9 (4 + 5), 13 (4 + 4 + 5), 18 (9 + 4 + 5; 13 + 5), 19 (13 + 4 + 2; 9 + 4 + 4 + 2) and 20 (9 + 4 + 5 + 2). The double counting of Grandmother, Grandfather, and Blood Girl would bring the total cast of characters to exactly fifty two! There are other characters in the drama, but these appear to have been added later and are not given speaking parts in the Classical section of the text.

In general calendrical structure, *The Hero Twins* is strongly reminiscent of the Yucatecan *Ceremonial of the Baktun* (Edmonson n.d.t). It does not seem too outrageous to propose that it may have been the *baktun* ceremonial of 10.0.0.0.0 (A.D. 830), or even earlier. Scenes from the *baktun* ceremonial appear to be reflected in the Classic text in two cycles in the same order as in the Yucatecan ceremonial. The acts of the *baktun* ceremonial and the seeming correspondences to it in the

110

Popol Vuh may be listed as follows: Act 1: Mead (Edmonson 1971: line 1675); Act 2: Mask (lines 1855, 3413); Act 3: Cycle (lines 2013, 3430); Act 4: Fire (line 2039); Act 5: Bird (line 3460); Act 6: Heart (line 2159); Act 7: Rain (line 2283); Act 8: Circuit (line 2300); Act 9: Katun (missing); Act 10: Year (line 2321); Act 11: Pacing (missing); Act 12: Dawn (line 4025); Act 13: Sacrifice (line 2341); Act 14: Examination (line 2485); Act 15: Word (line 2561); Act 16: Penance (line 2611); Act 17: Commemoration (line 2790); Act 18: Counting (lines 2819, 4059); Act 19: Farce (line 4140); Act 20: Sermon (lines 2867, 4560).

3. EARLY POSTCLASSIC PERIOD. Sometime in the tenth century there appears to have been an incursion of Nahua speakers into the western Guatemalan area. They added words to the Quiche vocabulary and motifs to Quiche mythology, and they importantly revised the tradition that was to lead to the *Popol Vuh*. The significant words added were reshaped to fit the pattern of Mayan pronunciation, and hence are sometimes difficult to recognize as Nahua. They include: Xpiacoc (*yexpaococcane*), Xmucane (*yexpaomoccane*), Cipacna (*cipactonalli*), and Cipacyalo (*cipactli-alo*). Other, less distorted, Nahuatlisms may have been introduced at this time: Tepev (*tepeuh*), Toltecat (*toltecatl*), Naval (*nahualli*), Tamazul (*tamazollin*). They are arguably all names of gods, priests, or spirits.

The impact of this first Nahua influence in western Guatemala appears to have been primarily religious, and I believe it imposed a new cosmological structure on the *Popol Vuh*: one of five creations instead of four. This had the effect of revising our received version of the first three creations.

3.1. MYTH. The Early Postclassic alterations in the tradition introduce Quetzalcoatl to the Quiche and substitute him for (or unite him with) the Former and Shaper of the older Mayan tradition, inserting an extra creation about Seven Parrot and his sons and altering the cycles of creation along the following lines.

3.1.1. QUETZAL SERPENT. Quetzalcoatl appears in the *Popol Vuh* under his Quiche name, Q'uq' Kumatz, though Late Postclassic texts refer to him in Nahuat as Quetzalcoat and as Nacxit. He is identified with the ancestral creator gods of the Quiche, Former and Shaper, the Mother and Father, Grandmother and Grandfather, and is poetically paired with Tepev and obliquely aligned with Hummingbird. Quetzalcoatl and Tepev appear together in the water "wrapped in quetzal and dove feathers," and through the power of the Word they produce the First Creation, the creation of animals. By implication, Quetzalcoatl was accompanied by Huitzilopochtli. The animals still prove to be incapable of prayer and the first creation is ended (Edmonson 1971: lines 1–189).

3.1.2. THE MUD PEOPLE. Except for the reidentification of Former and Shaper by their Nahuat names, Xpiacoc and Xmucane, the Second Creation remains intact (Edmonson 1971: lines 325–484).

3.1.3. THE DOLLS MADE OF WOOD. Xpiacoc, Xmucane, and Quetzalcoatl are all introduced into the Third Creation, though they drop out of the account of the flood that ends it (Edmonson 1971: lines 667–820).

3.1.4. SEVEN PARROT. Seven Parrot is a distinctly Nahuat character. Though he is named in Quiche, he appears to have had a Nahuat day name, probably Seven Cozcacuauhtli, and his two sons also had calendric names: Cipactonal (Mayanized to Cipacna) and Ome Icxit (Maya Kab r Aqan). Their mother was Chimalmat (the mother of Quetzalcoatl as well).

With the assistance of the grandparental gods, the Hero Twins achieve the destruction of Seven Parrot and his sons for the sin of pride. The Twins are somewhat confusingly identified as the grandchildren of Xpiacoc and Xmucane, and Hunter (Hun Ah Pu) and Jaguar Deer (Ix Balam Keh) are thus converted into the central figures of both the Fourth and Fifth creations (Edmonson 1971: lines 821–1674).

3.1.5. THE HERO TWINS. The Early Postclassic version of the saga of the Twins rather confounds the Classic version in three respects: (1) it adds an extra generation to the

111

story, (2) it inserts the *Fable of the Louse* (Chapter 29), and (3) it ends the account of this creation with the transformation of the Twins into the Sun and Moon (Chapter 42). Otherwise the Classic version appears to have survived into the sixteenth century pretty much intact (Edmonson 1971: lines 1687–1978, 3219–3348, 4659–4708).

3.2. POETRY. I do not perceive any massive change in the poetry and rhetoric of the Early Postclassic literature. It is to be expected that Nahuat influence should introduce the Quiche to couplet kenning (*difrasismos*), and that appears to have happened (Edmonson 1970; 1973). Thus the first couplet of the *Popol Vuh* contains two levels of meaning:

This is the root of the former word.
    Here is Quiche by name.
              (Edmonson 1971: lines 1–2)

This may be taken to mean that the origin of the hieroglyphic tradition was esoterically referred to as 'many trees' (Qui. *K'iche*; Nah. *quauhtlamallan*; eventually Sp. *Guatemala*).

3.3. DRAMA. Although it is more schematic, the account of *Seven Parrot* and his sons suggests drama in nearly the same degree as the earlier story of *The Hero Twins*. It is highly iconic and makes frequent use of direct discourse. The characters in the drama are (in order of appearance):

    Seven Parrot, a Lord
    Hunter, the older Twin
    Jaguar Deer, the younger Twin
    Alligator, older son of Seven Parrot
    Shield Bearer, wife of Seven Parrot
    Two Leg, younger son of Seven Parrot
    Grandmother, of the Twins, Coati
    Grandfather, of the Twins, Pig
    Four Hundred Sons, gods of wine and the Milky Way

Since the "Four Hundred Sons" act as a unit, the play has nine roles. In connection with this drama and in other passages of this apparent date, the manuscript makes free use of direct discourse, but there are no examples of formal oratory. While prayers are referred to several times, none are directly quoted.

3.4. RHETORIC. There is no abrupt change in the rhetoric. Respect forms continue in use. The Grandparents, for example, use polite address to Seven Parrot throughout, addressing him as Lord, and he uses familiar address to them, though addressing them as "our grandfathers" (Edmonson 1971: line 1065). Alligator and the Four Hundred Sons use familiar address to each other, as do the Twins and Two Leg. There is notably less use of humor in *Seven Parrot* than in *The Hero Twins*, and punning is rare. The motif of trickery and loss of face is continued from the earlier period.

4. LATE POSTCLASSIC PERIOD. In the fifteenth century there was a fresh wave of Nahuat influence in western Guatemala. It is represented in the *Popol Vuh* in a large number of Nahuat words that have undergone very little modification as they were adopted into Quiche, presumably because there wasn't enough time: *acul, acutec, aztapulul, cahuiztan, cauizimah, chinamit, coatepec, iztayol, macutax, mexico, mixtam, nacxit, nanahuac, oloman, petatuyub, quetzalcoat, tatil, tecpan, tecum, tepepul, tinamit, tonatiuh, tulan, xpuch, yaqui, yolcoat, zuyua*. Most of the account of the Fourth Creation in the *Popol Vuh* is sprinkled with these terms, largely p rsonal names, place names, and political or military expressions.

It is quite possible that some modifications were made at this time to the received body of literary traditions, particularly those involving passages containing such words as *tepev, naval,* and *toltecat*. They appear, however, to have been minor in most cases. There may also have been something of a Mayan revival going on, recasting the mythology into the Four Creation model of Mayan cosmology, more or less as it stands in the *Popol Vuh*. This is suggested by the fact that twenty-two of the fifty-five chapters dealing with the Fourth Creation have no Nahuatlisms at all. The remaining thirty-three chapters contain the Nahuatlisms that have been listed above. The account of the Fourth Creation averages one Nahuatlism every 21 lines (as compared with one every 233 lines in the Third Creation, one every 27 in the Second, and one every 36 in the First). A number of the chapters without any at all may simply be too short to constitute a reasonable sample. I conclude nonetheless that the text on the Fourth Creation is probably a mixture of the Mayan myth of the origin of the Great Quiche and a Toltec myth of the origins and wanderings of their Nahuat-speaking conquerors. Both belong to the fifteenth century, though both doubtless contain older elements.

4.1. MYTH.

4.1.1. THE ORIGIN OF THE QUICHE. The people of the Fourth Creation were made from corn and water discovered by Former and Shaper at a place called Cleft Mountain, revealed to them by Wildcat, Coyote, Parakeet, and Crow. The people immediately gave thanks to the gods. They proceeded to divide into three groups, the Quiche, Tamub, and Ilokab, who were known as the Great Quiche. Together with the Cakchiquel, Rabinal, and Tzutuhil, they fasted and waited for the dawn. Then sacrifice was begun, giving rise to warfare (Edmonson 1971: lines 4747–4750; 4895–4954; 5647–5912; 6369–6462; 6782–6938).

4.1.2. THE ORIGIN OF THE TOLTECS. The four First Fathers, once they were created by Xpiacoc and Xmucane, went to Tula Zuyua, the place of Seven Caves and Seven Canyons, where they got their gods, fire, and incense, and began their wanderings, dividing into tribes, which captured and sacrificed each other. They eventually reached Fire Peak, obtained the insignia of royalty from Quetzalcoatl, and finally settled at Quiche (Edmonson 1971: lines 4709–4746; 4751–4894; 4955–5248; 5297–5646; 5913–6368; 6463–6781; 7071–7666).

4.1.3. THE QUICHE KINGDOM. The final segment of the *Popol Vuh* is historical rather than mythological. It presents the history of *The Quiche Kingdom*. As a segment of the

Popol Vuh, this account undoubtedly took its present form in the mid-sixteenth century. It may nonetheless have been composed in oral or in hieroglyphic form before the conquest of Guatemala, and all but a few lines of it are preconquest in reference.

In the early fifteenth century, around 1420, the city of Quiche (Q'umarik Ah, Utatlan) came under the rule of a lord called Quetzalcoatl (Q'uq' Kumatz), who is reported to have ruled alone, occupying both the first and second ranked positions in the Quiche hierarchy, perhaps from 1420 to 1450. Around 1450 he was succeeded by Blood (Kiq'ab), who enlarged the Quiche kingdom to its maximum extent and died in 1490, leaving the throne to Seven Incense (Nooh), 1490–1500. He was succeeded in turn by Grandfather (Tecum), 1500–1524, who was killed when Don Pedro de Alvarado (Tonatiuh) arrived to collect tribute (Edmonson 1971: lines 7667–8357).

4.2. POETRY AND RHETORIC. The account of the Fourth Creation in the *Popol Vuh* is understandably fuller than those of the preceding three, constituting nearly half of the surviving text. It is rich in legend and history as well as myth. It quotes formal prayers and snatches from the *Song of Tula*, and makes considerable use of direct discourse, but while sections of it are visually graphic, it contains no drama. It is relatively humorless and puns rarely if at all, and while it uses titles of respect, it does not employ polite address: even the gods are addressed throughout in the familiar. An additional feel for the content and style of fifteenth-century Quiche literature may be obtained from the following fragments and examples.

4.2.1. PRAYER TO ONE LEG.

Hail thou of the five days
  Thou One Leg,
Thou Heart of Heaven
  And Earth,
Thou giver of what is yellow
  And what is green,
And thou giver of daughters
  And sons:

113

Drip down,
  Pour down
Thy greenness,
  Thy yellowness;
Give thou, pray, life
  And sustenance
For my children,
  My sons,
That they may multiply,
  That they may continue
As nourishers to thee
  And supporters to thee,
Calling upon thee in the paths
  And roads,
At the rivers
  And canyons,
Under the trees
  And bushes.
Give them daughters
  And sons.
Let there be no disgrace
  Or captivity,
Fighting
  Or perversion.
Let no demons come behind them
  Or before them.
Let them not fall;
  Let them not be wounded;
Let them not fornicate;
  Let them not be sentenced;
Let them not fall below the road
  Or above the road.
Let nothing afflict
  Or assail them
Behind
  Or before.
Put them on the green path,
  The green road.
Let nothing disgrace them
  Or imprison them
By thy misfortune
  Or thy enchantment.
Good be
  Their essence
As nourishers to thee,

Supporters to thee,
Before thy mouth,
  Before thy face,
Thou Heart of Heaven,
  Thou Heart of Earth,
Thou Shrouded Glory,
  And thou, Storm,
Lord Jaguar,
  Fire Peak,
Womb of heaven,
  Womb of earth,
For the four creations,
  And the four destructions.
Let there just be light;
  Let there just be peace in them
Before thy mouth
  And before thy face,
O thou,
  God.

(Edmonson 1971: lines 8197–8268)

4.2.2. THE SONG OF TULA. Three brief fragments of the *Song of Tula*, known in Quiche as *It Is Hidden* (*Ka Muqu*), are quoted in the *Popol Vuh*:

Alas, it is not here that we shall see the dawn,
When the sun is born again,
  Brightening the face of the earth.

(Edmonson 1971: lines 5630–5632)

Alas! We were lost at Tula!
  We have broken ourselves up.
We have left behind again our older brothers
  Our younger brothers.
Where did they see the sun then?
  Where might they have been when it dawned?

(Edmonson 1971: lines 6065–6070)

O our sons,
We are going.
  But we shall return.
Bright words,
  Bright commands are our farewell to you.

(Edmonson 1971: lines 7110–7114)

114

The lyricism of these fragments is not characteristic of the text as a whole.

4.2.3. THE TULA SCRIPTURE. The question arises how these various traditions came down from antiquity. Some may have been oral, but some were almost certainly written. At least one fragment is explicitly identified as written (Edmonson 1971: lines 7280–7318), and the text calls it *The Tula Scripture* (*u tz'ibal Tulan*). It deals with the wanderings of the second generation of Toltec lords, Chief Two (Qo Kaib), Chief Acutec (Qo Acutec), and Chief Lord (Qo Ahau), who went to the sunrise to get the insignia of royalty from Quetzalcoatl (Nacxit):

. . . Canopy
  And throne,
Nose Bone
  And Earring (Nah. *champuchtli,*
    nacochtli),
Jade Labret (Nah. *tentetl*)
  And Gold Beads (Nah. *cozcapetlatl*),
Panther Claws
  And Jaguar Claws,
Owl Skull
  And Deer,
Armband of Precious Stones (Nah.
macuetlaxtli, matemecatl)
  And Snail Shell Bracelet (Nah.
    matzopeztli),
Bowing
  And Bending,
Filled Teeth
  And Inlay,
Parrot Feather Crest
  And Royal Crane Panache (Nah.
    aztapolloli, cuachictli).
      (Edmonson 1971: lines 7295–7312)

No less than seven of these elements parallel those of the Aztec emperor, and four of them appear in garbled Nahuat in the Quiche text. Since the Quiche word *tz'ibal* may mean either writing or painting, it is my conclusion that at least this passage and perhaps other parts of the Toltec mythology of this period were preserved in a Nahua picture manuscript which the Quiche called *The Tula Scripture.*

4.3. POPOL VUH: THE BOOK OF COUNSEL. By the coming of the Spanish, the *Popol Vuh* had already taken approximately its present form, and the postconquest accretions to the text are minor and brief. Spanish words occur in the text at lines 45–46, 7642, 8415, 8417–8418, 8495–8497 and 8584. When the anonymous author of the work as we have it organized and transcribed it around 1550–1556, he apparently added some comments to the first chapter and brought the work up to date by adding the last thirteen chapters (226 lines) to summarize it. (Presumably the anachronistic hispanicism of line 7642 was also added at this time.) The remainder of our text can be said to be aboriginal: moreover, it was derived from a written work which the author himself (lines 49, 8149) calls the *Popol Vuh* (*Book of Counsel*). Whether this was a "book" of paintings or of hieroglyphic writing may perhaps never be known, and even if it were glyphic, we have no way of knowing how much the sixteenth-century author added to it from oral sources or whether he changed the textual order of the received tradition. It seems clear nonetheless that there was a fifteenth-century *Popol Vuh* and that it contained all of the literary materials we have considered up to this point.

4.4. DRAMA.

4.4.1. THE KNIGHT OF RABINAL. Although the *Popol Vuh* does not give us any late Postclassic drama, I believe we have some—the entire 3100-line text of one, in fact: *The Knight of Rabinal* or *Rabinal Achi*, also called in Quiche *The Dance of the Drum* (*Xahoh Tun;* see Carmack 1973:325). Collected in Rabinal in 1850, and published in Quiche and French by Brasseur de Bourbourg (1862), the play contains no Spanish words, but it has frequent Nahuatlisms: Tepecanic, *teponovoz* (Nah. *teponaztli*), and repeatedly *yaquim*. It refers to quite a number of Quiche towns, naming them all in Maya. (There is good reason to suppose that the renaming of Quiche towns in Nahuatl did not begin until after the Spanish conquest.) The text also includes some indentifiable archaisms, such as the greeting *kala* (found as *q'ala* in the Classic version of *The Hero Twins*, as cited above).

The plot of the drama refers to a Postclassic battle between Quiche and Rabinal, possibly in the fourteenth century but probably even earlier, since many of the characteristic Nahuatlisms of the Late Postclassic (*chinamit*, *tinamit*, etc.) are given in Quiche. The language of the *Rabinal Achi* and its poetic style are completely traditional Maya. I conclude that René Acuña's (1975) claim that the drama was not even written by an Indian, let alone Precolumbian, is simply absurd. I date it to the fourteenth century and consider our text to be a late copy of a sixteenth-century manuscript recording of the earlier oral tradition.

The cast of characters of the *Rabinal Achi* (in order of appearance) is as follows:

Knight of Quiche, warrior of Quiche
Knight of Rabinal, son of Five Rain
Five Rain, Lord of Rabinal
Female Slave, of the Knight of Rabinal
Male Slave, of Five Rain

In addition there are these characters without speaking parts:

Queen, wife of Five Rain
Quetzal's Mother, wife of the Knight of Rabinal
Twelve Eagle Knights, warriors of Rabinal
Twelve Jaguar Knights, warriors of Rabinal

If we group the Knights, we get a nine-character structure, just as in the Early Postclassic drama of *Seven Parrot*.

In a sense the drama is mistitled, since its subject is the heroism, capture, and sacrifice of the Knight of Quiche, and it is his bravery that constitutes the center of the piece. Indeed the drama is sometimes called *K'iche Vinak*, the *Man of Quiche*. It is ably recorded and well (if grandiosely) translated into French by Brasseur (1862). Translations into Spanish also exist (see Monterde 1955). The dance continues to be performed in Rabinal with traditional masks, costumes, and associated music, some of which was written

out by Brasseur, and modern versions of which have been collected by Carroll E. Mace (1970).

The *Rabinal Achi* shows continuity with earlier dramatic tradition and with later plays as well, and I continue to believe that it is one of our very best windows on the aboriginal theater of Middle America. A section of the text follows.

The Knight of Quiche has been defeated by the Knight of Rabinal and speaks:

It has come to
  My ending—
The many days,
  The many nights
Here between heaven
  And earth.
Indeed, did nothing
  Come from
My courage,
  My manhood?
Ah heaven!
  Ah earth!
I shall go someplace into my mountain,
  My valley!
      (Edmonson n.d.m: lines 1031–1044)

He proves himself the perfect tragic hero, and at the end of the play he is sacrificed.

5. THE SIXTEENTH CENTURY.

5.1. TITLES. For historical and literary purposes we may begin "the sixteenth century" with the fall of the Quiche capital (Utatlan) in 1524. Its characteristic literary product in Quiche was the *Title* (*Título*), a document usually written to support claims to office and title in the Spanish system by appealing to the antiquity of nobility of the authors. The final section of the *Popol Vuh* itself may be considered to be such a *Title*, but there are many others. We possess the texts of twelve of these documents in Quiche or close translations. We know of five more because they were cited by Fuentes y Guzmán in the seventeenth century (Fuentes y Guzmán 1932–1933), and Carmack (1973) reports on the discovery of an additional eight, six of them in Spanish. All of the important

116

ones were produced in a single generation (1550–1583). The ones we have in Quiche text are as follows:

1. (1550–1556) *Title of the Kavek* (Kavek)
2. (1551) *Title of Sacapulas* (Toltekat)
3. (1556) *Title of the Lords of Totonicapan* (Kavek)
4. (1558) *Title of Izkin* (Nihay)
5. (1558) *Title of Ixcuin* (Nihay)
6. (1558?) *Title of Nihaib III* (Nihay)
7. (1560?) *Title of C'oyoi* (Ahav)
8. (1579) *Origin of the Lords of Zapotitlan* (Kavek)
9. (1580) *History of Juan de Torres* (Tam)
10. (1583) *Title of the Indians of Santa Clara la Laguna* (Kavek)
11. (?) *Paper of Francisco Gómez* (Tam)
12. (1600) *Title of Uchabaja* (Uchabaja [Tam])

The characteristic feature of the Quiche *Titles* presents a clear continuity with the Toltec literature of the late Postclassic. The way to prove your title is to begin with creation itself (the Fourth) and then document your own descent from the First Four Fathers, preferably from Tula on.

Titles are always identifiable by patrilineage, as in the above list, and from the point of view of the Kavek of Quiche the order of precedence was:

I. The Great Quiche (The Three Quiche)
  A. Quiche
    1. Kavek
    2. Nihay
    3. Ahav
    4. Zaqiq'
  B. Tam
  C. Ilokab
II. Cakchiquel
III. Tzutuhil

Titles exist for the Cakchiquel (Recinos 1950a; 1957) and Tzutuhil (Carmack 1973), but I am concerned with the four Quiche lineages for which we possess documentation for the period, the Kavek, the Nihay, the Ahav, and the Tam.

5.1.1. THE TITLES OF THE KAVEKS. Titles 1, 2, 3, 8, and 10 document the lineage claims of the number one lineage of the city of Quiche (Gumarcaah, Utatlan, later Santa Cruz Quiche)—the Kavek lineage.

Title 1, the *Title of the Kavek* (Edmonson 1971: lines 7667–8584, the last 917 lines of the *Popol Vuh*), lists the titles of the Kavek, Nihay, Ahav, and Zaqiq' lineages and retraces their ancestry from perhaps the beginning of the fifteenth century. It does not repeat the preceding generations already listed in the *Popol Vuh*, and indeed there are contradictions within the *Popol Vuh* and among the Quiche *Titles* about the count of generations from the First Fathers (Edmonson 1971:note to line 8552; Wauchope 1948; Carmack 1973). There are relatively detailed reviews of the careers of Quetzalcoatl (Qu'uq' Kumatz) and Blood (Kiq'ab) and a further review of the genealogy and ranks of the Quiche lords.

Title 2, *Title of Sacapulas* (Carmack 1973; Acuña 1968), has a relatively brief Quiche text giving four First Fathers in the approved Toltec fashion and listing the boundaries of the land claimed by their descendants of the Toltekat lineage of Sacapulas. It is not clear what relation they bore to the lineages of the central Quiche, but on the grounds that Ah Toltekat was a Kavek title, I suspect they may have been a sublineage of the Kavek.

Title 3, *Title of the Lords of Totonicapan* (Recinos 1950a; 1953; Edmonson n.d.p), known only from the 1834 Spanish translation by José Chonay, is nonetheless an important Kavek document, paralleling at length the latter part of the Fourth Creation in the *Popol Vuh*. It traces the same ancestors and agrees on the supremacy of the Kavek. Chonay's translation is sufficiently tight that it can be scanned in couplets.

Title 8, *The Origin of the Lords of Zapotitlan* (Edmonson n.d.j), gives in 134 lines a somewhat divergent twelve-generation genealogy of the Kavek lords from Jaguar Quiche to Eight Monkey, whose grandson is identified as a Great Elder of Rabinal who is applying to be mayor of the Royal Court. It is not clear what association it has with Zapotitlan.

Title 10, *Title of the Indians of Santa Clara la Laguna* (Recinos 1957; Edmonson n.d.q), in 280 lines, traces the ancestry of Santa

Clara la Laguna from the mid-fifteenth century (Blood and Eight Monkey) on, dating itself to 1583. This version was recertified at Quiche in 1640, and is largely a list of unidentified boundary markers.

5.1.2. THE NIHAY TITLES. There are four surviving *Titles* of the Great-Houses (Nihaib), three of them in Quiche. None of them goes back very far, and they are of relatively minor literary interest.

Title 4, *Title of Izkin* (Recinos 1957; Edmonson n.d.o), in 888 lines, identifies with a conquering ancestor named Dog (Izkin), claiming recompense for conquests made in the northern (Chixoy) area for the Quiche kings. It was executed at Santa Cruz del Quiche.

Title 5, *Title of Ixcuin* (Recinos 1957; Edmonson n.d.n), in 888 lines, identifies with a conquering ancestor named Dog (Ixcuin) who conquered the western Quiche towns from the Mam even before the rule of Blood (early fifteenth century). It is associated with Quezaltenango and Momostenango and was signed before Alvarado himself, or so it claims.

Title 6, *Title of Nihaib III* (Carmack 1973:349–352), dates itself to 1542, but that is unreasonably early, and I believe it to be more or less contemporary with the other Nihay titles, which it closely resembles. There is also a *Title of Nihaib IV*, but we have it only in Spanish and it is devoid of literary interest (see below). None of the Nihaib *Titles* claim Toltec ancestors: their claims to preference are based upon the right of conquest and service to the Quiche kings, though the use of the name Dog (Nah. *itzcuintli*) is significant. The Kavek documents identify the ancestry of the Nihay with the second ranking of the four Toltec Fathers.

5.1.3. THE AHAV TITLE. Title 7, *Title of C'oyoi* (Carmack 1973:265–345), is a lengthy and typically Toltec *Title* which Carmack believes to be Kavek, but which I am persuaded presents the land claims of the Ahav lineage, focusing on a territory just north of Quezaltenango. It is one of the longest *Titles* extant and is of substantial historical and lit-

erary interest. It includes a detailed description of the conquest.

5.1.4. THE TAM TITLES. Title 9, *The History of Juan de Torres* (Recinos 1957; Edmonson n.d.g), traces at length (1100 lines) the lineage and title of the descendants of the third of the First Fathers of the Kavek [*sic*], Nought (Mahqinalo). The divisions and subdivisions of the Tam are complex, and so are their wanderings from Tula, but both are listed in tedious detail by Juan de Torres, a member of one of the sublineages, to justify a 1580 land claim, the borders of which are listed but have not been identified.

Title 11, *Paper of Francisco Gómez* (Edmonson n.d.k), is a brief (143-line) and truncated Tam *Title* of unknown date. It lists four ancestors and traces the ancestral wanderings from Egypt instead of Tula. I would guess that it dates to around 1580. The Tam were more detached from the Kavek than were the Nihay and the Ahav, and their mythological history is correspondingly distinct.

Title 12, *Title of Uchabaja* (Carmack 1973), dating to the first year of the seventeenth century, shows clearly that the earlier *Title* tradition was definitively dead by 1600. It is a land claim, but no effort is made to give an aboriginal rationale for it, mythological or historical.

5.1.5. THE TÍTULOS OF FUENTES Y GUZMÁN. In his seventeenth-century *Recordación florida*, Francisco Antonio de Fuentes y Guzmán (1932–1933), an otherwise somewhat unsatisfactory historian, included footnotes, referring to five Quiche *Títulos* since lost. Two of them are datable, and something of the contents of four of them can be surmised despite the fact that Fuentes' reading of Quiche was badly flawed. The first four of them were apparently Tam.

Title 13, *Nobility of Santa Catarina Ixtahuacán*, identified with Francisco García, Calel Tesumpan Xauila, and plausibly dated by Fuentes to 1561, is clearly a Tam Title. (He also dates it to 1541 and 1544.) Although badly garbled, the original manuscript of at least twenty-three folio pages was clearly a Toltec origin myth beginning at Tula and tracing the ancestry of the Tam to Utatlan, covering the wars of Kiq'ab and the role of Tecum in the conquest. Somewhat less plausibly it is cited as telling of two Quiche princesses who fled to Santiago Atitlan (A Tzikina Hay) and provoked a war between the Quiche and the Tzutuhil.

Title 14, *The Manuscript of Juan de Torres Macario*, is dated to 1568 and associated with Totonicapan. It presents the status claim of Juan Macario, son of Juan de Torres, son of Nine Jaguar (Chignavicelut), and appears to have described in at least seventeen folio pages the Tam view of the migration from the sunrise, the genealogy and land claims of the western Quiche, and the same Quiche-Tzutuhil war mentioned in the preceding document, as well as the Mixco campaign against the Spanish.

Title 15, *Quiche Manuscript*, undated and in at least thirteen folio pages, was also Tam and presented a Toltec origin myth with four Founding Fathers, migrating to Chiapas, Verapaz, and Mam and Quiche country. Their grandsons provided kings for the Quiche, Cakchiquel, and Tzutuhil, and there is reference to wars in Nebaj, Uspantan, and with the Tzutuhils and Spanish. Juan de Torres is referred to, probably the one in Title 14 rather than the one in Title 9.

Title 16, *The Two Princesses*, a manuscript in thirteen folio pages by Juan Gómez (n.d.), dealt with the Tzutuhil-Quiche war, and in that it resembled Titles 13, 14, and 15. On this ground I suppose it to have been Tam.

Title 17, *The Xecul Manuscript of Counsellor Keham*, in at least seventeen folio pages, was a rather garbled and mythologized account of the Spanish conquest, and I rather doubt that it was a Quiche manuscript at all. It describes "Auitzol, eighth Montezuma" as warning Tekum u Mam of the Spanish invasion, then has Kiq'ab oppose it, makes Kiq'ab II the tenth king of Utatlan, identifies Iximche and Quezaltenango as persons, and then shifts attention to the Mam conquests of Gonzalo de Sandoval. Quiche titles appear as personal names, but none of it makes much sense.

5.1.6. THE TITLES OF CARMACK. Unquestionably the most significant contribution of recent date to our knowledge of the *Title* literature is the identification by Robert M. Carmack (1973) from documents in both Indian and Spanish archives of an additional ten *Titles*. The most significant of these for our present (literary) purposes is the *Title of C'oyoi*, already cited. The *Title of Nihay III* and the *Title of Uchabaja* have also been discussed. The remaining seven have been dated and amply described by Carmack (1973). None but the first of them can be identified by lineage, and all but numbers 18 and 24 are known only in Spanish translation. The documents are:

Title 18: (1555) *Title of Nihay IV*
Title 19: (1557) *Title of Retalhuleu*
Title 20: (1558) *Title of Paxtoca*
Title 21: (1567) *Title of Huitzitzil Tzunun*
Title 22: (1592) *Title of Chuachituj*
Title 23: (1595) *Title of Lamaquib*
Title 24: (1607) *Title of Chacatz-Tojin*

The *Title* literature of the sixteenth century is mostly dull, anxious, humorless, and repetitive. It depicts but does not even bother to mourn the Spanish conquest. It was rather a litigious and industrious attempt on the part of the doomed noble lineages to stave off their destruction by wearying Spanish courts with petitions and appeals, and it has all the charm of a collection of legal briefs. But a number of the *Titles*, particularly the lengthy ones, nonetheless display a clear link to the literature of the Late Postclassic. This is particularly true, of course, of the Kavek *Titles*, since the *Popol Vuh* is a Kavek document, and we do not have the corresponding sources for the other segments of Quiche tradition. Clearly the Ahav and Tam also refer back to their own versions of Toltec and earlier history.

5.2. POETRY. The continuity with the past is unmistakably marked in the continued use of semantic couplets. To be sure, matching place name with place name and ancestor with ancestor makes for rather dull couplets, and appeals to Spanish courts do not constitute a genre that lends itself to wit, but the sixteenth century was a disastrous period for the Quiche as a whole, and particularly so for the noble class that had been responsible for creating and preserving most of their literature up to that time. The Quiche had little to laugh about.

5.3. DRAMA. It is clear nonetheless that the dramatic tradition continued. The dance dramas of the past were written into the *Popol Vuh*: *Seven Parrot* (*K'ele Tz'u*), the *Shield Dance* (*Chanal, Pokob*), the *Armadillo Dance* (*Iboy*), the *Owl Dance* (*Puhuy*), the *Flower Dance* (*Tz'utubal*), the *Weasel Dance* (*Kux*). A few have survived to the present century: the *Stilt Dance* (*Chi Tik*), the *Monkey Dance*, the *Centipede Dance* (*Ix Tz'ul*), the *Jaguar Deer Dance* (*Ix Balam Keh*), and of course the *Rabinal Achi* (see Appendix). The existence of the *Rabinal Achi* (*Xahoh Tun*) in the sixteenth century is explicitly attested in the *Title of C'oyoi* under the name *Xahil Tun*, as is that of the *War Dance* (*Tzala Tun*) (Carmack 1973:295). But perhaps the best indicator of the vitality of the Quiche theater was the fact that the conquest itself was converted into not one, but two dramas—the *Conquest of Mexico* and the *Conquest of Guatemala*. The point is undocumentable, but it would be surprising if these were not taking shape by the end of the sixteenth century. Quiche drama remains, like the rest of Quiche literature, imperfectly documented, but it continued as a lively art, absorbing Spanish influences, both secular and religious, and preserving autochthonous elements at the same time that new ones were being created.

There is little to be said about the rhetoric and oratory of the sixteenth century. None has survived. It is impossible to judge whether there was any change in styles of expression. The uses to which literacy was put preclude comparison with either earlier or later periods. Even the segments of the *Popol Vuh* that belong to this time are dishwater compared with what had gone before, despite the obvious literary intelligence of the compiler of that work. The impact of the Spanish conquest was all but overwhelm-ing—perhaps as much because it made the physical preservation of books difficult as because it balked the imagination. Quiche literature survived, as did Quiche literacy, but by 1600 both were clearly in decline.

6. THE SEVENTEENTH CENTURY.

6.1. TITLES. Except for the land titles of 1600 and 1607 already cited and an additional land document from Sacapulas dated to 1613 (Carmack 1973), we confront a gap of nearly a century in the history of Quiche literacy from 1583 to 1663. In the violence, both natural and political, that characterizes Guatemala, much of the documentation of its history has been lost, Indian and non-Indian alike. But we know from the parallel history presented by the *Annals of the Cakchiquels* (*Memorial of Solola*) (Recinos 1950a; 1953) that the first thirty to forty years of this period saw a major transformation of the Indian towns of western Guatemala. The old Indian titles and the noble lineages that coveted them disappeared from history, along with intertribal and intertown alliances and warfare.

If Solola was a typical case, and I believe it was, the mechanism of the destruction of the lineages was to put them into competition for the posts of the new Spanish town organization and the *cofradías*. Jealousy being an ancient, chronic, and frequently acute Mayan disease, this policy had the effect of making the priest, often the only Spanish representative in the town, the decisive arbiter among the deadlocked lineages. The royal Zotz'il lineage lost out in Solola before the end of the sixteenth century, and the second-ranked Xahila did not last to the end of the *Annals* in the early seventeenth.

6.2. ORDINANCES. That the Quiche experience was parallel to that of the Cakchiquels is made stunningly clear in the only seventeenth-century Quiche document available to me: the 708-line *Ordinances of the Fraternity of the Rosary*, recorded by Pascual Vásquez in 1689 in some unidentified Quiche town. The document exhorts obedience to the ten commandments of God, the five commandments of the Church, and the nine(!) ordinances of the *cofradía*: (1) elections, (2) con-

120

tributions, (3) certification, (4) alms, (5) humility, (6) obedience, (7) mass, (8) prayer, and (9) instruction. The redundancy of the fifth and sixth ordinances makes it clear that hierarchy (and its corollary, jealousy) were a continuing problem for the Quiche. The fifth ordinance reads in part:

Or if someone is ordered
  By the *mayordomo*,
He should just obey
  And follow him.
He should not force him
  With constraint.
He should not glorify himself;
  He should not advertise himself.
And he should not utter
  Any evil words.
He should just be humble,
  Just a modest person
Before God
  The Great Lord,
And before his older brother,
  His younger brother.
          (Edmonson n.d.i: lines 227–242)

In other words, avoid the sin of Seven Parrot! And the second ordinance dictates:

They make a box
  And two keys.
One is kept;
  The second is kept by the *mayordomo*.
And the one that they keep
  For the older brothers
Is at the house of the priest,
  The teaching father,
And it is kept closed up there,
  Whatever is needed, in the box.
They all store there
  That the dues shouldn't bring about many
  fights there,
But be seen to be the same,
  Even.
          (Edmonson n.d.i: lines 83–96)

6.3. POETRY. The continuity of Quiche literature is attested by the orthography—un-

changed since 1583. It is also confirmed by the continuation of the poetic form, unaltered since Classic times, and by the prominence of the number nine. And despite the general orthodoxy of this text, it gives the First Commandment as "Do not give the evil eye to the saints." It is a great pity that the seventeenth century is so largely lost to us.

Other seventeenth-century documents do exist: the land titles already mentioned, the papers of the *Cofradía de San Nicolás* (1663–1852), and *Documents and Legal Papers from Totonicapán* (1689–1812), but I have not seen them.

6.4. DRAMA. Continuity in the drama is certain, and seventeenth-century plays must have included the *Rabinal Achi*, the *Spider Monkey Hunter Dance*, the *Stilt Dance*, the *Flying Pole Dance*, and the *Centipede Dance*, since they are attested both before and after this period. There is reason to suppose that *White Demon*, the *Monkey Dance*, the *Deer Dance*, and the *Conquest of Guatemala* also go back this far (see Appendix). From records of the Inquisition, Ernesto Chinchilla Aguilar (1953:290–291) reports a dance called *Tun Teleche* (he has *Tum*) in San Bartolome de Mazatenango in 1623. This was almost certainly the *Rabinal Achi*. It was apparently also called the *Ox Tun* (*Three Drums*).

7. THE EIGHTEENTH CENTURY. Presumably because we are closer to it, we can document the eighteenth century much better, and its content dispels any doubts about the continuity of the previous tradition. Fragmentary though it is, the Quiche literature of this period includes calendrical, dramatic, legal, and religious documents. The earliest of these gives clear evidence of the survival of the Quiche divinatory system and a substantial amount of its traditional mystique.

7.1. CALENDRICS.

7.1.1. THE COUNT OF THE CYCLE. The fragility of the hieratic political system of the Maya, with its almost suicidal conflict among lineages, did not eliminate the traditional religion. Truncated and driven underground, it maintained the ancient count of the 260- and 365-day cycles and continued to use both for

121

divinatory, religious, and magical purposes. Three interrelated eighteenth-century manuscripts prove it. The first is *The Count of the Cycle of the Days* (*Chol Poval Q'ih*), probably from Quetzaltenango and dated 1722, which identifies the first day of the Quiche year as occurring on 9 Deer (Keh) 1 First Elder (Nabe Mam), Sunday, May 3, 1722 (Calendario de los indios de Guatemala 1722). It lists the Mayan and European days of that year and the initial days of the Mayan months for the ensuing five years (1723–1727). What has come down to us is not the original but an 1877 copy of a 1770 copy in twenty-two folio pages, but it demonstrates continuity with the sixteenth-century Quiche calendar and with the one still in use. It has no literary merit, though it has a few notes of some interest.

7.1.2. THE NUMBERS OF THE DAYS. In the copy of the preceding work that we possess there follow two divining calendars, both called *The Numbers of the Days* (*Ahilabal Q'ih*). The earlier (*a*), in fourteen folio pages, dates to 1722; the later (*b*), in thirteen folio pages, to 1770. The first begins on 1 Alligator (Imox), the second on 1 Blood (Q'anil). As in the divining calendars of the *Dresden*, *Madrid*, and *Paris* codices, the days are grouped by "houses," five days to a house, each bearing the same numeral prefix. A note at the end of the earlier calendar explains:

These are the numbers of the days
  For worshiping everything.

The prognostications are concerned with worship, both Christian and pagan, but they are also concerned with violence, sex, crops, witchcraft, capture, trade, and other matters. There is general agreement between the two, but they are not identical, and occasionally they contradict each other. A typical prediction is that for 5 Alligator (Imox), Cane (Ah), Snake (Qan), Incense (Nooh) or Rain (Toh):

(a: 1722)

A man
  And a woman
Evil faced, are sinning.

They are committing evil
Because these are evil days,
  All five of them.

(b: 1770)

Great is the anger of the days
  And good and bad the office
Of eagle
  And jaguar
At the bottom of the canyons,
  And their sinners,
A man
  And a woman, are fornicating.

(Edmonson n.d.b)

7.2. DRAMA.
7.2.1. WHITE DEMON. The literary chef d'oeuvre of the eighteenth century was certainly the drama of *White Demon* (*Zaqi Q'axol*), the Dance of the Conquest of Mexico (Edmonson n.d.r). It is a play in four acts, eighteen scenes, and 3056 lines composed (in Quiche and Indianized Spanish but in Mayan couplets throughout) in 1726 or earlier. It is not clear where, but the provenience of the extant versions suggests Rabinal. There is a substantial discrepancy between the 1726 manuscript and all the later versions, but the list of characters and the general plot line are consistent with intermittently oral transmission and a retranscription in the early nineteenth century. The stage directions indicate the use of musical themes keyed to different characters and occasions, a distinctive feature of later (and probably of earlier) Quiche drama. Like most other Quiche plays it was danced masked. It has a cast of twenty-four (the order of appearance is indicated by letters, and the characters who do not have solo speaking parts are in parentheses):

Indians ("Lacandons")

B *Montezuma*, Emperor of Mexico
A Xuxinkitzal, his lieutenant
G Kopoka, King of Tlaxcala
K Quiche, King of Utatlan
C Chanal, Montezuma's spokesman
D (Messenger, a captain)
E (Messenger, a captain)

122

H Hummingbird, Kopoka's daughter
I Her Mother, Kopoka's wife
J Her Grandmother, Kopoka's mother-in-law
F Zaqi Q'axol, White Demon
L Gracejo, Clown

Spaniards

N *Cortés*, Spanish commander
O *Alvarado*, his lieutenant
S *Sandoval*, Cortés' officer
M Francisco, Cortes' officer
U (*Juan Díaz*, a priest)
V (*Martín de Valencia*, a priest)
W *Bartolomé de Olmedo*, a priest
P *Malinche*, Cortés' mistress
Q (Girl)
R (Girl)
T Lavariano, soldier
X Soliman

The characters identifiable from Spanish sources as participants in the conquest are italicized, but the plot has little to do with the historical event except that the Indians are defeated and converted. The title role is drawn from a god who appears in the Late Postclassic myth of *The Origin of the Toltecs*, where he is the only one of the gods who is not turned to stone with the rising Sun of the Fourth Creation (Edmonson 1971: line 6009). There as here he represents traditionalism. Since the play has not been published, a synopsis of it is perhaps appropriate.

Act I (First News)

Scene 1: Montezuma's court in Mexico. Xuxinkitzal and Chanal report the arrival of the Spaniards. Montezuma orders that Kopoka be summoned.

Scene 2: On the road to Tlaxcala. Xuxinkitzal, Chanal, and White Demon picnic.

Scene 3: The court of Kopoka in Tlaxcala. Xuxinkitzal and Chanal summon Kopoka and his women (Hummingbird and his wife and mother-in-law) to Mexico.

Scene 4: Montezuma's court in Mexico. Kopoka reports to Montezuma and is sent to find out the temper of the army.

Scene 5: The Fort of Mexico. Kopoka, act-ing as spokesman for Montezuma, orders Chanal and the other messengers to mobilize the army and send for Quiche.

Scene 6: The Fort of Quiche at Utatlan. Xuxinkitzal and Chanal summon Quiche, who orders mobilization of the Quiche army.

Act II (Interlude)

Scene 7: Montezuma's court in Mexico. Quiche reports to Montezuma, introducing White Demon, and Xuxinkitzal gets Montezuma's permission to take Hummingbird away from White Demon. Chanal eggs him on, acting as Xuxinkitzal's spokesman.

Scene 8: The forest of White Demon. Xuxinkitzal and Chanal court Hummingbird for the former. She demands brandy, i.e., marriage.

Scene 9: The forest of White Demon. Xuxinkitzal and Chanal entice White Demon through Hummingbird into joining the war. Although he has been tricked, he consents.

Scene 10: Montezuma's court in Mexico. White Demon is introduced by Xuxinkitzal to Montezuma, who orders the construction of a moat and decides to wait to find out whether the Spaniards want gold or conquest.

Act III (Arrival of Spanish)

Scene 11: The road to Mexico. The Spanish company (Cortés, Alvarado, Don Francisco, Gonzalo de Sandoval, Malinche and two female companions, Juan Díaz, Martín de Valencia, and Bartolomé de Olmedo) encounter Chanal, who exchanges insults with Malinche. As a spokesman, Chanal declares war.

Scene 12: The road to Mexico. Gonzalo de Sandoval and Lavariano agree to fight to victory.

Scene 13: Montezuma's court in Mexico. Cortés and Bartolomé de Olmedo offer to convert the Mexicans; Montezuma and his spokesman, Chanal, refuse and the insults of war are exchanged by Montezuma and Chanal, Cortés, Gonzalo de Sandoval, Don Francisco, a Father, and a Clown.

123

Scene 14: On the battlefield. Quiche and Xuxinkitzal urge Montezuma to fight.

Scene 15: On the battlefield. Cortés and Alvarado confront Kopoka and Chanal. Chanal and Xuxinkitzal persuade Montezuma to war.

Act IV (Battle)

Scene 16: On the battlefield. Chanal, Xuxinkitzal, and Clown give war speeches. Alvarado and Lavariano reply.

Scene 17: On the battlefield. Quiche, Chanal, Hummingbird, and Clown witness the battle.

Scene 18: In Mexico. Cortés preaches; Montezuma surrenders and asks for bap- tism. Chanal offers the crown to Kopoka, but after Montezuma asks them not to continue the war, Kopoka, Quiche, Chanal, and Xuxinkitzal surrender. All the Indians kneel and swear fealty to the King and Cortés except White Demon, who does not surrender. Sandoval and Soliman rejoice in the Spanish victory and hail Charles V.

To illustrate the use of Quiche and Spanish in the play, I quote from a section of Scene 13. Chanal, who elsewhere speaks Spanish, nonetheless addresses the Spaniards in this case in Quiche, while Montezuma speaks to them in Spanish. The problems presented by the Spanish text will, I think, be obvious.

Chanal:

Vakamik alaq ahavab kaxtilan taq vinaq.
  Alaq pu ri 'ahavab Markex,
A pa su va ri lo chabibal alaq,
  Tzihobal alaq?
Xa 'are na beq qa tzih nimalah koyevarik chi,

  Chi tata na alaq.
Ve 'are ch u biih,
  Ve pu lo ma na 'are tah ri ch u biih,
Chi tax tah,
  Ta na alaq, qey.

Montezuma (*ka ch'avik ch u vi tzaq kuy uloq*):

El corason me tiene robado d ese mayor Dias,
  Pues que darlo prometo mi corason y bida.
Los desoro que poseo
  Son ora penisimo.
Dare socorido:
  Yra tu jente.
Mira la grandesa
  De lo presente.
Consideyte mi poder,
  La multitud de mi jente.
Que (…) benido de mi jente
  Con armas para matar que mis basallos.
Yo de mi poder
  Cayda bais.
Y lugares, los reynos

Chanal:

Now then, ye lords of the Castilian people,
  And ye the lords of the Marquis,
What can all this chattering of yours be?
  And your lecturing?
But in a minute we shall be extremely furious with you,
  And with your fathers and mothers.
If this is what is said,
  Then probably it isn't what should be said,
So listen,
  Listen here!

Montezuma (leaning down from the fort):

This greater God has stolen my heart,
  For in giving it I promised heart and life.
The treasure I possess
  Is finest gold.
I shall give you ransom:
  Your people may go.
Look at the grandeur
  Of what is around you.
Consider my power,
  The multitude of my people.
Some of my own people have come
  With arms to kill my vassals.
I, from my power
  Will see you leave, fallen.
And as for places, the kingdoms

124

Y provinsias quiniente sujeto de mi corona	And provinces subject to my crown number five hundred
De a mi ympedio d esta rendido,	From my empire at this count,
Y que tengo sujeto	And I hold them subject
Por poder	By power
Por boluntad,	And will,
Y por fuerza	By force
Y a fuero	And privilege,
Compelido	Compelled
Que el deme e saserdota.	To fear the priests.

Other dramas of the eighteenth century were the *Stilt Dance* (*Tu*), *Spider Monkey Hunter, Centipede, Monkey, Deer*, and *Rabinal Achi*, but the evidence for this assertion is inferential. *The Dance of the Conquest of Guatemala* is also probably at least this old, as its modern performers still wear colonial costumes (Bode 1961).

7.3. ORDINANCES. Additional *cofradía* documents from the late eighteenth century include the untranslated *Ordinances of the Brotherhood of the Holy True Cross* (1777) and the *Ordinances of 1785* (translation in my possession).

7.4. LETTERS. A brief but interesting Quiche document of 1794 known as the *Petition to the Lord President* (*Petición r uq Ahav Presidente*) has been translated and published by Günther Zimmermann (1956). It apparently comes from various western Quiche towns and is actually a copybook of model letters, illustrating how to write a letter to the President of the Audiencia, a Head Mayor, a Bishop, a Parish Priest, an Inspector, a Lieutenant, the Auditor, a Ladino, a General, a Lady, a Governor, or a Sacristan. While these letters have apparently been collected as models, many of them have explicit local historical content as well. Because of the rarity of such materials in Quiche, I'll cite the love letter.

Thou,
　My lady,
Miss Juana,
　My love,
My darling,

Only thou art my lady.
I rejoice greatly in my soul
　That thou enjoyest complete health.
I am fine,
　To serve thee, my lady.
I am sending thee herewith this little fruit.
　Please forgive me.
I remain, praying God to love
　And Guard thee
Many
　Many years.
Quezaltenango, March 20, 1794.
　I kiss thy hands.

　　　　　　　　　　　　(Edmonson n.d.c)

So much for the Romantic Movement in Quiche.

7.5. WRITS. The late eighteenth century provides us with a collection of Mayan legal documents dating from 1750 to 1799. They include deeds of sale and mortgages of lands and houses, and testaments, recording particularly the career of Domingo Matías Santéliz, a highly successful man in an unknown Quiche town. It is of interest that, like all other Quiche documents, these legal instruments are composed in couplets:

So we have divided out to each and every one
　Whatever is in their testament.
And if anyone seek further
　To protest to them,
They will be taught by the Justices
　With sixty lashes.
And thus will be dropped

125

And forgotten this testament
In witness
Before God.

(From the Testament of Manuel Ziz,
May 12, 1773; Edmonson n.d.s)

There is an *Arte de Lengva Qiche* of 1793 which also contains legal documents.

8. THE NINETEENTH CENTURY.

8.1. WRITS, ORDINANCES, CALENDRICS, AND PRAYERS. The Colonial tradition of literacy lasted into the nineteenth century but did not survive it. Some of the earlier documents carry over into this period: the *Documents* of Totonicapan (1689–1812) and the book of the *Cofradía de San Nicolás* (1663–1852). We also have an Ixtlauacan *Calendar* dated 1854 (Bunting 1932) and a *Prayer of the Sun Priest at Rax Kim* from the same year (Edmonson n.d.l). The Sun Priest (Ah Q'ih) apostrophizes the Trinity and every spirit he can dream up a name for in either Quiche or Spanish or a mixture of the two, and implores them for his client:

Let him not find illness,
    Let him not find fleas,
Let him not find a seizure,
    Let him not find choking,
Let him not be bit by a serpent,
    Let him not encounter a fall,
Let not his anger come,
    Do not turn him into bones,
Let him not be bit by a dog,
    [*Line missing*]
For there is lightning in liquor:
    Let him not choke on it.
Buddies,
    Companions, let them not come to him,
For there is cutting
    And there is knifing from it.

(Edmonson n.d.l)

I am unable to examine the original orthography of any of these documents, and the point is of some interest. Nineteenth-century copies of the script of *White Demon* are written in the Colonial orthography down to 1875.

8.2. DRAMA. Besides *White Demon*, the drama of the nineteenth century certainly included the *Flying Pole Dance*, *Stilt Dance*, *Centipede Dance*, *Conquest of Guatemala*, *Huaxteco*, *Jaguar Deer Dance*, *Deer Dance*, *Monkey Dance*, *Spider Monkey Hunter*, *Rabinal Achi*, and probably a number of other plays, with or without texts (see Appendix). It should be noted that none of these dances was new in the nineteenth century except perhaps the *Huaxteco*. This was clearly a period of decadence in both literacy and literature, and while there was a subsequent revival, it was slow, fragmented, and very complex.

8.2.1. THE BULL DANCE. Survivals of Quiche literature into the twentieth century are largely a matter of drama and oral literature, and it is arguable that the earliest documented contribution to the modest literary renaissance of the Quiche may have been the *Bull Dance* of Cantel, probably composed between 1880 and 1900 (Edmonson n.d.a; Porras Vidal 1900). A version of it collected in 1911 "at the instance of" the German Vice Consul in Quezaltenango, the *Baile de Toritos*, presents both problems and points of interest. It is in a modern hand and a totally new orthography. (For example, it uses *sh* for *x* [š], and *j* for *h* [x].) But it is not clear whether it was written down from oral tradition, copied from an older manuscript or even translated from a Spanish original! It represents in any case the first appearance of Freemasons and steamboats in Quiche literature.

9. THE TWENTIETH CENTURY.

9.1. DRAMA. The *Bull Dance* remains a tantalizing bridge to the twentieth century, since the Quiche literature of our epoch presents the same ambiguities that the dance does. On the one hand we confront the unquestionable continuation of a native tradition of drama. On the other hand we have an increasing—even a burgeoning—intervention of non-Indians in the preservation of Quiche oral tradition.

Even to list the known twentieth-century dance dramas verges on the tedious, especially because they are a lively and continuing folk art that has been only very partially recorded. There are at least twenty that have not been previously mentioned in this account. The matter is complicated by the fact that some are danced masked with traditional music and dialogue, while others are in fact ballet, with or without masks. Some have Quiche texts, some Spanish, and some none, and available descriptions rarely specify which is which, though Celso Narciso Teletor's (1945) listing for Rabinal is more than ordinarily informative. An example of the pure dance (without script) is the *Baile de Convite* (*Dance of Invitation*) (Edmonson 1960–1961), involving men costumed as women from a number of neighboring towns to symbolize regional solidarity (women's dress being distinguished by *municipio* in 1960, while men's was not). Aside from brief Spanish praises to the patron saint, it has no text.

But it appears that dance dramas are still being composed (Armas Lara 1964), and the best example available to me is the farce from Rabinal called the *Flute Dance* (*Charamiyex* or *Baile de las Chirimías*) (Mace 1957; Edmonson n.d.d). Along with San Cristobal Totonicapan, Rabinal has long been a center of Quiche drama. I have been told that both rent masks, costumes, and scripts for particular *bailes* to dance groups from other towns, or even other language groups. The dance groups themselves contract to perform at particular fiestas in their own communities or elsewhere, so drama parallels trade in unifying the Quiche region.

9.1.1. THE FLUTE DANCE. Despite the fact that it has the ritual fourfold and fivefold redundancies of traditional drama, this comedy in 396 lines appears to me to have been composed in the twentieth century at Rabinal. It concerns an Old Man who is trying to arrange the marriage of his two sons to the daughters of María. After a sexually racy conversation with the Scribe, he appears before the three-man Council and pleads his case in comically mock Classic Quiche:

How the backs of their skirts bother me!
　How the fronts of their skirts bother me!

Hanging there,
　Or following behind!
So now speaks this my word.
　If they had nothing before them
Then also my word would speak
　To be able to pick those flowers:
Two of God's little angels
　Here and now.

(Edmonson n.d.d)

9.1.2. JAGUAR DEER. But if the *Flute Dance* is capable of "modernism" and of using "classicism" for comic effect, the fragmentary text of the 170-line *Jaguar Deer Dance* (*Baile del Tigre y Venado*), with its cast of thirteen characters, takes us abruptly back to the Classic in another (and partially calendrical) sense. Again the effect includes burlesque.

Old Man:

Boys there, hey, day-bearers,
　Light-bearers, boys there, hey!
Come on there, boys, are you all there?
　Are you all together, you twelve boys?
This then is what I say to you, boys:
　Let us make a celebration.
Listen to the murmur of our mountains,
　The murmur of our valleys, which
　they give.
Listen to the murmur
　And the dance.
And will you give it, boys?

All:

We shall give it, grandfather.
(They imitate overcoming a woman.)
(Edmonson n.d.h:lines 1–12)

The evocations of ancient Quiche tradition are muted and distant, but the echoes are undeniably there. The Quiche are even regaining their sense of humor.

For other examples of twentieth-century drama, see Appendix and specifically the *Bailes* of *Animals, Brujo castigado, Conquista, Costeño, Diablitos, Huaxteco, Huehuecho, Israelitos, Maner, Marineros, Mexi-*

127

canos, Monos y micos, Moros y cristianos, Negritos, Palo volador, San Jorge, San Jorge y Anix, San Pablo, and *Venadito*. Folk drama has become the history and scripture of the modern Quiche. It is linked closely with the religious calendar and is particularly tied to the fiestas of the saints. At the same time the traditional calendar is still maintained, and it is possible that human sacrifice was still occasionally practiced in very isolated areas as recently as the 1930's. Mostly, however, the Ah Q'ih (Sun Priest) is now a diviner and curer, and the dance groups that perpetuate the theater are even more secular.

9.2. ORAL LITERATURE.

9.2.1. POETRY. The perpetuation of Quiche oral tradition has been encouraged by an increasing pace of recording of texts by linguists, anthropologists, and folklorists. Literary ethnography is well represented in Leonhard Schultze Jena's (1933) Quiche materials, gathered on the model of Bernardino de Sahagún's ethnography, but rich in literary values. They include an extensive and varied body of texts on the life cycle, curing, ritual, drama, and other matters, carefully recorded, and reading in couplets, even in relatively prosaic contexts. The father of a newborn child describes his duties:

Early today a baby was born
    And his name is Juan Ah.
Let's go for the diviner to offer flowers;
    There might be illness for the
    newborn one.
Tell the godparents the child is born;
    Have the baptism with the priest.
Tell the midwife to wash his head,
    And make the sweatbath to wash the
    little child.
            (Schultze Jena 1933; my translation)

There are similar passages of literary ethnography in Ruth Bunzel's monograph on Chichicastenango. She quotes a prayer, for example:

It seems that our first ancestors
    Were made the watchers

And listeners
    And guardians of all these rites.
But these men
    And women
Have passed among the first gods,
    The first spirits.
But these rites did not descend with their hearts
    And minds
Beneath the earth
    And sand.
            (Bunzel 1952:234; my scansion)

My own manuscript on Francisco Tam is unambiguously a member of the same family. When I asked Francisco to tell me his life history, he began as follows:

My face made its appearance
    In my village.
In time I grew;
    I was raised
With my mother,
    With my father.
And now today
    I am already big.
I serve my father
    Because he raised me.
Also my mother—
    My mother raised me.
Now I respect her;
    I serve her.
            (Edmonson n.d.e:lines 1–14)

It was much later that I realized the importance of couplets, and the significance of his equating his person ("face") with his village as a primordial statement of identity.

9.2.2. TALES. We have come a long way since Sol Tax (1949) puzzled over why the Quiche had no folklore. Beginning with the extensive texts collected by Manuel J. Andrade (1971a) in the 1940's, linguists and folklorists have begun to assemble Quiche folklore at an increasing pace. We have some information on beliefs, superstitions, games, riddles, and customs, and the extensive folk drama has already been reviewed. For literary purposes the most significant additional materials are the folk tales. (It is curious that we have as yet no folk songs.)

We have accumulated at least thirty folk tales, many of them in Quiche text (see also Fox 1957). A partial list of titles follows (sometimes revised to emphasize the content):

The Clever Rabbit (Rabinal) (Shaw 1971: 227–230)

The Death of Tecum u Mam (Joyabaj, Santa Catarina Ixtahuacan) (de Urrutia 1974: 158–159; Shaw 1971:223–224)

The Devil Man (Joyabaj) (Shaw 1971: 221–222)

The Dumb Little Chick (Totonicapan) (Fox and Fox 1956b; Henne and Henne 1972b)

The King of the Animals (Santa Catarina Ixtahuacan) (de Urrutia 1974)

The King of the Quiches (Cubulco) (Shaw 1971:55–56)

The Man Who Became the Sun (Cantel dialect) (Shaw 1971:215)

The Man Who Was Swallowed by an Alligator (Santa Catarina Ixtahuacan) (Tepaz Raxuleu 1976)

The Man Who Was Swallowed by a Fish (Santa Catarina Ixtahuacan) (Mondloch 1978:192–203)

The Necklace That Bit a Man (Cantel dialect) (Shaw 1971:214, 458)

The Origin of Corn (Cubulco) (Búcaro Moraga 1959:1–19; Shaw 1971:41–43, 253–258)

The Origin of Illness (Cubulco) (Neuenswander and Shaw 1966)

The Origin of the Dance of the Serpent (Santa Catarina Ixtahuacan) (Búcaro Moraga 1959)

The Origin of the Patron Saint (Joyabaj, Santa Catarina Ixtahuacan) (Búcaro Moraga 1959)

People with Holes in Their Throats (Cubulco) (Shaw 1971:54–55)

The Poor Man and the Robbers (Joyabaj) (Shaw 1971:221)

The Rabbit and the Coyote (Santa Catarina Ixtahuacan) (de Urrutia 1974)

Satan as a Suitor (Cantel dialect) (Shaw 1971: 214, 459–461)

Separation of Santa Catarina and Nahuala (Santa Catarina Ixtahuacan) (de Urrutia 1974)

The Serpent and the Lightning Angels (Cubulco) (Shaw 1971:43–45, 259–264)

Sipac and the Three Corn Goddesses (Cubulco) (Shaw 1971:48–51)

Sipac the Mighty (Cubulco) (Shaw 1971:48)

The Son of a Widower (Santa Catarina Ixtahuacan) (de Urrutia 1974)

The Theft of Lake Atitlan (Quezaltenango) (Edmonson 1960–1961; Osborne 1965)

Three Rabbit Tales (Totonicapan) (Fox and Fox 1956a; Henne and Henne 1972a)

The Twisted Tree (Totonicapan) (Shaw 1971: 213, 455–457)

The Two-Headed Eagle (Santa Catarina Ixtahuacan) (Tzep López and Ajpacajá Tum 1979)

Why Our Teeth Decay (Cubulco) (Shaw 1971:46–48, 265–273)

Why There Was a Famine in Olden Times (Santa Catarina Ixtahuacan) (Mondloch 1978:204–222)

The Woman Who Became a Fish (Santa Catarina Ixtahuacan) (Tzep López and Ajpacajá Tum 1979)

Perhaps the most important general sources on Quiche folklore are Lilly de Jongh Osborne (1965), Mary Shaw (1971), and Raúl Pérez Maldonado (1966). I have examined all but the last. To illustrate the consistency of Quiche oral literature with the written sources we have examined, a sample is in order.

9.2.2.1. THE MAN WHO WAS SWALLOWED BY AN ALLIGATOR. Written by F. Lucas Tepaz Raxuleu of Santa Catarina Ixtahuacan and translated and published by William Norman (1976b), this fourteen-page tale is of particular interest because of its resonance with themes of earlier Quiche literature (Alligator and Deer), its absorption of Spanish motifs (Jonah and the Whale, Moors and Christians), and the fact that it illustrates the reinvolvement of the Quiche in writing their own literature. (See also Tzep López and Ajpacajá Tum 1979.)

The tale ends with a succinct summary of the plot, which also demonstrates the continuity of poetic form in Quiche tradition.

This is how it happened:
    First
He was swallowed by an Alligator.
    And then he was vomited by the Alligator.
Second
    He perforated the Moors;
And third
    He used the Deer to ride here.
That is how the man experienced it
    In the old tale.
Our fathers
    And mothers tell it.

>   (Norman 1976b:54, my translation
>   and scansion)

(I have no quarrel with Norman's translation, from which I have departed only slightly, but his object was linguistic and mine is literary.)

9.2.3. PROSPECTS. Quiche participation in their own literature is once again on the rise. Beginning with the collaboration of Flavio Rodas of Chichicastenango with Antonio Villacorta (Villacorta Calderón and Rodas N. 1927), there is increasing native interest in Quiche literature of the past, and particularly in the *Popol Vuh*. The career of Patricio Xec of San Cristobal Totonicapan is a case in point. Coauthor of a translation of the *Popol Vuh* (Burgess and Xec 1955), he also taught generations of Quiche children to read Quiche in general and the *Popol Vuh* in particular, and coauthored a Quiche dictionary (Xec and Maynard 1954). And recently we have arrived at the first Quiche solo performance at translating the old classic—by Adrián I. Chávez of San Francisco el Alto (Chávez 1979).

Like Humpty Dumpty, the Colonial tradition has not been and perhaps cannot be put together again. The Instituto Bíblico Quiché of San Cristobal Totonicapan, the most effective agent of literacy in the twentieth century, uses one alphabet. The Instituto Indi-

genista uses another. Most linguists use yet another, or invent their own. Adrián Chávez of the Academia Maya-Quiché of Quezaltenango has one all to himself (an achievement which bears comparison with the achievement of Sequoyah in Cherokee). But this technical problem should not be exaggerated. I have known Mayas who could read their native language in four or more orthographies with relative ease.

Quiche is rapidly becoming a modern language. It has been used in electoral campaigns in Guatemala since the 1950s, and is now heard regularly on radio and television. I should like to close by quoting the Coca Cola commercial, but I have not been in Guatemala lately. I'll bet it's in couplets.

10. CONCLUSIONS. Quiche literature, despite its fragmentary character, presents us with a continuous poetic, mythological, oratorical, historical, and dramatic tradition, traceable, at least in general terms, from the Middle Classic period to the twentieth century. At its inception it appears to have been cognate with the ancestral mythological tradition of the Yucatecan Maya, and probably that of other Mayan peoples as well. During the Postclassic it was exposed to at least two differentiable waves of Nahuat influence, one beginning in the tenth century, and the second, explicitly Toltec, in the fourteenth or fifteenth. From the middle sixteenth to the middle nineteenth centuries it enjoyed an indigenous and continuous tradition of literacy in a Latin-based orthography. In the late nineteenth or early twentieth century a slow and fragmented revival of literacy began, spurred at least in part by alien scholars and missionaries (and not a few individuals who were both).

Given the political disruption of contemporary Guatemala, the social, economic, and cultural pressures on the Quiche have never been more intense than they are today. But it will be some time before the measured formality, farcical and sometimes satirical humor, sense of tradition and duty, and sense of time disappear from the discourse of the heirs of the *Popol Vuh*.

APPENDIX. QUICHE DANCE-DRAMAS.

NAMES OF DANCES			SOURCES
Spanish	English	Quiche	
Animales	Animals	Koh balam	Correa and Cannon 1958
Armadillo	Armadillo	Xah iboy	Edmonson 1971: line 4267
Cautivo	Captive Drum	Tun teleche, Ox tun	Chinchilla Aguilar 1953: 290–291; 1963
Chico mudo	Mute	Ah met, Kaman q'eq	Mace 1957; 1970; Teletor 1955: 161–162
Chirimías	Flute	Charamiyex	Edmondson n.d.d; Mace 1957; 1970: 155–194
Ciempiés	Centipede	Ix tz'ul	Edmonson 1971: line 4268
Comadreja	Weasel	Xah kux	Edmonson 1971: line 4266
Conquista de Guatemala	Conquest of Guatemala	Xahoh r ech Tekum	Bode 1961; Bunzel 1952: 424; Coester 1941; Paret-Limardo 1962
Conquista de Mexico, Baile de Cortés	Conquest of Mexico, White Demon	Zaqi q'axol	Mace 1957. See also Zaccicoxol, in Bibliography
Convite	Invitation		Edmonson 1960–1961
Costeño	Coast People		Ayala 1943; Mace 1957; Teletor 1955: 173–176
Culebra	Serpent	Kumatz	Búcaro Moraga 1959; Schultze Jena 1933: 204–212; Termer 1930
Diablitos	Little Devils		Correa 1955, 1958
Escudo	Shield	Chanal, Pokob	Carmack 1973: 295
Flores	Flower	Tz'utubal	
Guerra	War	Tzala tun, E zal vach	Carmack 1973: 295
Huaxteco		Maxtekat	Galiego Suyen 1891
Huehuecho	Goiter	Patzka	Mace 1961; 1970: 19–153; Teletor 1955:.163–165
Israelitos			Teletor 1945
Lechuza	Screech Owl	Xah puhuy	Edmonson 1971: line 4265
Mando	Commandment	Pixab	Teletor 1945
Maner	Beggar	Maneropicio	Bunzel 1952: 426–427
Marineros	Sailor		Teletor 1945
Mexicanos	Mexicans		Teletor 1945
Mico	Spider Monkey Hunter	Hun ah pu q'oy	Edmonson 1971: line 2790
Monos y micos	Monkey		Edmonson 1960–1961; Dieseldorff Collection, Tulane University Library
Moros y cristianos	Moors and Christians		Paret-Limardo 1963
Negrito	Black-man	Ah q'eq	Blaffer 1972; Mace 1957
Palo volador	Flying Pole	Guajxaquib batz, Ah u vi che	Fuentes y Guzmán 1932–1933: 6: 363–366;

NAMES OF DANCES			SOURCES
Spanish	English	Quiche	
			Goubaud Carrera 1935; Schultze Jena 1933:212–218; Termer 1931
Rabinal Achí	Knight of Rabinal, Dance of the Drum	Xahoh tun, K'iche vinak, Rabinal achi	Brasseur de Bourborg 1862; Carmack 1973:325; Mace 1967; 1970; Monterde 1955
San Jorge	St. George		Mace 1957; Teletor 1955:165–168; Termer 1957
San Jorge y Anix	St. George and Aniceto		Teletor 1945
San Pablo	Great Dance	Nima xahoh	Teletor 1945, 1955:182
Siete guacamaya	Seven Parrot	K'ele tz'u	Edmonson 1971:lines 821–1674
Tigre y venado	Jaguar Deer	Ix balam keh	Edmonson n.d.h; Mace 1957; Teletor 1955:168–173
Toritos	Bull		Bunzel 1952:199–200; Edmonson n.d.a; Porras Vidal 1900
Tzules		Xahoh ah tzulab	Ordóñez Ch. 1968
Venadito	Deer	Mazat	Schultze Jena 1933:218–228; Bunzel 1952:424; Paret-Limardo 1970
La Virgen	Virgin Girl	Qapoh ix t'an	
Zancos	Stilt	Chi tik, Tu	Edmonson 1971:line 4269

6. Cyclical Patterns in Chorti (Mayan) Literature

JOHN FOUGHT

1. INTRODUCTION. The Chorti live on the slopes around the market towns of Camotan, La Union, Olopa, and especially, Jocotan, in Chiquimula state, eastern Guatemala.[1] There are about thirty thousand speakers, at a conservative estimate; adults are bilingual in Spanish and Chorti.

In the course of my work on the language, I have so far collected more than two hundred texts, of which fully three-fourths are also of significant interest for their ethnographic and folkloristic content. Several dozen informants are represented, including adults and children, males and females, coming mostly from a group of hamlets lying west of Jocotan.

Until this collection can be expanded by a more systematic survey of the Chorti territory, and until the editing and analysis of the old and new material is farther advanced, comments on the scope and content of the tradition as a whole, or on the degree to which the texts now on hand are representative of it, would be mostly speculation. Instead, I will concentrate here on exploring some characteristic features of Chorti rhetoric, attempting to present a few texts against a background of the linguistic and cultural resources used, in order to show their verbal artistry, for which my admiration continues to grow.

It will be obvious that my approach here is closely similar to that of Dell Hymes, developed in a series of publications on the verbal art of the Northwest (see Hymes 1977; 1981).

2. CYCLICAL PATTERNS. A well-known trait of Mayan culture since ancient times is the elaboration of cyclical patterns, especially in those areas having close connections with religion and ritual: arithmetic, numerology, the calendar, myth, ceremony, etc. The Mayan calendar is perhaps the best-known example of this predilection for cyclical patterns. The *tzolkin*, a ritual cycle of 260 days, is generated by the interaction of two smaller cycles, one of 13 numbers, and the other of 20 day names. To return to the same combination of number and day name, say 1 Imix, takes 13 × 20 or 260 days, since after Imix come 19 other day names, so that the next occurrence of Imix in the cycle bears the number 8, and the one after that is 2 Imix, and so on. This 260-day cycle is itself a component of a larger cycle, together with the 365-day solar year, or *haab* (composed of 18 named months of 20 numbered days each, plus a special sequence of 5 days). The cycle

133

generated by the *tzolkin* and *haab* together is the Calendar Round of 73 *tzolkin* or 52 *haab*, or 18,980 days. The Calendar Round is itself a repeating cycle.

The calendar is far more complex than this, of course, but the Calendar Round by itself is enough to establish the point I wish to make. Just as important as the arithmetic structure of the calendar for the present study, moreover, is the binomial structure of the dates it expresses. In both the *tzolkin* and the *haab*, a particular day is designated by means of a name and a number; in the Calendar Round, two such expressions together designate each day in the cycle: 4 Ahau 13 Ch'en, for instance. Paired expression elements, and pairs of pairs, up to a considerable level of complexity, will be shown to play a crucial role in the formation of Chorti verbal art.

Studies of Mayan belief systems have pointed out another prominent role played by cycles in the Mayan conception of time. In a number of traditions, including the Chorti, there are myths of the cyclical creation and destruction of the world, by flood, by fire, and by other means. Gary Gossen's study of Chamula Tzotzil cosmology (1974b) is an especially striking and well-articulated instance of cyclical patterns interacting in many ways within the content of Chamula myths and legends. In a study of time structuring in Chorti narrative (Fought 1976), I examined a small-scale example of cyclical patterning in the events related in a folktale.

A cyclical conception of time, then, as composed of a number of repeating, interlocking periods or sequences of events, is reflected in the *form* of the Mayan calendar and likewise in many aspects of the *content* of Mayan tradition as it touches on the nature of time and its consequences. This relationship immediately suggests another line of inquiry, one which has so far been little explored, namely, the search for cyclical patterns in the *form* of Mayan verbal art as well as in its content.

While examining Chorti traditional verbal art for the occurrence of such patterning, it will be useful to bear in mind some general properties of cycles and epicycles generated by the interaction of a number of constituent factors. First, even quite long *sequences* of items may be a part or the whole of a cycle generated in this way, provided that each item is a composite of the factors. If the total number of items making up some actual manifestation of the pattern is smaller than any of the constituent factors, the sequence may not appear to be cyclical in nature, as it would if the number of items were large enough to include a repetition of one of the constituent epicycles. Thus, a sequence of eight or nine days from the Calendar Round, unless it included a transition from the end of one or both number series back to the beginning, would not appear to be part of a cycle; it would look like a list. A participant in the culture who recognizes it as manifesting part of a larger cyclical pattern will however accept it on quite a different basis.

Another point to remember is that each factor, a closed list of some specific number of items, will introduce an epicycle with that number as its period into the larger pattern. The smaller the number of the factor, the more repetitive the pattern will seem. Where one factor is a list of two elements, every other expression in the cycle will repeat one or the other, for example:

> A1, B2, C1, D2, E1,
> A2, B1, C2, D1, E2 . . .

Here there are two factors, one of five elements (A–E), and the other of two (1–2); in the cycle of ten composite items there are two epicycles with periods of five and two.

Now, this pattern is strikingly similar to one variety of the *couplet* form so often found in Mayan oral literature. Although these couplets are very familiar, their possible connection with cyclical patterns of the ritual and calendrical type has not been noticed before, so far as I know. A major aim of this chapter is to examine the connection between the two as part of an analysis of formal patterns in Chorti literature.

3. MAYAN COUPLETS. A Mayan couplet, generally defined, is a simple paradigmatic

COUPLETS IN TZOTZIL		COUPLETS IN YUCATEC	
šči ʔuk hnup	'With my spouse,	*cat sihi ximbal u cah*	'Then it was born. It progresses,
šči ʔuk hči ʔil	With my companion;	*sut u cah*	It turns back,
šči ʔuk avob	With your guitar,	*chacal hilib*	The red extractor,
šči ʔuk asot	With your gourd rattle'	*sacal hilib*	The white extractor,
		sut u cah	It turns back,
		chacal nuhcap	The red joiner,
		sacal nuhcap	The white joiner,
		sut u cah	It turns back,
		ximbal u cah	It progresses.'

FIGURE 6-1. Couplets in two Mayan languages.

structure composed of two pairs of elements, such that one element is common to both pairs and one element is unique to each pair:

A1   A1

or

B1   A2

Examples are known from many periods and in many languages. Figure 6-1 includes an example from modern Tzotzil (Gossen 1974b:203) and another from the earlier Yucatec Maya of the *Ritual of the Bacabs* (Roys 1965:38, 92). The Tzotzil couplets are linked by the repeated first elements into a list-like structure. Notice, however, the shift in the pronominal prefixes between the two pairs of lines. In the Yucatec example, a more complex hierarchical structure is clearly evident, with couplets serving as single elements in larger-scale couplet structures. Some of this structure is shown by the indentations in Figure 6-1, which are not found in the original. In discussions of the couplet form in the literature of Mayan studies, it is usually the semantic relationships among the elements which attract attention. The content seems to be easier to appreciate than the form. Of the passage cited in Figure 6-1, Roys remarked, for instance, "Pairing of words with contrary meanings appears to be a favorite rhetorical device in this manuscript" (1965:38n90). However, Mayan couplets arise directly from the exploitation of the most basic syntactic resources of the Mayan

languages, and lend themselves equally well to the development of any desired semantic linkages among elements.[2]

In Chorti, there are two fundamental types of predication. One is equational and intransitive: two items are juxtaposed, placed on a symmetrical and equal footing. This type is used for attributive constructions, such as adjective-noun pairings, and for appositive constructions, such as noun phrase–noun phrase pairings. In the possessive type of predication, the other main variety, the possessed constituent bears a prefix (or occurs with a specialized particle) which subordinates it to the possessor. These constructions, of either type, may be combined hierarchically, in sequential or nesting patterns. Here is a Chorti couplet built out of two attributive constructions, each marked by the *·in-* attributive prefix, as found in Text 20 of Fought 1972:[3]

e in-iax ruede	'The green-blue ring,	(A1)
e in-sak ruede	The white ring'	(B1)

The possessive construction is used more frequently to form couplets in that same text, however, as in this example, where the first element in each line is the third person possessive prefix, marking the first element as possessed by the second, and the second in turn bears a possessive prefix, second person plural, referring to the group of spirits to whom the text is addressed:

u-mak-txan-ir	'The rainbow of your	(A1)
iu-ut	appearance,	
u-mak-txan-ir	The rainbow of your	(A2)
iu-eroh	expression'	

The most natural, immediate product of either of these two types of construction, the equational or the possessive, is a two-part construct. A pair of these constructs will form a couplet so long as one constituent is repeated in the second construct and the other is not.

4. COUPLET STRUCTURES IN A RITUAL TEXT: CURING. The skillful use of the couplet form in the Curing text will be more fully appreciated if it is shown against the background of its symbolic context. Except for the first five pause groups of introductory matter, this text consists of an exhortation addressed to a number of spirits whose actions or body parts are thought to be involved in the illness of the patient over whom the words are spoken.

Adult-child pairings run through the text. Normally a Chorti curer (*ah nirom*) employs a child as a medium: the child touches the patient during the treatment, and the curer touches the child.[4] Built into the customary setting of the performance of this text, then, is an association between adult and child figures, both serving together as intercessors on the human side of the contest between humans and spirits for the soul of the patient. It is no coincidence that the Chorti culture hero, the Kumix Anhel, is also a child: many Chorti refer to the child who works with a curer as his *anxer*, an earlier borrowing of Spanish *angel*, like the less adapted form *anhel*. Furthermore, the final line of Text 20 charges the 'Lightning Aimer, Thunder Aimer' with removing the offending spirits to distant wilderness; these attributes belong especially to the Kumix Anhel.

The intercessors are also matched with San Gregorio, named twice in slightly different ways. The first mention is vague and may refer to an adult, but the second is definitely a child. There is also repeated reference made to the seemingly adult spirits in the exhortation as a whole. Likewise, at some later points in the text, the spirit of the patient is likened to a helpless child, to be defended by the curer. Multiple pairings of adult and child figures, which intersect with relations between humans and spirits, form the basic symbolic background. There is a progression through the text from the opening passages, which speak of the gathering of spirits in the heavenly pool, through a detailed itemizing of the associations between them and specific diseases, to a section describing their malicious mistreatment of the spirit of the patient, to a reassertion of control by the curer, who banishes the spirits in the name of the gods. In step with this development, there is an opposition running through the text between second person plural forms (*i-*, *ix-*, and *-ox*) referring to the celestial spirits and third person forms (*u-*) referring to San Gregorio, one of the names of the ascending Sun and probably an avatar of the Kumix as Sun God, to the spirit of the patient, and perhaps to the spirit of the medium as well. First person plural forms (*ka-*, *-on*) come into play in the last sections, referring to the curer and the medium, and perhaps more vaguely to both and to the patient and spirits as well.

The text is made up mostly of couplets. Through the first half of it, up to 20.90, there are thirty different possessive couplets, but only six different pairs of second elements: appearance-expression, appearance-walking, walking-running, arm-leg, presence-coming, and ghosts-spirits. Obviously, most of the cyclical patterning is manifested by the end pairs of the couplets.

Only the couplet structure of the first part of the text will be examined in any detail here, but the larger scale of internal organization will be discussed in dealing with other texts in which the use of couplets formed at the grammatical level is less noteworthy. The portion of the text shown in Figure 6-2 is arranged to display its internal structure. There are several levels of couplet organization. The passage as a whole falls into two parallel segments. In the first, 20.6–15, the final sequence of three couplets refers, by the sec-

I   (6) *ah ti-txan-er hustixi-ox*   O heavenly judges,

      (7)   *tiaa uar ix-as-i ua-to-ox*   where you are coming to play

               tama ee in-iax ruede   in the green-blue ring,

               e in-sak ruede   the white ring,

      (9)   *tuee saŋ gregorio di agua*   of San Gregorio of Water,

               taka u-mak-txan-ir iu-ut   with the rainbow of your appearance,

               u-mak-txan-ir iu-eroh   the rainbow of your expression,

     (12)   *u-tikau-ir*   *iu-ut*   the warmth of your appearance,

               u-tikau-ir   *iu-eroh*   the warmth of your expression,

               u-le ʔkꞏon-ir   *iu-ut*   the heat of your appearance,

     (15)   *u-le ʔk-on-ir*   *i-xam-ʔp-ar* the heat of your walking;

II (16)   *tiaa i-noh-komon-i i-ʔpa*   where you pile yourselves together,

               ix-as-i ua-to-ox   coming to play

               tama e in-iax pila   in the green-blue basin,

               e in-sak pila   the white basin,

     (19)   *ia a-as-i e ninio san gregorio* there where the Child San Gregorio plays,

               taka u-ʔtsa ʔp-ta-r u-ut   with the reflection of his appearance,

               u-ʔtsa ʔp-ta-r ui-eroh   the reflection of his expression,

     (21)   *uu-arar-ir*   *u-ut*   the beams of his appearance,

               uu-arar-ir   *u-xam-ʔp-ar* the beams of his walking,

               u-tikau-ir   *u-ut*   the warmth of his appearance,

     (23)   *u-tikau-ir*   *ui-eroh*   the warmth of his expression;

Figure 6-2. Couplet structure in Text 20.

I   *[tiaa]* *[(uar) (ix- ... -ox)]*

      [tama] *[(iax/sak) (ruede)]*

        [tuaa] *[San G. de A.]*

          [taka] *[(u- ...) (i- ...)]*

II *[tiaa]* *[(komon) (ix- ... -ox)]*

      [tama] *[(iax/sak) (pila)]*

        [ia] *[N. San G.]*

          [taka] *[(u- ...) (u- ...)]*

Figure 6-3. Structures in Text 20.

ond person pronouns on the end elements, to the spirits; the second segment, 20.16–23, also ends in three couplets, whose end elements have third person pronouns referring to San Gregorio. In Figure 6-3, the same portion of text is condensed into outline form, with bracketings to make the hierarchical patterns clear. Each line in the first segment of Figure 6-3 forms a couplet when paired with the corresponding line of the second segment. The second part of each line, the portion within the second set of square brackets, likewise forms a couplet when paired with the corresponding second portion from the second segment. The first and second lines of the first segment, taken together, form a couplet when paired with the first and second lines of the second segment. The same is true of the last two lines of the first and second segments, and of the first segment as a whole when paired with the second segment as a whole. All of this is in addition to the lowest level of couplet structure, as already noted.

Worked into this already rich hierarchical form is another repeating pattern of affixes, readily visible in Figure 6-2. This sort of repetition is almost unavoidable, given the reliance of the narrator on grammatically parallel construction and the nature of Chorti morphology. Still, it contributes powerfully to the unity of the text, establishing further metrical and phonological regularities that can be heard in recitation to have a most impressive incantatory effect.

Overall, Text 20 has four parts, arranged symmetrically: short-long-long-short. The first of these has already been discussed. The second part is a long list of couplets, from 20.24 to 20.79, similar in structure to the six possessive couplets in the first part. They have a *u-* prefix on the first element and an *i-* prefix on the second, and are addressed to the same spirits. The couplet structure of the first part and of the beginning of the second is schematized in Figure 6-4, which covers the text as far as 20.54. From there, the text continues in much the same way for the rest of part 2; little would be added by extending Figure 6-4 to cover it. In Figure 6-4, a letter is assigned to each beginning element in a couplet half, and a number to each ending element, as before. Note that the only recurrence of a beginning element is between the two portions of part 1, as noted. Ending pairs, on the other hand, recur in a strongly cyclical pattern, which Figure 6-4 is designed to reveal. The parenthesized numbers refer to the pause group of the immediately following element. An asterisk marks the place of each occurrence of the preposition *taka* 'with, at', whose appearance marks the beginning of a new text segment in this portion of the text. Gaps were left in the figure to line up couplets with their earlier structural counterparts. The two large circles mark the mentions of San Gregorio; nothing in later segments corresponds to that, so gaps are left. The fourth and sixth segments lack the central group of couplets found in the others, so a gap is left between the opening couplet and the closing couplet in those segments. The fifth segment begins in the usual way, but has an odd number of elements in the chain of couplets and lacks the segment-ending pair. Figure 6-4 displays quite clearly the structural theme and variations of the segments. In particular, it shows how the marking of the overtly cyclical aspects of the structure of Text 20 is left to the ending pairs of the couplets. These do not serve as individual items from a list which repeats, as do the days in

the *tzolkin*; instead, pairs of items having desired semantic relationships are used as units to form patterns of sameness or difference of sound and sense in grouping larger sequences of couplets together within the text.

The third part of Text 20, from 20.80 to 20.144, is also addressed to the spirits, but is somewhat different in form. The list of couplets is largely made up of transitive verbal expressions having an *i-* second person plural prefix on the first part and an object with a *u-* third person prefix referring to the patient's spirit as the second part:

20.102   *uar i-leu-leu-r-es u-meein*
        'You are softening his spirit'

20.103   *uar i-leu-leu-r-es u-ʔpak-er*
        'You are softening his bones'

The fourth and last part is short, like the first, and contains the actual injunction to the spirits to leave the patient and his spirit alone. It includes the forms for 'now', 'today', and 'we', as mentioned above. In this, it parallels strikingly the organizational plan of folktales of the kind to be examined in the remainder of this chapter, which commonly end with a brief section returning the action of the narrative to the present and reminding the listeners of what they are expected to notice about the relevance of the tale. Like the first part, the end of Text 20 consists of two parallel passages, and, again like the beginning, it evokes the adjoining long section from the middle of the text by the repetition of certain key forms and images from it.

It seems likely that Text 20 represents a fragment of what may once have been an extensive and quite complex system for generating associations between spirits, their actions, and their body parts on the one hand and the symptoms and syndromes of an elaborate disease taxonomy on the other. If so, it would be a natural use of the projective body part metaphors by which the Chorti, like other Mayan peoples, classify and label parts of artifacts, geographical features, and even other body parts, making analytical use of terms for 'head', 'neck', 'face', and 'heel',

I	II	III	IV	V	VI		VII
(6)	(16)	(24)	(32)	(36)	(43)		(47)
A1	A5	*H4	*L4	*N4	*S6		*U4
B1	B5	H6	L6	N6	S4		U6
○	○						
*C2	*F2	I7		N9		(49)	*V10
C3	F3	I8		09			V11
D2	G2	J7		P9		(51)	*W10
D3	G4	J8		Q9			W11
E2	D2	K2	M2	R9	T4	(53)	*X4
E4	D3	K3	M3		T6		X6

Figure 6-4. Segments of couplet sequences in Text 20. (Read from top to bottom, then from left to right.)

among others, in a productive system of nomenclature.

5. SEGMENTAL AND COUPLET PATTERNS IN MAYA HIEROGLYPHIC TEXTS. Before looking at Chorti rhetorical patterns on a larger scale, it is worth noting that segmental and couplet structures of the sort just discussed are readily evident in the hieroglyphic texts of the ancient Mayas. Without having to enter into details of the writing system as it is now understood, one can see clear patterns evident on the basis of sameness and difference of glyph groups in portions of texts.

Many suitable examples can be found in the hieroglyphic codices. Figure 6-5 shows two from a portion of the *Dresden Codex*. Each segment begins with a bar and dot numeral in the upper left, above a column of day signs from the *tzolkin*. In this portion of the *Dresden Codex*, segmentation is based on the *tzolkin*, and in each segment, the period of 260 days is subdivided in various ways by the black, or interval numbers, which separate the red numbers of dates in the cycle.

Divisions between segments, and subdivisions within segments of this type in the codices, then, are based on the structure of the *tzolkin* cycle. Further calendrical details are not relevant here.

In the segment in the upper portion of Figure 6-5 a Chicchan serpent stretches beneath the glyphic text. The order of reading of the glyphs in this text is unusual, but there can be little doubt of what it must be. The first glyph group on the left is repeated across the top of the text; evidently it is to be read in single columns rather than the more usual double columns from left to right. Given the repeated top glyph groups, this produces a chain of A1-A2 type. The pattern is

A1 A A A A A A
2 1 3 4 5 6

and thus quite similar to some of the segments of Text 20. I am not making any claims about the content of the hieroglyphic text—unfortunately it is not well enough understood for that—but only about the formal resemblance to structures already pointed out in Text 20.

The lower segment in Figure 6-5 is more typical in its structure. It too is based on the *tzolkin* cycle and contains four pictures of gods or other creatures, each with four glyph groups above it and each corresponding to a paired black and red numeral, marking a date in the *tzolkin*. Each of these subdivisions is called a frame in the literature of hieroglyphic studies. The glyph groups are to be read in double columns, from left to right. If letters and numbers are assigned as before on the basis of patterns of sameness and difference among the glyph groups, the following structure is found:

A1 A1 A1 A1
B2 C3 D4 E5

Once again a couplet structure of a familiar kind is found in the frame-to-frame relationships within the segment. Once again, the content of the text is not well enough understood to allow us to determine what the exact relationship is between the gods and the text in each frame, but for present purposes that is not essential. It is clear enough that the very same kinds of patterning found in modern Chorti ritual texts and in other Mayan oral literatures were present in the hieroglyphic writings. Indeed, other varieties of internal organization can also be seen in the *Dresden* and in other hieroglyphic texts: a

139

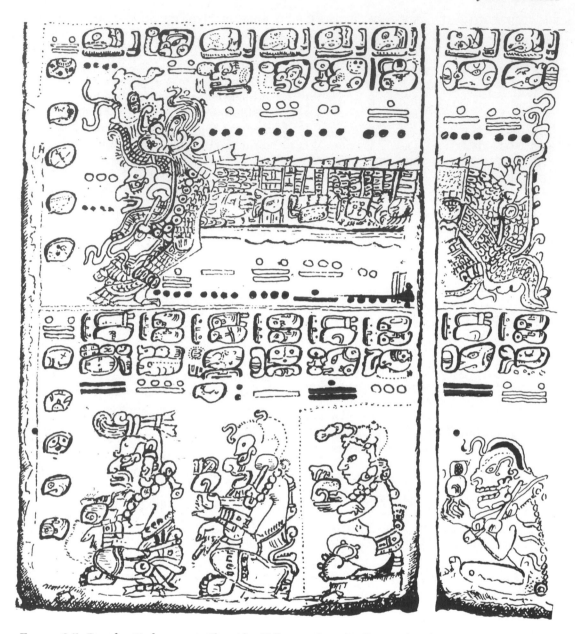

FIGURE 6-5. *Dresden Codex*, pp. 4–5bc. After Villacorta C. and Villacorta (1933).

very common one is the repetition of the second and third, that is, the middle glyph groups of the four in the text of a frame, and there are numerous other patterns.

6. COUPLETS IN FOLKTALE DIALOGUE: COYOTE AND RABBIT. Among Chorti narratives I have heard so far, Lorenza Martínez' telling of the Coyote and Rabbit tale ranks as the outstanding narrative performance. She uses a wide range of vocal dynamics, gives each animal character's lines in a special voice, and sets the stage so effectively that both adults and children in the audience are delighted to listen.[5]

The text is made up of two episodes, of which the first is a Tar Baby variant, with sugar syrup serving as the sticky substance, and the second is the Big Cheese episode, in which Coyote is tricked into bursting his stomach by trying to drink a pond dry to get at the reflection of the moon in it, which he has been told is a cheese. Although the tale is strongly influenced by European elements, it nevertheless contains a clear though slightly looser variety of the couplet form in its organization, together with the usual division into segments through the use of discourse particles and other markers acting with them.

As the passage quoted in Figure 6-6 opens, Rabbit has just come upon Coyote, and both become aware of a jar of sugar syrup cooling near a temporarily unguarded sugar mill in the fields. The syllable at the top of the left column is Rabbit's exclamation, followed by his opening remark to Coyote. Comparing this with its near echo by Coyote shows that they form an A1-B1 couplet, with the second line of each character corresponding to the repeated item, though the echo is not perfect in this instance.

Moving down through the dialogue, in the left-hand portion of Figure 6-6, one finds a number of very clear A1-B1 couplets, such as *ane e berda*, *uar berda*, or Rabbit's lines in pause groups 26 and 28. And if each line of dialogue is paired with its quotative particle to the right, another layer of A1-B1 patterning is seen, where the repeated *txa-aii* (an assimilation of *txe* 'he said' and Spanish *allí*

'there') forms a chain linking the whole passage together. The couplet form, then, even in its complex hierarchical manifestations, is not confined to one type of text, nor to the work of one narrator.

7. PAIRED SEGMENTS IN A LEGEND: THE SESIMITE OF TA PILA. The example to be considered next does not involve grammatically formed couplets in any significant role, but it does show the segmental plan of organization and a number of pairings of thematic elements fitted into a characteristic progression of plot from a general (and implicitly cyclical) statement, through increasingly specific instances of the general pattern, to a final dramatic reversal of this pattern as a resolution.

This is the story of the Sesimite of Ta Pila. The *ʔkeʔtxuh* or Sesimite are long-haired ogresses with feet turned rearward and dangerous teeth put frequently into the service of their insatiable appetites. They visit human habitations to get food by cunning or by force. They are able to assume human form, either to offer sexual temptation as young women or to arouse sympathy as old crones, but they do not always remember to correct their feet. They live in caves or water sources, and keep snails as humans keep chickens.[6] Ta Pila is a muddy spring hole near Pelillo Negro.

The structures of interest in this text encompass the whole of it, but do not involve the forms of the Chorti expressions themselves. A close translation will serve the purposes of this study well enough. The translation is divided into thirteen paragraphs, lettered A–M; each one corresponds to a segment in the organization of the Chorti original. These segments are marked off by the use of intonation contours, discourse particles, and certain other rhetorical devices, as explained in Fought 1976.

The Sesimite of Ta Pila
(Isidro González)

A. There is a story that was told in times past by the old people.

B. They said that where we live in Pelillo there is a mud hole we call Ta Pila. They say

	+ *txa-aii e koneho haax-ir e im-ʔpahr* +
+ *aa*	*txa-aii* + (10)
tar-a uar a-txahp-e-eie txaap +	
	txa-aii aaraaiee -- koiote + (13)
+ *a-koom-ʔp-ah*	*txa-aii* + (14)
uar a-txahp-a-ra pues	*txa-aii* +
+ *ane e berda*	*txa-aii* + (17)
+ *uar berda* +	*txa-aii* +
peree maa -- peree maa to --	
haax ta-ʔkan +	*txa-aii* + (23)
+ *tsihts-i to* +	*txa-aii* +
+ *pero ia mero a-tur-an*	+ *txa-aii ier ee -- koneho* + (28)
haax-ir ia meru a-tur-an	*txa-aii* +
a-kohk-o to koora +	*txa-aii* + (31)
txe-en to n-tia a-ier ora koora +	
+ *ia ia a-tur-an*	*txa-aii* +

Figure 6-6, Part 1. Dialogue between Coyote and Rabbit.

that in that place in times past there were snails, because they say that a Sesimite used to live there.

C. And that Sesimite went out to all the houses in the hamlets. When she found a house with no people in it, and a baby lying swaddled, what she did was eat it.

D. They said that that Sesimite became like an old woman with children; she went visiting houses. When she came to a house, she would say to the wife, "Go get me some water. I'll watch things." And those who didn't know she was a Sesimite would leave their children lying there. And when they came back from the water, they didn't find them there. They would have been eaten already by the Sesimite.

E. There was a woman, they say, approached and spoken to by the Sesimite: "Woman, go get some water, because it's already late. I'll take care of your child." The woman wrapped up the baby, put it down, and left. And when she returned, it had been all eaten up by the Sesimite, except for one foot left behind.

F. Then it became known that the woman who went around visiting was not human.

G. Then everyone was very frightened in the hamlets. They no longer would leave their children alone then.

H. One day, they say, the Sesimite entered a house, and the wife had wrapped up a stone *mano* in cloths and laid it on the bed where she slept. And the Sesimite saw it when she entered, lying on the bed like a wrapped-up baby. She jumped over and grabbed it up. And since it was inedible, she began to yell about her teeth, because she broke off her teeth in the *mano* she had mistaken for a baby. And the woman, who was watching from behind the house, heard her, as soon as she began yelling. And the Sesimite said, "Ah, I thought it was your little child on the bed. I wanted to give it a kiss, and I broke my teeth."

I. Then the woman laughed.

J. And another time the Sesimite came to a house. A baby had been left lying there. When the woman came back, it had been all eaten up by the Sesimite. What the woman did was set fire to the thatch all around the house. The fire at once surrounded the house, and everything was burned up in the fire.

	Said the Rabbit next,
Ah!	He said, (10)
Here is some syrup boiling.	
	Said the -- Coyote, (13)
Really!	He said, (14)
It's boiling along, all right.	He said,
That's the truth,	He said, (17)
It's the truth.	He said,
But -- But -- it --	
isn't done.	He said, (23)
It's not finished.	He said.
But it's just about ready.	He said -- the little Rabbit. (28)
It's almost ready.	He said,
Wait a little!	He said, (31)
Take a little time.	
There, it's ready!	He said.

Figure 6-6, Part 2. English translation of Part 1.

K. And when the fire had passed away from the house, they went to see, and there was a big stone lying where it had burned.

L. And that stone lies there today, where Alberto Pérez lives. They say it is the Sesimite who was burned up. And the stone lies there today, and the place is called Sesimite Stone. And the snail shells which were there in times past, there, all dried out, and turned to stone, they are, because people say that their owner died.

M. That is why there are no longer so many snails nowadays; but in times past, it is said there were many of them. Because we see their shells in the stone. Just snail shells, but all turned to stone. Because their owner died.

Segment *A* is the traditional opening formula for any kind of traditional narrative. Segment *B* gives the factual setting of the story; this will be echoed at the end. Segments *C* and *D* state the habitual pattern of action of this Sesimite: they form the general statement of the cycle of events making up the core of the story. Segment *E* gives a specific instance of this cycle, with one key

detail added that is not present in the general statement, the baby's foot left behind by the Sesimite. (This foot, by the way, appears in several different stories about other Sesimites in the same position within the development of the action.) These three segments form two couplets, in an A1-B1-B2 sequence, since *C* and *D* differ in their statements of how the common ending element, the eating of the baby, was achieved, and *E* supplies a distinctive final detail in this ending, but is almost exactly like *D* up to that point.

Segments *F* and *G* are the pivot of the plot. Before them, everything goes the Sesimite's way; after them, the humans gradually reassert control. Segment *G* states the moral of the story, in the middle of its development as do so many of the Chorti tales. Here the moral is "Don't leave your child unattended." This segment also prepares the hearers for the prudent mother of the next segment.

In segment *H*, the mother's countermeasures are introduced after each step in the Sesimite's habitual procedure. This interspersing of Sesimite and human moves is one stage in the process of the reversal of control, which shifts more and more to the humans in the second part of this text. This progression is matched in many other Chorti tales. The swaddled *mano* motif, like the baby's foot, reappears in many Sesimite stories, including the important cycle of myths of the Kumix Anhel.

Segment *I*, very brief, but very clearly separated from its neighbors, answers dramatically to the fear mentioned in Segment *G*.

Segment *J* begins with the eating of the baby, where the others end. This reversal of order is part of the symmetry of the plot, however: the process of human ascendancy is continuing. The woman destroys the water demon with fire, echoing the symbolism of the Kumix Anhel myth, in which the Sun God is raised by a Sesimite foster mother whom he destroys with lightning. With only one inconclusive exception, when humans kill a Sesimite it is with fire.

The motif of the Sesimite Stone, in segments *K*, *L*, and *M*, is a brilliant success, unifying and concentrating the levels of the story's symbolism into one tangible detail. I have not seen this stone, but I am confident that it is really there. It provides the desired authentication of the events of the plot; it is a plausible compacting and hardening effect of fire on the body of the Sesimite, literally full of snails; it explains the nature and origin of fossils, and the present dearth of live (soft, wet) snails; and finally, it deftly evokes the stone "baby," the swaddled *mano*, used earlier to deceive the Sesimite.

To summarize the symbolism, then, there is mud opposed to stone, water opposed to fire, live snails to stone snails, live babies to stone babies, and the old Sesimite, with her snails swaddled in their shells, opposed to the young women with their babies swaddled in cloths.

Comparison with another Sesimite text, the story of the Sesimite of Uis Haa, reveals strikingly similar organization in both texts. The Sesimite of Uis Haa also makes the rounds of nearby hamlets over a period of a year (specific hamlets are named). The portion of the text occupied in the Ta Pila story by the stone *mano* and the fired house are

similarly filled in the Uis Haa text, where the Sesimite offers sex to a boy she meets as he rides a horse along the path between hamlets. When he approaches her, she abruptly turns her ankle-length hair into a net and carries him off to her home, but he escapes. She is trapped by some boys as she walks along a stream-bed, and they set fire to her hair. The swaddled *mano* motif also appears in this text in roughly the same position. Both tales were told by the same informant at different times and places; together they provide a good example of the use of circumstantial touches to differentiate and localize versions of the same basic plot. In both, the dramatic resolution is provided by fire: in the Ta Pila story, a woman is sent to fetch water, and returns with fire; in the Uis Haa story, the ogress has her feet in the water of her home while her head is in flames.

8. SUMMARY AND CONCLUSIONS. Besides the segmentation of narratives into groups of event clauses separated from each other by discourse particles and other related means of boundary marking, as explained in Fought 1976, there is another kind of patterning in Chorti verbal art. The Mayan couplet form, a simple but powerful paradigmatic system based on paired expressions sharing a common portion and differing in their remaining portions, is used in ritual speech by the modern Chorti and by other Mayan peoples. Mayan couplets arise directly from their foundation in basic Mayan syntax and are used to construct complex cyclical patterns in Mayan verbal art.

These cyclical patterns occur on several levels simultaneously in some of the examples discussed here. They are similar to but not exactly the same as the cyclical patterns in the Mayan calendar, and they bear a still closer resemblance to patterns of sameness and difference among glyph groups in some portions of the Mayan hieroglyphic codices. All of these appear to be related applications of a very general and productive system for generating interlocking cyclical patterns in art and ritual that the Mayan peoples have exploited for ages.

NOTES

1. My work on Chorti was at first supported by the National Science Foundation and directed by Floyd G. Lounsbury. I relied especially on the help and friendship of Isidro González in learning about the culture and language of his people. Working with this remarkable man has been a delight, as well as an advantage. For a collection of Chorti texts with a descriptive introduction to the language and an appraisal of earlier works on the language and culture, see Fought 1972; the phonology and morphology of Chorti are treated in more detail in Fought 1967.

2. The Mayan languages are *ergative* in type, unlike the familiar *accusative* organization common to the Indo-European languages (and to many others). In an accusative language, there is a clear and fundamental distinction marked between the subjects of both transitive and intransitive verbs on the one hand (the nominative case category) and the objects of transitive verbs on the other (the accusative case), with the possessor of a noun marked in a third way (by the genitive case). In an ergative language, however, the clear and fundamental distinction is made between subjects of transitive verbs and, usually, possessors of nouns on the one hand (the ergative case) and the subjects of intransitive verbs and the objects of transitive verbs on the other (the absolute case). There are many ramifications of this typological difference. For a fuller discussion of ergativity in Chorti and in Mayan generally, see Fought 1969 (published in 1973); it is sufficient here to underline the importance of the possessive construction (used both in possessive noun phrases and in transitive "verb" clauses) and the distinction drawn in such systems between transitive and intransitive predications, whose "subjects" (though alike to us) are marked differently. In Chorti, this different marking is quite straightforwardly shown in the different pronoun sets used; in the other languages, distinct combinations of pronouns and derivational suffixes must be taken into account.

3. The forty texts in Fought 1972 are numbered sequentially. Future published collections will continue this sequence. Within each text, reference is by *pause groups*, each one a group of syllables separated by pauses from neighboring pause groups. Pauses are symbolized by + (regular or planned pause) and -- (hesitation or unplanned pause), never by space. Thus, 20.6 is the sixth pause group in Text 20. In Fought 1972, each *utterance*, a sequence of pause groups usually ending with a terminal intonation contour, begins with a pause group number in the printed version. Count groups from the nearest such number to find the desired reference.

Transcriptions in this chapter will be simplified by the omission of stress markings and vocalic laryngealization (symbolized elsewhere by prevocalic $^?$); preconsonantal $^?$ indicates that the following stop or cluster is laryngealized and ejective, thus $^?p$, $^?t$, $^?k$, $^?ts$, and $^?tx$ in place of most other Mayanists' p', t', k', c', and $č'$. Although the reasons for this transcription are rooted in phonological theory and are important to me, it is not necessary to air them here. See Fought 1967, 1972, and 1982 for full discussion.

4. Isidro González learned the text of this exhortation while serving as the medium for his grandfather, a well-known curer, but so far as I know, he never entered practice later on his own. His memory of the text is obviously very good, but just as obviously not perfect. He therefore preferred to dictate it from notes rather than attempt a performance without memory aids. His slight distance from the working version of the text should be remembered during the discussion of the details of its structure.

5. Transcribing this text was a serious challenge. It was spoken rapidly, and the special voices required the development of some special notational conventions. Besides that, Martínez' involvement with the performance was so complete that she sometimes assigned a line of dialogue to the wrong character (and sometimes the wrong voice, too). Everyone except me knew the text well enough to make the necessary corrections while enjoying the

performance. Isidro González helped with the translation and corrections of his aunt's story later on. The full text will appear, with annotations and special conventions, in the next series of Chorti texts.

6. Laughlin 1977 is an interesting collection of Tzotzil texts with many parallels to the Chorti literature, including the Longhairs, or Sesimites. Laughlin's notes and bibliography are indispensable.

BIBLIOGRAPHY

For a scholarly and accurate identification of native manuscripts, their publication histories, and their alternative titles, see the annotated bibliography by Gibson and Glass (1975).

ACUÑA, RENÉ
1968   Título de los señores de Sacapulas. *Folklore Américas* 28:1–45.

1975   *Introducción al estudio del "Rabinal Achi."* Centro de Estudios Mayas, Cuaderno 12. Mexico City: Universidad Nacional Autónoma de México.

ALVARADO TEZOZOMOC, FERNANDO
1949   *Crónica mexicayotl.* Translated by Adrian León. Instituto de Historia, 1st ser., no. 10. Mexico City: Universidad Nacional Autónoma de México and Instituto Nacional de Antropología e Historia. (Reprinted in 1975.)

ANALES:
Anales antiguos
n.d.   Anales antiguos de México y sus contornos. Archivo del Museo Nacional de Antropología, Colección Antigua, vols. 273, 274. Mexico City.

Cuauhtitlan
1945   In *Códice Chimalpopoca: Anales de Cuauhtitlan y Leyenda de los Soles.* Translated by Primo Feliciano Velázquez. Instituto de Historia, 1st ser., no. 1, pp. 3–118. Mexico City: Universidad Nacional Autónoma de México. (Reprinted in 1975.)

Mexicanos
1903   Anales mexicanos: México-Azcapotzalco,

1426–1589. *Anales del Museo Nacional de México* 7:49–74.

México y Tlatelolco
n.d.   In Anales antiguos de México y sus contornos, pp. 587–632. Archivo del Museo Nacional de Antropología, Colección Antigua, vols. 273, 274. Mexico City.

Tlatelolco
1948   *Anales de Tlatelolco: Unos annales históricos de la nación mexicana y Códice de Tlatelolco.* Edited by Heinrich Berlin and R. H. Barlow. Fuentes para la Historia de México 2. Mexico City: Porrúa.

Tula
1979   *Anales de Tula: Cód. 359, Museo Nacional de Antropología, Mexico City.* Commentary by Rudolf A. van Zantwijk. Graz: Akademische Druck- und Verlaganstalt.

ANDERSON, ARTHUR J. O., FRANCES BERDAN, AND JAMES LOCKHART
1976   (eds. and trans.) *Beyond the Codices: The Nahua View of Colonial Mexico.* Berkeley and Los Angeles: University of California Press.

ANDERSON, THOR R.
1975   Kruston: A Study of House and Home in a Maya Village. B.A. honors thesis, Department of Anthropology, Harvard College.

147

ANDRADE, MANUEL J.

1971a Quiché (Maya) Texts. Translated by Remigio Cochojil-González. Microfilm Collection of Manuscripts on Cultural Anthropology, ser. 20, no. 111. Chicago: University of Chicago Library.

1971b Yucatec (Maya) Texts. Translated by Refugio Vermont-Salas. Microfilm Collection of Manuscripts on Cultural Anthropology, ser. 19, no. 108. Chicago: University of Chicago Library.

ANONYMOUS

1939a Bix tuculnahi huntul zacothel iix bix tu bootah u ppax huntul mazeual [What a whiteskin thought and how a peasant paid his debt]. *Yikal Maya Than* 1(1): 9–10. Merida: Imprenta Oriente.

1939b Xtabay iix xtabentun [Xtabay and xtabentun]. *Yikal Maya Than* 1(1):15, 20.

1939c Bix u tabzah xtabay [How the xtabay deceives]. *Yikal Maya Than* 1(2):7.

1939d Aac maac uxmali [Turtle man of Uxmal]. *Yikal Maya Than* 1(16):7.

1953 Juan del Monte. *Yikal Maya Than* 14: 143–144.

AQUINO CH., ZENAIDO

1973a *In lacal hual quimictic in sierpe* [The man who killed a serpent]. Mexico City: Dirección General de Educación Extraescolar del Medio Indígena.

1973b *In ome compadres* [The two godfathers]. Mexico City: Dirección General de Educación Extraescolar del Medio Indígena.

1973c *In quinami quipanuc se xucuatulon* [The fat man who went in search of a wife]. Mexico City: Dirección General de Educación Extraescolar del Medio Indígena.

1973d *Se lacal monamictia* [A man got married]. Mexico City: Dirección General de Educación Extraescolar del Medio Indígena.

ARBUZ, GEORGES S.

1963 La Construction de la guitare et du violin à Chamula. MS, Harvard Chiapas Project, Peabody Museum, Harvard University.

ARMAS LARA, M.

1964 *El renacimiento de la danza guatemalteca y el orígen de la marimba.* Guatemala City: Ministerio de Educación Pública.

ARTE

1793 Arte de lengva Qiche. MS in Bibliothèque Nationale, Paris; photocopy in Ayer Collection, Newberry Library, Chicago.

ARZÁPALO, RAMÓN

1970 The Ceremony of Tsikul T'an Ti' Yuntsiloob at Balankanche. Appendix II of *Balankanche, Throne of the Tiger Priest*, by E. Wyllys Andrews IV, pp. 79–182. Middle American Research Institute, Tulane University, Pub. 32. New Orleans.

AYALA, M. ANGEL

1943 El costeño. MS, Archivo de Materiales Culturales del Instituto Indigenista Nacional, Guatemala City.

BAER, MARY E.

1970 The Rabbit and Mountain Lion: A Lacandon Myth. *Tlalocan* 6:268–275.

BARRERA VÁSQUEZ, ALFREDO

1957 (ed. and trans.) *Códice de Calkini.* Biblioteca Campechana, no. 4. Campeche: M. Porrúa.

1961 Contrata de un maya de Yucatan, escrita en su lengua materna, para servir en Cuba, en 1849. *Estudios de Cultura Maya* 1:199–210.

1965 (ed. and trans.) *El libro de los cantares de Dzitbalché.* Série Investigaciones, Instituto Nacional de Antropología, no. 9. Mexico City.

1980 (director) *Diccionario Maya Cordemex: Maya-español, español-maya.* Merida: Ediciones Cordemex.

BARRERA VÁSQUEZ, ALFREDO, AND SILVIA RENDÓN

1948 (eds. and trans.) *El libro de los libros de Chilam Balam.* Mexico City: Fondo de Cultura Económica.

BAUDOT, GEORGES

1978 Un *huehuetlatolli* desconocido, de la Biblioteca Nacional de México. *Estudios de Cultura Nahuatl* 13:69–87.

BAUTISTA, JUAN

ca. 1600 *Huehuetlatolli.* Mexico City. (1901 ed., edited by Antonio Peñafiel, vol. 3 of *Colección de documentos para la historia mexicana.* Mexico City: Secretaría de Fomento.)

BINDERMAN, WILLIAM N.
1960 Contemporary Oral Tradition of the Mexican Revolution. MS, Harvard Chiapas Project, Peabody Museum, Harvard University.

BLAFFER, SARAH C.
1972 *The Black-man of Zinacantan: A Central American Legend.* Austin: University of Texas Press.

BODE, BARBARA
1961 The Dance of the Conquest of Guatemala. In *The Native Theater in Middle America*, pp. 204–292. Middle American Research Institute, Tulane University, Pub. 27. New Orleans.

BRASSEUR DE BOURBOURG, CHARLES ETIENNE
1862 (ed.) *Grammaire de la langue quiché.* Paris: A. Bertrand. (Spanish ed., 1961. Guatemala City: Ministerio de Educación Pública.)
1869–1870 *Manuscrit Troano.* Paris: Imprimerie Imperiale.
1872 *Dictionnaire, grammaire et chrestomathie de la langue maya.* Paris: Maisonneuve.

BRETON, ADELA C.
1919–1922 Maya Documents. British Museum, MSS 13, 974, and others.

BRICKER, VICTORIA REIFLER
1968 The Meaning of Laughter in Zinacantan: An Analysis of the Humor of a Highland Maya Community. Ph.D. dissertation, Department of Anthropology, Harvard University.
1973a Algunas consecuencias religiosas y sociales del nativismo maya del siglo XIX. *América Indígena* 33:327–348.
1973b *Ritual Humor in Highland Chiapas.* Austin: University of Texas Press.
1973c The Structure of Classification and Ranking in Three Mayan Communities. *Estudios de Cultura Maya* 9:161–103.
1973d Three Genres of Tzotzil Insult. In *Meaning in Mayan Languages: Ethnolinguistic Studies*, edited by Munro S. Edmonson, pp. 183–203. The Hague: Mouton.
1974a The Ethnographic Context of Some Traditional Mayan Speech Genres. In *Explorations in the Ethnography of Speaking*, edited by Richard Bauman and Joel Sherzer, pp. 368–388. London: Cambridge University Press.
1974b Some Cognitive Implications of Informant Variability in Zinacanteco Speech Classification. *Language and Society* 3:69–82.
1976 Some Zinacanteco Joking Strategies. In *Speech Play: Research and Resources for Studying Linguistic Creativity*, edited by Barbara Kirshenblatt-Gimblett, pp. 51–62. Philadelphia: University of Pennsylvania Press.
1977 Historical Dramas in Chiapas, Mexico. *Journal of Latin American Lore* 3: 227–248.
1978 Symbolic Representations of Protohistoric Social Stratification and Religious Organization in a Modern Maya Community. In *Codex Wauchope: A Tribute Roll*, edited by Marco Giardino, Barbara Edmonson, and Winifred Creamer. *Human Mosaic* (Tulane University) 12:39–56. New Orleans.
1979a Aztec and Mayan Ritual Humor. In *Forms of Play of Native North Americans*, edited by Edward Norbeck and Claire R. Farrer, pp. 153–169. St. Paul, Minn.: West.
1979b Movimientos religiosos indígenas en los altos de Chiapas. *América Indígena* 39:17–45.
1979c Yucatec Maya Text. In *Mayan Texts II*, edited by Louanna Furbee-Losee, pp. 27–37. Native American Texts Series, vol. 3. Chicago: International Journal of American Linguistics.
1979d Tzotzil Text. In *Mayan Texts II*, edited by Louanna Furbee-Losee, pp. 122–135. Native American Texts Series, vol. 3. Chicago: International Journal of American Linguistics.
1980 The Function of Humor in Zinacantan. *Journal of Anthropological Research* 36:411–418.
1981 *The Indian Christ, the Indian King: The Historical Substrate of Maya Myth and Ritual.* Austin: University of Texas Press.

BRINTON, DANIEL G.
1882 (ed. and trans.) *The Maya Chronicles.* Library of Aboriginal American Literature, no. 1. Philadelphia.
1887 (trans.) *Ancient Nahuatl Poetry.* Library

of Aboriginal American Literature, no. 7. Philadelphia.

BRUCE S., ROBERTO D.

1968   *Gramática del Lacandón.* Departamento de Investigaciones Antropológicas, Instituto Nacional de Antropología e Historia, Pub. 21. Mexico City.

1974   *El libro de Chan K'in.* Colección Científica, Lingüística, no. 12. Mexico City: Instituto Nacional de Antropología e Historia.

1976   (ed.) *Textos y dibujos lacandones de Naja.* Colección Científica, Lingüística, no. 45. Mexico City: Instituto Nacional de Antropología e Historia.

BÚCARO MORAGA, JAIME ISMAEL

1959   (compiler) Leyendas, cuentos, mitos y fábulas indígenas. Mimeographed. Guatemala City: Instituto Indigenista Nacional.

BUNTING, ETHEL-JANE W.

1932   (trans.) Ixtlavacan Quiché Calendar of 1854. *Maya Society Quarterly* 1:72–75.

BUNZEL, RUTH

1940   The Rôle of Alcoholism in Two Central American Cultures. *Psychiatry* 3: 361–387.

1952   *Chichicastenango, a Guatemalan Village.* American Ethnological Society, Pub. 12. Locust Valley, N.Y.: Augustin.

1959   Chichicastenango and Chamula. In *Drinking and Intoxication: Selected Readings in Social Attitudes and Controls,* edited by Raymond G. McCarthy, pp. 73–86. New Haven: Yale Center of Alcohol Studies.

1960   El papel del alcoholismo en dos culturas centroamericanas. *Boletín del Instituto Nacional Indigenista* 3:27–81. Mexico City.

BURGESS, DORA M. DE, AND PATRICIO XEC

1955   (trans.) *Popol Wuj.* Quezaltenango, Guatemala: Noticiero Evangélico.

BURNS, ALLAN F.

1983   *An Epoch of Miracles: Oral Literature of the Yucatec Maya.* Austin: University of Texas Press.

BURSTEIN, JOHN N.

1975   The King Tales in Translation. B.A. honors thesis, Department of Anthropology, Harvard College.

1977a   (ed.) *Li'e skuenta sa' k'op vo'ne k'alal imeltzaj ach'rasone* [Here is an account of

political conflict at the time of the Revolution]. San Cristobal de las Casas: Instituto de Asesoría Antropológica para la Región Maya, Asociación Civil.

1977b   (ed.) *Sk'in ninyo ta Tzinakantan xchi'uk Chamula* [Christmas festivities in Zinacantan and Chamula]. San Cristobal de las Casas: Instituto de Asesoría Antropológica para la Región Maya, Asociación Civil

1978a   (ed.) *Ja' slo'il jun vinik Chamula k'uxi ch'i tal* [An account by a Chamula man: How I grew up]. San Cristobal de las Casas: Instituto de Asesoría Antropológica para la Región Maya, Asociación Civil

1978b   (ed.) *Li'e skuenta k'in xan chavaxchan ta Tzinakanta* [About the Fiesta of San Sebastián in Zinacantan]. San Cristobal de las Casas: Instituto de Asesoría Antropológica para la Región Maya, Asociación Civil.

CAB BAZ, LILIO

1950   X-yaax Ich. *Yikal Maya Than* 11:194–195. Merida: Imprenta Oriente.

CACALCHEN, PARISH BOOK OF

1647–1826   Documentos de Cacalchen en lengua maya. MS in Museum of the American Indian, Heye Foundation, New York.

CALENDARIO

1722   Calendario de los indios de Guatemala, 1722: Kiché. Copied by C. H. Berendt, 1877. MS, Berendt Linguistic Collection, University of Pennsylvania, Philadelphia.

CAMPBELL, LYLE

1978   Quichean Prehistory: Linguistic Contributions. In *Papers in Mayan Linguistics,* edited by Nora C. England, pp. 25–54. *Studies in Mayan Linguistics,* vol. 2. University of Missouri Miscellaneous Publications in Anthropology, no. 6. Columbia.

CAMPBELL, LYLE, AND TERRENCE S. KAUFMAN

1976   A Linguistic Look at the Olmecs. *American Antiquity* 41:80–89.

CAMPBELL, LYLE, ET AL.

1978   *Bibliography of Mayan Languages and Linguistics.* Institute for MesoAmerican Studies, Pub. 3. Albany: State University of New York.

CANCIAN, FRANK

1965   *Economics and Prestige in a Maya Com-*

munity: The Religious Cargo System in Zinacantan. Stanford: Stanford University Press.

CANTARES MEXICANOS
1904 *Cantares en idioma mexicano: Reproducción facsimilar del manuscrito original existente en la Biblioteca Nacional,* edited by Antonio Peñafiel. Mexico City: Secretaría de Fomento.
See also Garibay K. 1965; 1968.

CÁRDENAS, LÁZARO
1937 *Itlahtol in Mexihcayo tlalnantecuhtli tlacatecatl Lazaro Cardenas intechcopa in Mexihcayo altepeme.* Mexico City: Departamento Autónomo de Prensa y Publicidad.

CARMACK, ROBERT M.
1973 *Quichean Civilization: The Ethnohistoric, Ethnographic and Archaeological Sources.* Berkeley and Los Angeles: University of California Press.

CARMACK, ROBERT M., AND FRANCISCO MORALES
1984 (eds.) *Nuevas perspectivas sobre el Popol Vuh.* Guatemala City: Editorial Piedra Santa.

CAROCHI, HORACIO
1645 *Arte de la lengua mexicana con la declaración de los adverbios della.* Mexico City: Iuan Ruyz. (1904 ed., in *Colección de gramáticas de la lengua mexicana* 1:395–536. Mexico City: Museo Nacional de México.)

CASTELLANOS, ROSARIO
1957 *Balún-Canán.* Mexico City: Fondo de Cultura Económica.
1960 *Ciudad real: Cuentos.* Xalapa: Universidad Veracruzana.
1962 *Oficio de Tinieblas.* Mexico City: J. Mortiz.

CASTILLO, CRISTÓBAL DEL
1908 *Fragmentos de la obra general sobre historia de los mexicanos, escrita en lengua náhuatl.* Translated by Francisco del Paso y Troncoso. Biblioteca Náuatl 5. Florence: S. Landi.

CHARENCEY, CHARLES FÉLIX HYACINTHE GOUHIER
1866 Abrigé de grammaire de la langue tzotzil avec textes d'après le manuscript du R. P. Don Manuel Hidalgo. *Revue de Lingüistique et de Philologie Comparée* 19:170–188.

1885 Vocabulaire de la langue tzotzil. *Mémoires de l'Académie Nationale des Sciences, Arts et Belles-lettres de Caen,* pp. 251–289.
1889 Vocabulario tzotzil-español: Dialecto de los indios de la parte oriental del estado de Chiapas. *Revue de Lingüistique et de Philologie Comparée* 22:247–273.
1891 *Chrestomathie maya d'après la chronique de Chac-Xulub-Chen. Actes de la Société Philologique* 19, 20. Paris.
1910 Sur la langue tzotzile et sa numération. In *Verhandlungen des XVI. Internationalen Amerikanisten-kongresses* (Vienna, 1908) 2:597–610.
1912 De la formation des voix verbales en tzotzil. In *Actas del XVII° Congreso Internacional de Americanistas* (Buenos Aires, 1910), pp. 167–175.

CHASE, ARLEN F.
n.d. Contextual Implications of Pictorial Vases from Tayasal, Peten. In *Fourth Palenque Round Table, 1980,* edited by Elizabeth P. Benson. Forthcoming.

CHÁVEZ, ADRIÁN I.
1979 *Pop Wuj.* Centro de Investigaciones Superiores del Instituto Nacional de Antropología e Historia. Mexico City: Casa Chata.

CHILAM BALAM, BOOKS OF:
Ixil
n.d. Facsimile copy bound with Tizimin facsimile. Latin American Library, Tulane University, New Orleans.

Kaua
n.d. Facsimile copies in Arbeitsstelle für Altamerikanische Sprachen und Kulturen, Hamburg, and Iberoamerikanisches Institut, Berlin.

Nah
n.d. Gates Collection. Latin American Library, Tulane University, New Orleans.

Tusik
1944 Partial transcription by Alfredo Barrera Vásquez. Latin American Library, Tulane University, New Orleans.

CHIMALPAHIN QUAUHTLEHUANITZIN, DOMINGO FRANCISCO DE SAN ANTON MUÑON
1889 *Annales de Domingo Francisco de San Anton Muñon Chimalpahin Quauhtlehuanitzin: Sixième et septième relations (1258–1612).* Edited and translated by

Rémi Siméon. Bibliothèque Linguistique Américaine, vol. 12. Paris: Maisonneuve et C. Leclerc.

1958 *Das Memorial breve acerca de la fundación de la ciudad de Culhuacan.* Aztec text, translated into German by Walter Lehmann and Gerdt Kutscher. Quellenwerke zur alten Geschichte Americas 7. Stuttgart: W. Kohlhammer.

1965 *Relaciones originales de Chalco Amaquemecan.* Translated by Silvia Rendón. Biblioteca Americana, Serie de Literatura Indígena. Mexico City: Fondo de Cultura Económica.

CHIMAY, MARCOS DE

1925 Payalchi. In *Calendario de Espinosa para el año de 1925,* p. 127. Merida: Librería de Espinosa.

CHINCHILLA AGUILAR, ERNESTO

1953 *La Inquisición en Guatemala.* Guatemala City: Instituto de Antropología e Historia de Guatemala.

1963 *La danza del sacrificio y otros estudios.* Guatemala City: Ministerio de Educación Pública.

CHINO L., PORFIRIO

1975 *Tlajtoli de Vicente Guerrero ijcuac nemiya* [The story of Vicente Guerrero when he was alive]. Mexico City: Dirección General de Educación Extraescolar del Medio Indígena.

CODICES:

Aubin

1963 *Codex Aubin: Historia de la nación mexicana.* Translated by Charles E. Dibble. Madrid: J. Porrúa.

Azcatitlan

1949 *Journal de la Société des Américanistes de Paris,* n.s. 38:101–135. Commentary by Robert Barlow.

BORBONICUS

1974 *Codex Borbonicus, Bibliothèque de l'Assemblée Nationale, Paris.* Commentaries by Karl A. Nowotny and J. de Durand-Forest. Graz: Akademische Druck und Verlag.

Cozcatzin

n.d. Bibliothèque Nationale de Paris, MS. mexicain 41-45.

Cruz

1942 *Códice en Cruz.* Edited by Charles E. Dibble. Mexico City: Talleres Linotipográficos "Numancia."

Florentino

1979 *El códice florentino,* by Bernardino de Sahagún. Facsimile copy of Manuscript 218-20 of the Palatino Collection in the Laurentian Library, Florence. 3 vols. Mexico City: Secretaría de Gobernación.

Matritenses

1905–1907 Códices Matritenses de la Real Academia de la Historia. Vols 6(2)–8 of *Historia general de las cosas de Nueva España,* by Bernardino de Sahagún. Edited by Francisco del Paso y Troncoso. Madrid: Hauser y Menet.

Mendoza

1979 *Códice Mendoza (Códice Mendocino), manuscrito mexicano del siglo XVI que se conserva en la Biblioteca Bodleiana de Oxford.* Mexico City: San Angel Ediciones.

Mexicanus

1952 Commentaire du Codex Mexicanus, Nos. 23–24 de la Bibliothèque Nationale de Paris, by Ernest Mengin. *Journal de la Société des Américanistes,* n.s. 41: 387–498.

Moctezuma

n.d. Museo Nacional de Antropología, MS 35-26. Mexico City.

Telleriano-Remensis

1964 *Códice Telleriano-Remensis: Antigüedades de México, basadas en la recopilación de Lord Kingsborough.* Commentary by José Corona Núñez. 4 vols. Mexico City: Secretaría de Hacienda y Crédito Público.

Tlotzin and Quinatzin

1875 Examen des anciennes peintures figuratives de l'ancien Mexique. In *Archives de la Société Américaine de France,* 2d ser. 1:283–296.

Xolotl

1951 *Códice Xolotl.* Edited by Charles E. Dibble. Instituto de Historia, 1st ser., no. 22. Mexico City: Universidad Nacional Autónoma de México.

Xolotl y Quinatzin

1975 In *Memorias de las obras del sistema de drenaje profundo del Distrito Federal* 4: pls. 10–38. Mexico City.

COE, MICHAEL D., AND GORDON WHITTAKER

1893 (eds.) *Aztec Sorcerers in Seventeenth Century Mexico: The Treatise on Superstitions by Hernando Ruiz de Alarcón.*

Institute for MesoAmerican Studies, Pub. 7. Albany: State University of New York.

COESTER, ALFRED L.

1941 The Danza de los Conquistadores at Chichicastenango. *Hispania* 24:95–100.

COFRADÍAS

See Ordinances of cofradías; Vásquez, Pascual.

COLBY, LORE M.

1960 Tzotzil Dictionary. MS, Harvard Chiapas Project, Peabody Museum, Harvard University.

1964 Zinacantan Tzotzil Sound and Word Structure. Ph.D. dissertation, Department of Linguistics, Harvard University.

1966 Esquema de la morfología tzotzil. In *Los zinacantecos: Un pueblo tzotzil de los Altos de Chiapas*, edited by Evon Z. Vogt. Colección de Antropología Social, Instituto Nacional Indigenista 7:373–395. Mexico City.

COLLIER, GEORGE A., AND VICTORIA R. BRICKER

1970 Nicknames and Social Structure in Zinacantan. *American Anthropologist* 72:289–302.

COLLIER, JANE F.

1968 Courtship and Marriage in Zinacantan, Chiapas, Mexico. In *Contemporary Latin America*, pp. 139–201. Middle American Research Institute, Tulane University, Pub. 25. New Orleans.

1973 *Law and Social Change in Zinacantan.* Stanford: Stanford University Press.

COLOQUIOS DE LOS DOCE

1927 Coloquios de los doce: Coloquios y doctrina christiana con que los doze frayles de San Francisco embiados por el Papa Adriano Sesto y por el Emperador Carlos Quinto convertieron a los indios de la Nueva Espanya, en lengua mexicana y española. *Revista Mexicana de Estudios Históricos* 1(4)·101–116; 1(5):117–141, 7 pls.; 1(6): 6 pls.

CORNYN, JOHN HUBERT

1932a Ixcit Cheel. *Maya Society Quarterly* 1:47–55.

1932b X'tabay—the Enchantress. *Maya Society Quarterly* 1:107–111.

CORREA, GUSTAVO

1955 El espíritu del mal en Guatemala. In *Nativism and Syncretism*, pp. 37–104. Middle American Research Institute, Tulane University, Pub. 19. New Orleans.

1958 Texto de un Baile de Diablos. In *The Native Theatre in Middle America*, pp. 97–103. Middle American Research Institute, Tulane University, Pub. 27. New Orleans.

CORREA, GUSTAVO, AND CALVIN CANNON

1958 La Loa en Guatemala. In *The Native Theatre in Middle America*, pp. 1–96. Middle American Research Institute, Tulane University, Pub. 27. New Orleans.

COWAN, MARION M.

1956 *Ta jchantik castellano (Aprendamos castellano: Una gramática castellana-tzotzil).* Mexico City: Instituto Lingüístico de Verano.

1958a Morphological and Syntactic Structure of Tzotzil, San Andres Dialect. MS, Summer Institute of Linguistics, Norman, Oklahoma.

1958b *Segunda y tercera cartillas tzotzil: Dialecto de Huixtan.* Mexico City: Instituto Lingüístico de Verano.

1960 *Primera cartilla tzotzil: Dialecto de Huixtan.* Rev. ed. Mexico City: Instituto Lingüístico de Verano.

1961 Huixteco (Maya Tzotzil) Place-Names. In *Los Mayas del sur y sus relaciones con los Nahuas meridionales: VIII Mesa Redonda*, pp. 195–200. Mexico City: Sociedad Mexicana de Antropología.

1967 The Devils and the Young Boys: A Tzotzil Myth. *Tlalocan* 5:222–226.

1968a *Ja sc'opilal numeroetic (Los números en tzotzil de Huixtan).* Mexico City: Instituto Lingüístico de Verano.

1968b *Oraciones sencillas en huixteco y español.* Mexico City: Instituto Lingüístico de Verano.

1969 *Tzotzil Grammar.* Summer Institute of Linguistics, Publications in Linguistics and Related Fields, no. 18. Norman, Oklahoma.

1970 *Chib lo ʔil (Dos cuentos).* Mexico City: Instituto Lingüístico de Verano.

1972a *Ja lo'iletic yu'un ti coyotee (Cuentos de coyotes).* Mexico City: Instituto Lingüístico de Verano.

1972b *Ja ti lo ʔil yu'un jun vinic mazahua schi' uk sburro* [A story about a Mazahua man and his burro]. Mexico City: Instituto Lingüístico de Verano.

1975 *Cuaderno de trabajo: Tzotzil.* Rev. ed. Mexico City: Instituto Nacional Indigenista and Secretaría de Educación Pública.

COWAN, MARION M., AND KENNETH JACOBS
1975   *Cartilla tzotzil.* Rev. ed. Mexico City: Instituto Nacional Indigenista and Secretaría de Educación Pública.

COWAN, MARION M., AND WILLIAM R. MERRIFIELD
1968   The Verb Phrase in Huixtec Tzotzil. *Language* 44:284–305.
1971   Huixtec Tzotzil. MS, Summer Institute of Linguistics, Norman, Oklahoma.

CRAINE, EUGENE R., AND REGINALD C. REINDORP
1979   (eds. and trans.) *The Codex Pérez and the Book of Chilam Balam of Maní.* Norman: University of Oklahoma Press.

CRUZ, MARTÍN DE LA
1964   Libellus de Medicinalibus Indorum Herbis . . . según traducción latina de Juan Badiano. Mexico City: Instituto Mexicano del Seguro Social.

CUADERNO DE TEABO
1868   Copied by C. H. Berendt. MS, Berendt Linguistic Collection, University of Pennsylvania, Philadelphia.

DAVIS, VIRGINIA DALE
1978   Ritual of the Northern Lacandon Maya. Ph.D. dissertation, Department of Anthropology, Tulane University. Ann Arbor: University Microfilms (79-01486).
1979   Lacandon Song Texts. In *Mayan Texts II*, edited by Louanna Furbee-Losee, pp. 18–26. Native American Texts Series, vol. 3. Chicago: International Journal of American Linguistics.

DE URRUTIA, ANA MARÍA
1974   Cuentos populares de Santa Catarina Ixtahuacan. *Tradiciones de Guatemala* 2:131–159. Guatemala City: Universidad de San Carlos de Guatemala.

DELGATY, ALFA
1961   Notes on Dependent versus Independent Nouns in Tsotsil. In *A William Cameron Townsend en el vigésimoquinto aniversario del Instituto Lingüístico de Verano*, edited by Benjamin F. Elson and Juan Comas, pp. 413–419. Mexico City.

DELGATY, ALFA HURLEY VDA. DE, AND AGUSTÍN RUIZ SÁNCHEZ
1978   *Diccionario tzotzil de San Andres, con variaciones dialectales: Tzotzil-español, español-tzotzil.* Serie de Vocabularios y Diccionarios Indígenas Mario Silva y Aceves, no. 22. Mexico City: Instituto Lingüístico de Verano.

DELGATY, COLIN C.
1953   Tzotzil Phonemes. MS, Summer Institute of Linguistics, Norman, Oklahoma.
1956   Word List. MS, Summer Institute of Linguistics, Norman, Oklahoma.
1961   Tzotzil Verb Phrase Structure. *Mayan Studies* 1:81–123. Norman: Summer Institute of Linguistics.
1964   *Vocabulario tzotzil de San Andres, Chiapas.* Serie de Vocabularios Indígenas Mariano Silva y Aceves, no. 10. Mexico City: Instituto Lingüístico de Verano.

DIBBLE, CHARLES E.
1971   Writing in Central Mexico. In *Handbook of Middle American Indians*, vol. 10, edited by Robert Wauchope, Gordon F. Ekholm, and Ignacio Bernal, pp. 322–332. Austin: University of Texas Press.

DICCIONARIO EN LENGUA SOTZIL
ca. 1600   MS copy, dating to early twentieth century, in Gates Collection, Princeton University Library, Princeton.

DOCUMENTS AND LEGAL PAPERS FROM TOTONICAPAN
1689–1812   MS, Gates Collection, Princeton University Library; photocopy (dated 1690–1808) in Ayer Collection, Newberry Library, Chicago.

DURÁN, DIEGO
1867–1880   *Historia de las Indias de Nueva España y Islas de Tierra Firme.* 2 vols. and atlas. Mexico City: Andrade y Escalante. (1967 ed., edited by Angel María Garibay K., Biblioteca Porrúa 36. Mexico City.)

EDMONSON, MUNRO S.
1960–1961   Field notes, Quezaltenango, Guatemala. MS in possession of author.
1964   Historia de las tierras altas mayas, según los documentos indígenas. In *Desarrollo cultural de los mayas*, edited by Evon Z. Vogt and Alberto Ruz L., pp. 273–302. Mexico City: Universidad Nacional Autónoma de México.
1967   Narrative Folklore. In *Handbook of Middle American Indians*, vol. 6, edited by Robert Wauchope and Manning Nash,

pp. 357–368. Austin: University of Texas Press.

1970 Metáfora maya en literature y en arte. In *Verhandlungen des XXXVIII. Internatialen Amerikanistenkongresses* (Stuttgart-Munich, 1968) 2:37–50. Munich.

1971 *The Book of Counsel: The Popol Vuh of the Quiche Maya of Guatemala.* Middle American Research Institute, Tulane University, Pub. 35. New Orleans.

1973 Semantic Universals and Particulars in Quiche. In *Meaning in Mayan Languages: Ethnolinguistic Studies*, edited by Munro S. Edmonson, pp. 235–246. The Hague: Mouton.

1974 (ed.) *Sixteenth-Century Mexico: The Work of Sahagún.* School of American Research. Albuquerque: University of New Mexico Press.

1976 The Mayan Calendar Reform of 11.16.0.0.0. *Current Anthropology* 17:713–717.

1982a *The Ancient Future of the Itza: The Book of Chilam Balam of Tizimin.* Austin: University of Texas Press.

1982b The Songs of Dzitbalche: A Literary Commentary. *Tlalocan* 9:173–208.

in press *Heaven-Born Merida and Its Destiny: The Book of Chilam Balam of Chumayel.* Austin: University of Texas Press.

n.d.a El Baile de Toritos. MS in Iberoamerikanisches Institut, Berlin; translation in possession of author.

n.d.b The Count of the Cycle and the Numbering of the Days. From Calendario 1722; translation in possession of author.

n.d.c Quiche Documents: A Collection of Wills and Other Legal Papers in Quiche, 1775–1787. Photocopy of MS in Tulane University Latin American Library; translation in possession of author.

n.d.d Flute Dance. From Mace 1957; translation in possession of author.

n.d.e Francisco Tam: The Life History of a Quiche Indian. MS in possession of author.

n.d.f Goiter Dance. From Mace 1957; translation in possession of author.

n.d.g History of Juan de Torres. From Recinos 1957; translation in possession of author.

n.d.h Jaguar Deer Dance. From Mace 1957; translation in possession of author.

n.d.i Ordinances of the Fraternity of the Ros-

ary. Original in Vásquez 1689; partial translation in possession of author.

n.d.j Origin of the Lords of Zapotitlan. From Recinos 1950a, 1950b; translation in possession of author.

n.d.k Paper of Francisco Gómez. From Fuentes y Guzmán 1933; translation in possession of author.

n.d.l Prayer of the Sun Priest at Rax Kim. Translation in possession of author.

n.d.m Rabinal Achi. From Brasseur de Bourbourg 1862; partial translation in possession of author.

n.d.n Title of Ixcuin. From Recinos 1957; translation in possession of author.

n.d.o Title of Izkin. From Recinos 1957; translation in possession of author.

n.d.p Title of the Lords of Totonicapan. From Recinos 1950a; translation in possession of author.

n.d.q Title of the Indians of Santa Clara la Laguna. From Recinos 1957; translation in possession of author.

n.d.r White Demon. Translation in possession of author. Original: *See* Zaccicoxol.

n.d.s Writs of Domingo Matías Santéliz and Related Papers, 1750–1799. Translation in possession of author.

n.d.t The Baktun Ceremonial of 1618. In *Fourth Palenque Round Table*, edited by Elizabeth P. Benson. Forthcoming.

ENGLAND, NORA CLEARMAN

1978 (ed.) *Papers in Mayan Linguistics.* Vol. 2 of *Studies in Mayan Linguistics.* University of Missouri Miscellaneous Publications in Anthropology, no. 6. Columbia.

EROSA Y SIERRA, ELIGIO

1941 Ca dzit oc (El hombre). *Yikal Maya Than* 2:21. Merida.

ESCALONA RAMOS, ALBERTO

1935 *Historia de los mayas por sus crónicas.* Merida: Universidad Nacional del Sureste.

FABREGA, HORACIO, AND DANIEL B. SILVER

1973 *Illness and Shamanistic Curing in Zinacantan: An Ethnomedical Analysis.* Stanford: Stanford University Press.

FIELD, DENISE Z.

1975 With a Flower, with a Candle, with a Prayer: An Ethnography of Prayer in Chamula. B.A. honors thesis, Department of Anthropology, Radcliffe College.

FOUGHT, JOHN G.
1967 Chorti (Mayan): Phonology, Morphopho-
nemics, and Morphology. Ph.D. dissertation, Languages and Literatures, Yale
University. Ann Arbor: University Microfilms (67-10706).
1969 Chortí Semantics: Some Properties of
Roots and Affixes. Paper presented at the
68th annual meeting of the American Anthropological Association, New Orleans.
Published in *Meaning in Mayan Languages: Ethnolinguistic Studies*, edited
by Munro S. Edmonson, pp. 59–83.
The Hague: Mouton (1973).
1972 *Chorti (Mayan) Texts: I.* Edited by Sarah
S. Fought. Philadelphia: University of
Pennsylvania Press.
1976 Time Structuring in Chorti (Mayan) Narratives. In *Mayan Linguistics*, edited by
Marlys McClaran, 1:228–242. Los Angeles: University of California American
Indian Studies Center.
1982 A Note on Voice and Ergativity in Chortí.
Journal of Mayan Linguistics 3(2):35–37.

FOWLER, H. W.
1926 *A Dictionary of Modern English Usage.*
1st ed. London: Oxford University Press.

FOX, DAVID G.
1957 A Quiche Text in Multiple Stage Translation. *El Traductor* 5:1–7.

FOX, DAVID G., AND CAROL FOX
1956a *Oxib tzijobelil re ri imul (Tres cuentos
del conejo).* Guatemala City: Instituto
Lingüístico de Verano.
1956b *Ri conalaj ch'iw (El tonto pollito chiquito).* Guatemala City: Instituto Lingüístico de Verano.

FRAKE, CHARLES
1961 The Diagnosis of Disease among the
Subanum of Mindanao. *American Anthropologist* 63:113–132.

FUENTES Y GUZMÁN, FRANCISCO ANTONIO DE
1932–1933 *Recordación florida.* Biblioteca
"Goathemala," Sociedad de Geografía e
Historia, vols. 6–8. Guatemala City:
Tipografía Nacional.

GALIEGO SUYEN, PEDRO
1891 Guaxteco Rabinal. MS, Archivo de Materiales Culturales del Instituto Indigenista Nacional, Guatemala City.

GARCÍA DE LEÓN, ANTONIO
1970 Vocabulario y textos de los parajes Sisim

(Chalchihuitan) y Pasté (Zinacantan). Unpublished fieldnotes.
1971 *Los elementos del tzotzil colonial y moderno.* Centro de Estudios Mayas, Cuaderno 7. Mexico City: Universidad Nacional Autónoma de México.

GARCÍA ICAZBALCETA, JOAQUÍN
1941 (ed.) *Nueva colección de documentos
para la historia de México,* 2d ed. 5 vols.
Mexico City: Salvador Chávez Hayhoe.

GARCÍA QUINTANA, JOSEFINA
1978 Exhortación del padre que así amonesta
a su hijo casado, *tlazopilli. Estudios de
Cultura Náhuatl* 13:49–67.

GARIBAY K., ANGEL MARÍA
1943 Huehuetlatolli: Documento A. *Tlalocan*
1:31–53, 81–107.
1953–1954 *Historia de la literatura náhuatl.* 2
vols. Mexico City: Porrúa.
1958 (ed.) *Veinte himnos sacros de los nahuas.* Compiled by Bernardino de Sahagún. Fuentes Indígenas de la Cultura
Nahuatl, Informantes de Sahagún, no. 2.
Mexico City: Universidad Nacional Autónoma de México.
1964 (ed.) *Romances de los señores de la
Nueva España: Manuscrito de Juan Bautista de Pomar, Texcoco, 1582.* Poesía
Náhuatl, Instituto de Historia, vol. 1.
Mexico City: Universidad Nacional Autónoma de México.
1965 (ed.) *Cantares mexicanos: Manuscrito de
la Biblioteca Nacional de México, primera parte.* Poesía Náhuatl, Instituto de
Historia, vol. 2. Mexico City: Universidad Nacional Autónoma de México.
1968 (ed.) *Cantares mexicanos: Manuscrito de
la Biblioteca Nacional de México, segunda parte.* Poesía Náhuatl, Instituto
de Historia, vol. 3. Mexico City: Universidad Nacional Autónoma de México.

GATES, WILLIAM E.
1935a *The Maya Calkini Chronicle; or, Documents Concerning the Descent of the Ah-
Canul, or Men of the Serpent, Their Arrival and Territory.* Facsimile copy. Maya
Society Pub. no. 8. Baltimore.
1935b *The Chilan Balam of Tekax.* Facsimile copy. Maya Society Pub. no. 11.
Baltimore.

GELWAN, ELIOT M.
1972 Some Considerations of Tzotzil-Tzeltal

Ethnoastronomy. MS, Harvard Chiapas Project, Peabody Museum, Harvard University.

GIBSON, CHARLES.
1975 A Survey of Middle American Prose Manuscripts in the Native Historical Tradition. In *Handbook of Middle American Indians*, vol. 15, edited by Robert Wauchope and Howard F. Cline, pp. 311–321. Austin: University of Texas Press.

GIBSON, CHARLES, AND JOHN B. GLASS
1975 A Census of Middle American Prose Manuscripts in the Native Historical Tradition. In *Handbook of Middle American Indians*, vol. 15, edited by Robert Wauchope and Howard F. Cline, pp. 322–400. Austin: University of Texas Press.

GLASS, JOHN B.
1975 A Survey of Native Middle American Pictorial Manuscripts. In *Handbook of Middle American Indians*, vol. 14, edited by Robert Wauchope and Howard F. Cline, pp. 3–80. Austin: University of Texas Press.

GÓMEZ, FRANCISCO
n.d. Paper of Francisco Gómez. In *Recordación florida*, by Francisco Antonio de Fuentes y Guzmán. Guatemala City: Tipografía Nacional (1933).

GÓMEZ, JUAN
n.d. El robo de las princesas. In *Recordación florida*, by Francisco Antonio de Fuentes y Guzmán, 7:37–40. Guatemala City: Tipografía Nacional (1933).

GÓMEZ TAKIWAH, MARIANO
1977 Chonbilal ch'ulelal. Microfilm Collection of Manuscripts on Cultural Anthropology, ser. 43, no. 231. Chicago: University of Chicago Library.

CONZÁLEZ CASANOVA, PABLO
1976 Ciclo legendario del Tepoztécatl. In *Estudios de filología y lingüística náhuatl*, edited by Ascensión H. de León-Portilla, pp. 209–266. Mexico City: Universidad Nacional Autónoma de México.

GORDON, GEORGE BYRON
1913 Introduction to *The Book of Chilam Balam of Chumayel*. Museum of Anthropology Publications, vol. 5. Philadelphia: University of Pennsylvania.

GOSSEN, GARY H.
1970 Time and Space in Chamula Oral Tradition. Ph.D. dissertation, Department of Anthropology, Harvard University.

1972a Chamula Genres of Verbal Behavior. In *Toward New Perspectives in Folklore*, edited by Américo Paredes and Richard Bauman, pp. 145–167. Bibliographical and Special Series, American Folklore Society, vol. 23. Austin: University of Texas Press.

1972b Temporal and Spacial Equivalents in Chamula Ritual Symbolism. In *Reader in Comparative Religion*, 3d ed., edited by William Lessa and Evon Z. Vogt, pp. 135–148. New York: Harper and Row.

1973 Chamula Tzotzil Proverbs: Neither Fish nor Fowl. In *Meaning in Mayan Languages: Ethnolinguistic Studies*, edited by Munro S. Edmonson, pp. 205–233. The Hague: Mouton.

1974a A Chamula Solar Calendar Board from Chiapas, Mexico. In *Mesoamerican Archaeology: New Approaches*, edited by Norman Hammond, pp. 217–253. Austin: University of Texas Press.

1974b *Chamulas in the World of the Sun: Time and Space in a Maya Oral Tradition*. Cambridge: Harvard University Press. (Spanish ed., 1979, *Los Chamulas en el mundo del sol*. Serie de Antropología Social, Instituto Nacional Indigenista, no. 58. Mexico City.)

1974c To Speak with a Heated Heart: Chamula Canons of Style and Good Performance. In *Explorations in the Ethnography of Speaking*, edited by Richard Bauman and Joel Sherzer, pp. 389–413. London: Cambridge University Press.

1975 Animals Souls and Human Destiny in Chamula. *Man*, n.s. 10: 448–461.

1976a Language as Ritual Substance: Chamula Views of Formal Language. In *Language in Religious Practice*, edited by William Samarin, pp. 40–60. Rowley, Mass.: Newbury House.

1976b Verbal Dueling in Chamula. In *Speech Play: Research and Resources for Studying Linguistic Creativity*, edited by Barbara Kirshenblatt-Gimblett, pp. 121–146. Philadelphia: University of Pennsylvania Press.

1977 Translating Cuscat's War: Understanding Maya Oral History. *Journal of Latin American Lore* 3:249–278.

1978 The Popol-Vuh Revisited: A Comparison with Modern Chamula Narrative Tradition. *Estudios de Cultura Maya* 11:267–283.

1979 Cuatro mundos del hombre: Tiempo e historia entre los Chamulas. *Estudios de Cultura Maya* 12:179–190.

1980 Two Creation Myths from Chamula Municipio, Chiapas, Mexico. *Tlalocan* 8:131–165.

1984 El Popol Vuh, revisitado: Una comparación con la tradición oral contemporánea de San Juan Chamula, Chiapas. In *Nuevas perspectivas sobre el Popol Vuh*, edited by Robert M. Carmack and Francisco Morales Santos, pp. 305–329. Guatemala City: Editorial Piedra Santa.

GOSSEN, GARY H., AND ELEANOR A. GOSSEN

n.d. Four Creations of Man: A Maya Narrative Account of the Human Experience. In preparation.

GOSSEN, GARY H., AND MARIANO LÓPEZ MÉNDEZ

1979 *Kuento yuʔun ʔololetik* [Children's stories]. San Cristobal de las Casas: Instituto de Asesoría Antropológica para la Región Maya, Asociación Civil.

GOUBAUD CARRERA, ANTONIO

1935 El "Guajxaquip B'áts": Ceremonia calendárica indígena. *Anales de la Sociedad de Geografía e Historia de Guatemala* 12:39–50.

GRAMÁTICA DEL TZOTZIL

1818 San Cristobal de las Casas: José María Sánchez.

GUITERAS-HOLMES, CALIXTA

1961 *Perils of the Soul: The World View of a Tzotzil Indian*. Chicago: University of Chicago Press.

HARRISON, FRANK, AND JOAN HARRISON

1968 Spanish Elements in the Music of Two Maya Groups in Chiapas. *Selected Reports* 1(2):1–44. Los Angeles: Institute of Ethnomusicology of the University of California.

HAVILAND, JOHN B.

1966 Vob: Traditional Music in Zinacantán. MS, Harvard Chiapas Project, Peabody Museum, Harvard University.

1971 Gossip, Gossips, and Gossiping in Zinacantan: K'al tana mu xpah slo'iltael (Gossip about Him Will Never Cease). Ph.D. dissertation, Department of Anthropology, Harvard University.

1976 Sk'op sotz'leb: El Tzotzil de San Lorenzo Zinacantan. MS, Harvard Chiapas Project, Peabody Museum, Harvard University.

1977a Gossip as Competition in Zinacantan. *Journal of Communication* 27(1):186–191.

1977b *Gossip, Reputation, and Knowledge in Zinacantan*. Chicago: University of Chicago Press.

HENNE, DAVID, AND MARILYN HENNE

1972a *Oxib tzijobelil re ri imul (Tres cuentos del conejo)*. Rev. ed. Guatemala City: Instituto Lingüístico del Verano.

1972b *Ri conalaj ch'iw (El tonto pollito chiquito)*. Rev. ed. Guatemala City: Instituto Lingüístico del Verano.

HERNÁNDEZ, PEDRO MARCIAL

1905 (trans.) *De los primeros habitantes de la venturosa yucateca*. Merida.

HIDALGO SABANILLA, BARTOLOMÉ

1977a Cuentos tzotziles de San Bartolomé de los Llanos (Venustiano Carranza), Chiapas, Mexico. Edited by Harvey B. Searles. Microfilm Collection of Manuscripts on Cultural Anthropology, ser. 51, no. 274. Chicago: University of Chicago Library.

1977b Palabras y frases útiles del tzotzil San Bartoleño. Microfilm Collection of Manuscripts on Cultural Anthropology, ser. 43, no. 234. Chicago: University of Chicago Library.

HIRES, MARLA

1981 The Book of Chilam Balam of Chan Kan. Ph.D. dissertation, Department of Anthropology, Tulane University. Ann Arbor: University Microfilms (81-18367).

HISTORIA TOLTECA-CHICHIMECA

1976 Translated by Paul Kirchhoff, Lina Odena Güemes, and Luis Reyes García. Mexico City: Instituto Nacional de Antropología e Historia.

HOLLAND, WILLIAM

1961a Relaciones entre la religión tzotzil contemporánea y la maya antigua. *Anales del Instituto Nacional de Antropología e Historia* 13:113–131. Mexico City.

1961b El tonalismo y el nagualismo entre los tzotziles. *Estudios de Cultura Maya* 1:167–181.

1963 *Medicina maya en los altos de Chiapas: Un estudio del cambio socio-cultural.* Translated by Daniel Cazes. Colección de Antropología Social, Instituto Nacional Indigenista, no. 2. Mexico City.

1965 Contemporary Tzotzil Cosmological Concepts as a Basis for Interpreting Prehistoric Maya Civilization. *American Antiquity* 29:301–306.

HOPKINS, NICHOLAS A.

1967 A Short Sketch of Chalchihuitán Tzotzil. *Anthropological Linguistics* 9(4):9–25.

1977a A Phonology of Zinacantan Tzotzil. Microfilm Collection of Manuscripts on Cultural Anthropology, ser. 51, no. 272. Chicago: University of Chicago Library.

1977b Some Loan Words in Chalchihuitan Tzotzil. Microfilm Collection of Manuscripts on Cultural Anthropology, ser. 51, no. 271. Chicago: University of Chicago Library.

HORCASITAS, FERNANDO

1968 (ed. and trans.) *De Porfirio Díaz a Zapata: Memoria náhuatl de Milpa Alta.* Mexico City: Universidad Nacional Autónoma de México.

1969 Proclama en náhuatl de don Carlos María de Bustamante a los indígenas mexicanos. *Estudios de Cultura Náhuatl* 8:271–272.

1974 *El teatro náhuatl: Epocas novahispana y moderna.* Serie de Cultura Náhuatl, Instituto de Investigaciones Históricas, Mono. 17. Mexico City: Universidad Nacional Autónoma de México.

1978 Introduction to *Tira de Tepechpan, códice colonial procedente del Valle de México*, edited by Xavier Nóguez, pp. xiii–xiv. Biblioteca Enciclopédica del Estado de México, vol. 64. Mexico City: Mario Colin.

1980 Las danzas de Coatetelco. *Estudios de Cultura Náhuatl* 14:239–286.

HORCASITAS, FERNANDO, AND SARA O. DE FORD

1979 *Los cuentos en náhuatl de doña Luz Jiménez.* Mexico City: Universidad Nacional Autónoma de México.

HUNT, EVA

1977 *The Transformation of the Hummingbird: Cultural Roots of a Zinacantecan Mythical Poem.* Ithaca: Cornell University Press.

HYMES, DELL H.

1977 Discovering Oral Performance and Measured Verse in American Indian Narrative. *New Literary History* 8:431–457.

1981 *In Vain I Tried to Tell You: Essays in Native American Ethnopoetics.* Philadelphia: University of Pennsylvania Press.

JACOBS, KENNETH

1960 *Chonetic (Animales).* Mexico City: Instituto Lingüístico de Verano.

JACOBS, KENNETH, AND ROBERT E. LONGACRE

1967 Patterns and Rules in Tzotzil Grammar. *Foundations of Language: International Journal of Language and Philosophy* 3:325–389.

JUANA INÉS DE LA CRUZ, SISTER

1969 *Obras completas.* Mexico City: Fondo de Cultura Económica.

JUAN DE LA CRUZ

1851 Letter to Miguel Barbachano, August 20, 1851. MS, Crescencio Carrillo y Ancona Collection, Biblioteca General del Estado "Manuel Cepeda Peraza," Merida.

KARTTUNEN, FRANCES, AND JAMES LOCKHART

1980 La estructura de la poesía náhuatl vista por sus variantes. *Estudios de Cultura Náhuatl* 14:15–64.

KAUFMAN, TERRENCE

1970 Posición del tzeltal y del tzotzil en la familia lingüística mayance. In *Ensayos de antropología en la zona central de Chiapas*, edited by Norman A. McQuown and Julian Pitt-Rivers, pp. 171–183. Mexico City: Instituto Nacional Indigenista.

1972 *El proto-tzeltal-tzotzil: Fonología comparada y diccionario reconstruido.* Centro de Estudios Mayas, Cuaderno 5. Mexico City: Universidad Nacional Autónoma de México.

KIM DE BOLLES, ALEJANDRA

1972 *Tzicbaltabi ti in mama uch cachi: Stories My Mother Was Told Long Ago.* Komchen, Yucatan.

KÖHLER, ULRICH

1969 *Gelenkter Kulturwandel im Hochland von Chiapas: Eine Studie zur angewandten Ethnologie in Mexiko.* Freiberger Studien zur Politik und Gesellschaft überseeischer Länder, vol. 7. Bielefeld: Bertelsmann Universitätsverlag. (1975 ed., *Cambio cultural dirigido en los Altos de Chiapas*, translated by Waltraud Hangert. Mexico City: Instituto Nacional Indigenista.)

1970 Zur Geschichte und Ethnografie der Chiapaneken. In *Verhandlungen des XXXVIII. Internationalen Amerikanistenkongresses* (Stuttgart-Munich, 1968) 2:413–422. Munich.

1974a Grundzüge des religiösen Denkens der Pableros im Hochland von Chiapas, Mexiko. In *Atti del XL Congresso Internazionale degli Americanisti* (Rome-Genoa, 1972) 2:321–328. Genoa.

1974b Zur Jagd auf die Schemel der Berggötter: Ein Gebetstext auf Tzotzil (Maya). *Indiana* 2:193–207. (Spanish abstract.)

1975 Ein Zauberspruch auf Maya-Tzotzil zur Heilung von Schlangenbissen. *Zeitschrift für Ethnologie* 100:238–247.

LAUGHLIN, ROBERT M.

1962 El símbolo de la flor en la religión de Zinacantán. *Estudios de Cultura Maya* 2:123–139.

1966 Oficio de tinieblas: Como el zinacanteco adivina sus sueños. In *Los zinacantecos: Un pueblo tzotzil de los Altos de Chiapas*, edited by Evon Z. Vogt, pp. 396–413. Colección de Antropología Social, Instituto Nacional Indigenista, no. 7. Mexico City.

1969 The Tzotzil. In *Handbook of Middle American Indians*, vol. 7, edited by Robert Wauchope and Evon Z. Vogt, pp. 152–194. Austin: University of Texas Press.

1975 *The Great Tzotzil Dictionary of San Lorenzo Zinacantán*. Smithsonian Contributions to Anthropology, no. 19. Washington, D.C.

1976 *Of Wonders Wild and New: Dreams from Zinacantán*. Smithsonian Contributions to Anthropology, no. 22. Washington, D.C.

1977 *Of Cabbages and Kings: Tales from Zinacantán*. Smithsonian Contributions to Anthropology, no. 23. Washington, D.C.

1979 Tzotzil Texts. In *Mayan Texts II*, edited by Louanna Furbee-Losee, pp. 136–146. Native American Texts Series, vol. 3. Chicago: International Journal of American Linguistics.

1980 *Of Shoes and Ships and Sealing Wax:*

Sundries from Zinacantan. Smithsonian Contributions to Anthropology, no. 25. Washington, D.C.

LAUGHLIN, ROBERT M., AND W. S. MERWIN

1972 Two Zinacanteco Poems. *Review: Latin American Literature and Art* (Winter), pp. 48–49. New York: Center for Inter-American Relations.

LECCIONES ESPIRITUALES

1841 *Lecciones espirituales para las tandas de ejercicios de San Ignacio, dadas a los indios en el idioma mexicano, compuestas por un sacerdote del obispado de la Puebla de los Angeles*. Puebla: Imprenta Antigua en el Portal de las Flores.

LEGTERS, D. BRAINERD

1937 Story of a Hunter. *Investigaciones Lingüísticas* 4:302–307.

LEHMANN, WALTER

1920 *Zentral-Amerika*, part 1, *Die Sprachen Zentral-Amerikas in ihren Beziehungen zueinander sowie zu Süd-Amerika und Mexiko*. 2 vols. Berlin: Dietrich Reimer.

1938 (trans.) *Die Geschichte der Königreiche von Colhuacan und Mexiko*. Quellenwerke zur alten Geschichte Amerikas 1. Stuttgart: W. Kohlhammer.

LEÓN-PORTILLA, ASCENSIÓN H. DE

1980 Algunas publicaciones recientes sobre lengua y literaturas nahuas. *Estudios de Cultura Náhuatl* 14:419–432.

LEÓN-PORTILLA, MIGUEL

1961 *Los antiguos mexicanos a través de sus crónicas y cantares*. Mexico City: Fondo de Cultura Económica.

1963 *Aztec Thought and Culture: A Study of the Ancient Nahuatl Mind*. Translated by Jack Emory Davis. Norman: University of Oklahoma Press.

1966 *La filosofía náhuatl estudiada en sus fuentes*. 3d ed. Serie de Cultura Náhuatl, Instituto de Investigaciones Históricas, Mono. 10. Mexico City: Universidad Nacional Autónoma de México.

1967 *Trece poetas del mundo azteca*. 1st ed. Serie de Cultura Náhuatl, Instituto de Investigaciones Históricas, Mono. 11. Mexico City: Universidad Nacional Autónoma de México.

1968 *Tiempo y realidad en el pensamiento maya: Ensayo de acercamiento*. Serie de Culturas Mesoamericanas, Instituto de Investigaciones Históricas, no. 2. Mexico City: Universidad Nacional Autónoma de México.

1969 *Pre-Columbian Literatures of Mexico.* Translated by Grace Lobanov and Miguel León-Portilla. Norman: University of Oklahoma Press.

1971 Pre-Hispanic Literature. In *Handbook of Middle American Indians,* vol. 10, edited by Robert Wauchope, Gordon F. Ekholm, and Ignacio Bernal, pp. 452–458. Austin: University of Texas Press.

1972 *Nezahualcóyotl: Poesía y pensamiento.* Texcoco, State of México: Gobierno del Estado.

1977 Una denuncia en náhuatl. *Tlalocan* 7:23–30.

1978a (ed.) *Los manifiestos en náhuatl de Emiliano Zapata.* Mexico City: Universidad Nacional Autónoma de México.

1978b *Trece poetas del mundo azteca.* 2d ed. Serie de Cultura Náhuatl, Instituto de Investigaciones Históricas, Mono. 11. Mexico City: Universidad Nacional Autónoma de México.

1980 Carta de los indígenas de Iguala a don Luis de Velasco. *Tlalocan* 8:13–19.

LÉVI-STRAUSS, CLAUDE
1963 *Structural Anthropology.* Translated by Claire Jacobson and Brooke Grundfest Schoepf. New York: Basic Books.

LEWIS, VIVIAN
1969 The Myths of the Flood. MS, Harvard Chiapas Project, Peabody Museum, Harvard University.

LEYENDA DE LOS SOLES
1903 Leyenda de los soles, continuada con otras leyendas y noticias: Relación anónima escrita en lengua mexicana el año 1558. Edited and translated by Francisco del Paso y Troncoso. *Biblioteca Náuatl* 5(1):1–40. Florence: S. Landi.

LIBRO EN QUE SE TRATA DE LA LENGUA TZOTZIL
1832 Microfilm of MS, Museo Nacional de Antropología, Serie Chiapas, spool 70. Mexico City.

LIENZO DE TLAXCALA
1892 In *Homenaje a Cristóbal Colón: Antigüedades mexicanas publicadas por la Junta Colombina de México* 1:ii–80; 2. Mexico City: Secretaría de Fomento.

LINN, PRISCILLA RACHUN
1977 The Religious Office Holders in Chamula: A Study of Gods, Ritual, and Sacrifice. D.Phil. dissertation, Institute of Social Anthropology, Oxford University.

LÖNNROT, ELIAS
1963 (compiler) *The Kalevala; or, Poems of the Kalevala District.* Translated by Francis P. Magoun, Jr. Cambridge: Harvard University Press.

LÓPEZ AUSTIN, ALFREDO
1967 Términos del nahuallatolli. *Historia Mexicana* 17:1–36.

LÓPEZ (PÉREZ) TZINTAN, ANTONIO
1976 Textos tzotziles de Zinacantan, Chiapas, Mexico. Edited by Nicholas A. Hopkins. Microfilms of Manuscripts on Cultural Anthropology, ser. 51, no. 275. Chicago: University of Chicago Library.

LORD, ALBERT
1960 *The Singer of Tales.* Cambridge: Harvard University Press.

LUXTON, R. N.
1978 The Mayan Concept of Time. Ph.D. dissertation, University of Essex.

MACE, CARROLL E.
1957 A Collection of Dances from Rabinal. MS, Tulane University Latin American Library, New Orleans.

1961 The Patzcá Dance of Rabinal. *El Palacio* 68:151–167.

1967 New Information about Dance-Dramas of Rabinal and the *Rabinal-Achi. Xavier University Studies* 6:1–19. New Orleans.

1970 *Two Spanish-Quiché Dance-Dramas of Rabinal.* Tulane Studies in Romance Languages and Literature, no. 3. New Orleans.

McQUOWN, NORMAN A.
1959 (ed.) Report on the "Man-in-Nature" Project of the Department of Anthropology of the University of Chicago in the Tzeltal-Tzotzil-speaking Region of the State of Chiapas, Mexico. 3 vols., hectographed.

1979 A Modern Yucatec Maya Text. In *Mayan Texts II,* edited by Louanna Furbee-Losee, pp. 38–105. Native American Texts Series, vol. 3. Chicago: International Journal of American Linguistics.

McQUOWN, NORMAN A., ET AL.
1977 Notes on the Tzotzil of San Bartolomé de los Llanos (Venustiana Carranza). Microfilm Collection of Manuscripts on Cultural Anthropology, ser. 43. no. 235. Chicago: University of Chicago Library.

MAKEMSON, MAUD W.
1951   *The Book of the Jaguar Priest: A Transla-tion of the Book of Chilam Balam of Tizimin, with Commentary.* New York: Henry Schuman.

MALINOWSKI, BRONISLAW
1926   *Myth in Primitive Psychology.* New York: W. W. Norton.

MANUSCRITO MEXICANO, NÚMERO 40
n.d.   MS, Collection Aubin-Goupil, Biblio-thèque Nationale, Paris.

MAPA DE SIGÜENZA
1810   In *Vues de cordillères et monuments des peuples indigènes de l'Amérique*, by Al-exander von Humboldt, pp. 223–230, Pl. 32. Paris: F. Schoell.

MAPAS DE CUAUHTINCHAN
1968   *Los mapas de Cuauhtinchan y la historia tolteca-chichimeca.* Edited by Bente Bittmann Simons. Serie Investigaciones, Instituto Nacional de Antropología e Historia, no. 15. Mexico City.

MARTÍ, SAMUEL
1961   *Canto, danza y música precortesia-nos.* Mexico City: Fondo de Cultura Económica.

MARTÍNEZ, APOLONIO
1910   *"Egloga cuarta de Virgilio," traducido al mexicano de la huaxteca potosina a los cien años de la Independencia de Mé-xico.* San Luis Potosí.

MARTÍNEZ HERNÁNDEZ, JOEL, ET AL.
1980   *Naua Masehualpakilistli* [Rejoicing of the Nahua people]. Patzcuaro, Michoa-can: Etnolingüística, Instituto Nacional Indigenista.

MARTÍNEZ HERNÁNDEZ, JUAN
1926   *Crónicas mayas: Crónica de Yaxkukul.* Merida: Ca. Tipográfica Yucateca.

MAUSS, MARCEL
1954   *The Gift: Forms and Functions of Ex-change in Archaic Societies.* Translated by Ian Cunnison. Glencoe, Ill.: Free Press.

MENDELSON, E. MICHAEL
1967   Ritual and Mythology. In *Handbook of Middle American Indians*, vol. 6, edited by Robert Wauchope and Manning Nash, pp. 392–415. Austin: University of Texas Press.

MENDOZA, VICENTE T.
1956   *Panorama de la música tradicional de México.* Estudios y Fuentes del Arte en México, Instituto de Investigaciones Es-

téticas, no. 7. Mexico City: Universidad Nacional Autónoma de México.

MENÉNDEZ-PIDAL, RAMÓN
1944–1946   *Cantar de Mío-Cid: Texto, gram-ática y vocabulario.* 2d ed. 3 vols. Ma-drid: Espasa-Calpe.
1953   *Romancero hispánico.* Vol. 1. Madrid: Espasa-Calpe.

MEXIHKATL ITONALAMA
1950   *Mexihkatl Itonalama, el periódico del mexicano.* Azcapotzalco, Mexico: M. Ba-rrios Espinosa.

MEXIHKAYOTL
1946   Mexico City: Sociedad Pro Lengua Ná-huatl Mariana Jacobo Rojas.

MODIANO, NANCY
1973   *Indian Education in the Chiapas High-land.* New York: Holt, Rinehart and Winston.

MODIANO, NANCY, NANCY DILEANIS, GARY H. GOSSEN, AND ROBERT WASSERSTROM
1977   *Los tzeltales y tzotziles en el pasado, Fo-lleto 1: Antes de la conquista.* San Cristo-bal de las Casas: Escuela de Desarrollo Regional, Instituto Nacional Indigenista.

MOLINA, ALONSO DE
1555   *Aquí comiença un vocabulario enla lengua castellana y mexicana.* Mexico City: Casa de Juan Pablos.
1571a   *Arte de la lengua mexicana y castellana.* Mexico City: Casa de Pedro Ocharte.
1571b   *Vocabulario en lengua castellana y mexicana.* Mexico City: Casa de Antonio de Spinosa.
1970   *Vocabulario en lengua castellana y mexi-cana y mexicana y castellana.* Introduc-tion by Miguel León-Portilla. Mexico City: Porrúa.

MONDLOCH, JAMES L.
1978   *Basic Quiche Grammar.* Institute for Mesoamerican Studies, Pub. no. 2. Al-bany: State University of New York.
1984   Una comparación entre los estilos de habla del quiché moderno y los en-contrados en el Popol Vuh. In *Nuevas perspectivas sobre el Popol Vuh*, edited by Robert M. Carmack and Francisco Morales Santos, pp. 88–108. Guatemala City: Editorial Piedra Santa.

MONTERDE, FRANCISCO
1955   Prologue to *Teatro indígena prehispá-nico (Rabinal Achi).* Biblioteca del Estu-diante Universitario 71. Mexico City:

Universidad Nacional Autónoma de México.

MORLEY, SYLVANUS G.

1920 *The Inscriptions at Copan.* Carnegie Institution of Washington Pub. 219. Washington, D.C.

MORLEY, SYLVANUS G., AND RALPH ROYS

1941 The Xiu Chronicle. MS, Carnegie Institution of Washington, Division of Historical Research, Peabody Museum, Harvard University.

MOSCOSO PASTRAÑA, PRUDENCIO

1972 *Jacinto Pérez "Pajarito": El último líder chamula.* Colección Chiapas, no. 1. Mexico City: Gobierno del Estado de Chiapas.

MOTOLINÍA, TORIBIO DE BENAVENTE

1971 *Memoriales: O, libro de las cosas de la Nueva España y de los naturales de ella.* Edited by Edmundo O'Gorman. 2d ed. Serie de Historiadores y Cronistas de Indias, Instituto de Investigaciones Históricas, no. 2. Mexico City: Universidad Nacional Autónoma de México.

NEUENSWANDER, HELEN, AND DEAN E. ARNOLD

1977 (eds.)*Cognitive Studies of Southern Mesoamerica.* Summer Institute of Linguistics Museum of Anthropology, Pub. 3. Norman, Oklahoma.

NEUENSWANDER, HELEN, AND MARY SHAW

1966 Orígen de las enfermedades en el mundo. *Folklore de Guatemala* 2:169–183. Guatemala City: Ministerio de Educación Pública.

NICHOLSON, HENRY B.

1971 Religion in Pre-Hispanic Central Mexico. In *Handbook of Middle American Indians*, vol. 10, edited by Robert Wauchope, Gordon F. Ekholm, and Ignacio Bernal, pp. 395–446. Austin: University of Texas Press.

1973 Phoneticism in the Late Pre-Hispanic Central Mexican Writing System. In *Mesoamerican Writing Systems*, edited by Elizabeth P. Benson, pp. 1–46. Washington, D.C.: Dumbarton Oaks.

NORMAN, WILLIAM

1976a Linguistic Aspects of Quiche Ritual. Paper presented at the Conference on the Anthropology of Prehispanic Quichean Cultures, State University of New York, Albany.

1976b (trans.) Quiché Text. In *Mayan Texts I*,

edited by Louanna Furbee-Losee, pp. 40–60. Native American Texts Series, vol. 1, no. 1. Chicago: International Journal of American Linguistics.

NOVELO EROSA, PAULINO

1941 Baaxten cu yilal chhic ti pek [Why Coati looks at Dog]. *Yikal Maya Than* 2:42. Merida: Imprenta·Oriente.

NOWOTNY, KARL A.

1956 Die Notation des "Tono" in den aztekischen Cantares. *Baessler-Archiv*, n.s. 4:185–189. Berlin: Dietrich Reimer.

OLMOS, ANDRÉS DE

1875 *Grammaire de la langue nahuatl ou mexique . . . publiée . . . par Rémi Siméon.* Paris: Imprimerie Nationale.

ORDINANCES OF COFRADÍAS

1663–1852 Cofradía de San Nicolás. MS, Gates Collection, Princeton University Library; photocopy in Ayer Collection, Newberry Library, Chicago.

1689 Cofradía del Rosario, edited by Pablo Vásquez. MS, Gates Collection, Princeton University Library; photocopies in Tulane University Latin American Library, New Orleans, and Ayer Collection, Newberry Library, Chicago.

1777 Cofradía de Santa Vera Cruz . . . de Totonicapan. MS, Gates Collection, Princeton University Library; photocopy in Ayer Collection, Newberry Library, Chicago.

n.d. Cofradía del Ssmo. Sacramento. MS, Gates Collection, Princeton University Library.

ORDÓÑEZ CH., MARTÍN

1968 Baile de los tzules. *Tradiciones de Guatemala* 1:35–37. Guatemala City: Universidad de San Carlos de Guatemala.

OSBORNE, LILLY DE JONGH

1965 *Folklore, supersticiones y leyendas de Guatemala.* Guatemala City. Comisión Permanente de Folklore, Etnografía y Etnología de la Sociedad de Geografía e Historia.

PACHECO CRUZ, SANTIAGO

1938 Payalchi ti u kah-ik [Prayer to the bitter wind]. *Investigaciones Lingüísticas* 5:75.

n.d. [1938?] *Hadzutz othelxoc* [Beautiful skin]. Merida: El Porvenir.

1940 *Teatro maya.* Merida: Imprenta Oriente.

PAREDES, IGNACIO

1759 (ed.) *Compendio del arte de la lengua*

mexicana del padre Horacio Carochi de la Compañia de Jesvs. Mexico City: Bibliotheca Mexicana.

PARET-LIMARDO DE VELA, LISE

1962 (compiler) Baile de la conquista. *Guatemala Indígena* 2(2):87–132.

1963 Original del baile de los moros. *Guatemala Indígena* 3:102–121.

1970 (compiler) La famosa y verdadera historia de venados para solemnizar la fiesta titular de Santa Catarina. *Guatemala Indígena* 4(3):103–121.

PECH, AH NAKUK

1936 Historia y crónica de Chac-Xulub-Chen. Edited by Héctor Pérez Martínez. Mexico City: Secretaría de Educación Pública.

PÉREZ M., PEDRO

1973 *Ja' yu'un chcojtiquintic ti Mexicoe (Conocer a México).* Mexico City: Instituto Lingüístico de Verano.

PÉREZ MALDONADO, RAÚL

1966 *Tales from Chichicastenango: Legends of the Maya-Quiché.* Translated by Joan Debarcli. 4th ed. Guatemala City: Unión Tipográfica.

PINKHAM, JESSIE E.

1970 Lévi-Straussian Analysis of the Zinacanteco Myth, "The Three Suns." MS, Harvard Chiapas Project, Peabody Museum, Harvard University.

POLK, MILBRY C.

1973 A Study of the Mythology concerning Rainbows in Zinacantan. MS; Harvard Chiapas Project, Peabody Museum, Harvard University.

POOT YAH, ELEUTERIO

n.d. Songs, Tales and Riddles. MS in possession of Munro S. Edmonson.

POPE. CAROLYN C.

1969 The Funerary Ceremony in Zinacantán. B.A. honors thesis, Department of Anthropology, Radcliffe College.

PORRAS VIDAL, P.

1900 Original del baile de toritos. MS, Archivos de Materiales Culturales del Instituto Indigenista Nacional, Guatemala City.

POZAS ARCINIEGA, RICARDO

1952 *Juan Pérez Jolote: Biografía de un Tzotzil.* Mexico City: Fondo de Cultura Económica.

1959 *Chamula: Un pueblo indio de los Altos de Chiapas.* Memorias del Instituto Nacional Indigenista, vol. 8. Mexico City. (Also, 1977, Clásicos de la Antropología Mexicana, nos. 1-I, 1-II. Mexico City: Instituto Nacional Indigenista.)

1962 *Juan the Chamula: An Ethnological Recreation of the Life of a Mexican Indian.* Translated by Lysander Kemp. Berkeley and Los Angeles: University of California Press.

PROCLAMA DEL DUQUE INFANTADO PRESIDENTE

1812 MS, Princeton University Library Rare Book Collection.

REAL ACADEMIA ESPAÑOLA

1970 *Diccionario de la lengua española.* 19th ed. Madrid: Espasa-Calpe.

RECINOS, ADRIÁN

1950a (ed. and trans.) *Memorial de Sololá: Anales de los cakchiqueles. Título de los señores de Totonicapán.* Mexico City: Fondo do Cultura Ecónomica.

1950b (trans.) *Popol Vuh: The Sacred Book of the Ancient Quiché Maya.* Translated into English by Delia Goetz and Sylvanus G. Morley. Norman: University of Oklahoma Press.

1953 (ed.) *The Annals of the Cakchiquels.* Translated by Adrián Recinos and Delia Goetz. *Title of the Lords of Totonicapán.* Translated by Dionisio José Chonay and Delia Goetz. Norman: University of Oklahoma Press.

1957 (trans.) *Crónicas indígenas de Guatemala.* Guatemala City: Editorial Universitaria.

1959 Literatura maya-quiché. *Esplendor del México Antiguo* 1:170–190. Mexico City.

REDFIELD, MARGARET PARK

1935 *The Folk Literature of a Yucatecan Town.* Contributions to American Archaeology, Carnegie Institution of Washington, no. 13. Washington, D.C. (Also, Carnegie Institution Pub. 456, pp. 1–50.)

REDFIELD, ROBERT, AND ALFONSO VILLA ROJAS

1934 *Chan Kom: A Maya Village.* Carnegie Institution of Washington Pub. 448. Washington, D.C.

REJÓN GARCÍA, MANUEL

1926 Ti X'iz: A Isidra. *Boletín de la Universidad Nacional del Sureste,* April, pp. 125–127. Merida.

RIESE, FRAUKE JOHANNA

1981 *Indianische Landrechte in Yukatan um*

die Mitte des 16. Jahrhunderts: Dokumentenanalyse und Konstruktion von Wirklichkeitsmodellen am Fall des Landvertrages von Mani. Beiträge zur mittelamerikanischen Völkerkunde, no. 16. Hamburg: Museum für Völkerkunde.

RINCÓN, ANTONIO DEL
1595 *Arte mexicana*. Mexico City: Pedro, Balli. (1885 ed., edited by Antonio Peñafiel. Mexico City: Secretaría de Fomento. 1967 facsimile copy of 1885 ed. Guadalajara: Edmundo Aveña Levy.)

RODAZ, JUAN DE
1688 Arte de la lengua tzotzlem o zinacanteca con explicación del año solar y un tratado de las quentas de los indios en lengua tzotzlem. Microfilm of MS, Museo Nacional de Antropología, Serie Chiapas, spool 94. Mexico City.

ROMANCES DE LOS SEÑORES. *See* Garibay 1964.

ROMERO CASTILLO, MOISÉS
1965 Tres cuentos mayas. *Anales del Instituto Nacional de Antropología e Historia* 17: 303–320. Mexico City.

ROSADO VEGA, LUIS
1929 *El sueño de Chichen*. Mexico City: Talleres Gráficos de la Nación.

ROSALDO, RENATO I.
1968 Metaphors of Hierarchy in a Mayan Ritual. *American Anthropologist* 70: 524–536.

ROYS, RALPH L.
1931 *The Ethno-Botany of the Maya*. Middle American Research Series, Tulane University, Pub. no. 2. New Orleans.
1933 *The Book of Chilam Balam of Chumayel*. Carnegie Institution of Washington Pub. 438. Washington, D.C.
1939 *The Titles of Ebtun*. Carnegie Institution of Washington Pub. 505. Washington, D.C.
1943 *The Indian Background of Colonial Yucatan*. Carnegie Institution of Washington Pub. 548. Washington, D.C.
1965 (ed. and trans.) *Ritual of the Bacabs*. Norman: University of Oklahoma Press.

RUIZ DE ALARCÓN, HERNANDO
1900 Tratado de las supersticiones de los naturales de esta Nueva España. *Anales del Museo Nacional de México* 6: 123–223. (1953 ed., in *Tratados de las idolatrias, superstisciones, dioses, ritos, hechicerias, y otras costumbres gentilicas de las razas*

aborigenes de Mexico 2: 17–180. Mexico City: Ediciones Fuente Cultural.)
1983 *Treatise on the Heathen Superstitions*. Edited by J. Richard Andrews and Ross Hassig. Norman: University of Oklahoma Press.

RUSSELL, FRANK
1908 The Pima Indians. In *Twenty-Sixth Annual Report of the Bureau of American Ethnology, 1904–1905*, pp. 3–389. Washington, D.C.

SAHAGÚN, BERNARDINO DE
1956 *Historia general de las cosas de Nueva España*. Edited and translated by Angel María Garibay K. 4 vols. Mexico City: Porrúa.

SÁNCHEZ, JOSÉ MARÍA
1895 *La lengua tzotzil en Chiapas*. San Cristobal de las Casas: El Trabajo.

SANTOS V., LEODEGARIO
1975a *In quenin oquiahuiltique in tecuhtli* [How they mocked a gentleman]. Mexico City: Dirección General de Educación Extraescolar del Medio Indígena.
1975b *In tlacatl aquin oquipolo se cuacue* [The man who lost an ox]. Mexico City: Dirección General de Educación Extraescolar del Medio Indígena.

SCHULLER, RUDOLF
1925 La lengua ts'ots'il. *International Journal of American Linguistics* 3: 193–218.

SCHULTZE JENA, LEONHARD
1933 *Indiana I: Leben, Glaube und Sprache der Quiché von Guatemala*. Jena: Gustav Fischer.

SCHUMANN G., OTTO
1971 *Descripción estructural del maya itzá del Petén, Guatemala, C.A.* Centro de Estudios Mayas, Cuaderno 6. Mexico City: Universidad Nacional Autónoma de México.

SELER, EDUARD
1904 Die religiösen Gesänge der alten Mexikaner. In *Gesammelte Abhandlungen zur amerikanischen Sprach- und Altertumskunde* 2: 959–1107. Berlin: A. Asher. (Reprinted, 1960. Graz: Akademische Druck-u. Verlagsanstalt.)

SERNA, JACINTO DE LA
1900 Manual de ministros de Indios para el conocimiento de sus idolatrias, y extirpacion de ellas. *Anales del Museo Nacional* 6: 261–480. Mexico City. (Also, 1955, in

Tratado de las idolatrias, supersticiones, dioses, ritos, hechicerias y otras costumbres gentilicas de las razas aborigines de Mexico 1:41–368. Mexico City: Ediciones Fuente Cultural.)

SHAW, MARY
1971 (ed.) *According to Our Ancestors: Folk Texts from Guatemala and Honduras.* Summer Institute of Linguistics Pub. no. 32. Norman, Oklahoma.

SILVER, DANIEL B.
1966 Shamanism in Zinacantan. Ph.D. dissertation, Department of Anthropology, Harvard University.

SMAILUS, ORTWIN
1975 *Textos mayas de Belice y Quintana Roo: Fuentes para una dialectología del maya yucateca.* Indiana, Supplement 3. Berlin: Gebr. Mann.

SOLÍS ALCALÁ, ERMILIO, JR.
1949 (trans.) *Códice Pérez.* Merida: Imprenta Oriente.

SOUZA NOVELO, NARCISO
1947 Ch'it-kuuk: Leyenda maya. *Yikal Maya Than* 8:81–83. Merida: Imprenta Oriente.

STEPHENS, JOHN L.
1843 *Incidents of Travel in Yucatan.* 2 vols. New York: Harper and Brothers.

STEVEN, HUGH
1976 *They Dared to Be Different.* Irvine, Calif.: Harvest House Publishers.

STEVENSON, ROBERT
1968 *Music in Aztec and Inca Territory.* Berkeley and Los Angeles: University of California Press.

TABI, DOCUMENT OF
1569–1821 Documentos de tierras de la Hacienda Sn. Juan Bautista Tavi en idioma maya o yucateca. 5 vols. MS in Latin American Library, Tulane University, New Orleans.

TAX, SOL
1944 Information about the Municipio of Zinacantan, Chiapas. *Revista Mexicana de Estudios Antropológicos* 6:181–195.

1949 Folk Tales in Chichicastenango: An Unsolved Puzzle. *Journal of American Folklore* 62:125–135.

TEABO, NOTEBOOK OF
1868 Berendt copy, pp. 93–96, in Berendt Linguistics Collection, University of Pennsylvania, Philadelphia.

TEDLOCK, DENNIS
1984 Las formas del verso quiché. In *Nuevas perspectivas sobre el Popol Vuh,* edited by Robert M. Carmack and Francisco Morales Santos, pp. 123–132. Guatemala City: Editorial Piedra Santa.

TELETOR, CELSO NARCISO
1945 Bailes que representan los indígenas en Baja Verapaz. *Anales de la Sociedad de Geografía e Historia de Guatemala* 20:51–52.

1955 *Apuntes para una monografía de Rabinal (B.V.) y algo de nuestro folklore.* Guatemala City: Ministerio de Educación Pública.

TEPAZ RAXULEU, F. LUCAS
1976 Quiché Text. Translated by William Norman. In *Mayan Texts I,* edited by Louanna Furbee-Losee, pp. 40–60. Native American Texts Series, vol. 1, no. 1. Chicago: International Journal of American Linguistics.

TERMER, FRANZ
1930 Los bailes de culebra entre los indios quichés en Guatemala. In *Proceedings of the Twenty-third International Congress of Americanists* (New York, 1928), pp. 661–667.

1931 Der Palo Volador in Guatemala. *El Mexico Antiguo* 3:13–23.

1957 *Etnología y etnografía de Guatemala.* Seminario de Integración Social Guatemalteca, Pub. no. 5. Guatemala City: Ministerio de Educación Pública.

TEXTOS DE CHAMULA
n.d. Textos de Chamula (Tzotzil de los parajes de Chamula) (Estado de Chiapas, Mexico): Escritos en idioma tzotzil por informantes escribientes chamulas y traducidos al español por los mismos. [Data collected 1960–1962.] Microfilm Collection of Manuscripts on Cultural Anthropology, ser. 43, no. 232. Chicago: University of Chicago Library.

THOMPSON, J. ERIC S.
1930 *Ethnology of the Mayas of Southern and Central British Honduras.* Field Museum of Natural History Pub. 274. Chicago.

1937 *A New Method of Deciphering Yucatecan Dates, with Special Reference to Chichen Itza.* Carnegie Institution of Washington Pub. 483. Washington, D.C.

(Also, Carnegie Contributions to American Archaeology, no. 22.)

1950 *Maya Hieroglyphic Writing: An Introduction.* Carnegie Institution of Washington Pub. 589. Washington, D.C.

1970 *Maya History and Religion.* Norman: University of Oklahoma Press.

THOMPSON, STITH

1961 (trans.) *The Types of the Folktale: A Classification and Bibliography,* by Antti Aarne. 2d revision. Folklore Fellows Communications, no. 184. Helsinki: Suomalainen Tiedeakatemia.

TIRA DE LA PEREGRINACIÓN

1964 Tira de la peregrinación (Explicación del Códice Boturini). In *Antigüedades de México, basadas en la recopilación de Lord Kingsborough* 2:7–29. Mexico City: Secretaría de Hacienda y Crédito Público.

TIRA DE TEPECHPAN

1978 *Tira de Tepechpan: Códice colonial procedente del Valle de México.* Edited by Xavier Noguez. Biblioteca Enciclopédica del Estado de México, vols. 64–65. Mexico City: Mario Colin.

TÍTULOS DE LOS REYES DE GUATEMALA EN QUICHE

n.d. MS, Gates Collection, Princeton University Library.

TONALAMATL DE AUBIN

1981 Introductory study by Carmen Aguilera. Tlaxcala: Ediciones del Gobierno de Tlaxcala.

TOZZER, ALFRED MARSDEN

1907 *A Comparative Study of the Mayas and the Lacandones.* New York: MacMillan.

1921 *A Maya Grammar.* Papers of the Peabody Museum, Harvard University, vol. 9. Cambridge.

TRAVEN, B.

1971 *March to the Montería.* New York: Hill and Wang.

TUROK, MARTA

1976 Diseño y símbolo en el huipil ceremonial de Magdelenas, Chiapas. *Boletín del Departamento de Investigación de las Tradiciones Populares* 3:123–136. Mexico City: Dirección General de Arte Popular, Secretaría de Educación Pública.

TZEP LÓPEZ, JOSÉ, AND FLORENTINO P. AJPACAJÁ TUM

1979 *Ri k'aatel koot pa ch'aabal k'iche?.* Hue-

huetenango, Guatemala: Proyecto Lingüístico Francisco Marroquín.

ULRICH, MATTHEW AND ROSEMARY

1966 Mopán-Maya. Translated by Julio Vielman. In *Lenguas de Guatemala,* pp. 355–382. Seminario de Integración Social Guatemalteca, Pub. no. 20. Guatemala City.

UNOS ANNALES HISTÓRICOS DE LA NACIÓN MEXICANA

1945 Facsimile ed. Vol. 2 of *Corpus Codicum Americanorum Medii Aevi,* edited by Ernst Mengin. Copenhagen: Einar Munksgaard.

VÁSQUEZ, PASCUAL

1689 (ed.) Ordenanzas de la Cofradía del Rosario. MS, Gates Collection, Princeton University Library; copy in Tulane University Latin American Library, New Orleans.

VILLACORTA CALDERÓN, JOSÉ ANTONIO, AND FLAVIO RODAS N.

1927 (eds. and trans.) *Manuscrito de Chichicastenango (Popol buj): Estudios sobre las antiguas tradiciones del pueblo quiché.* Guatemala City: Sánchez & DeGuise.

VILLACORTA C., J. ANTONIO, AND CARLOS A. VILLACORTA

1933 *Códices mayas.* . . . Guatemala City: Tipografía Nacional. (2d ed., 1976.)

VILLA ROJAS, ALFONSO

1968 Los conceptos de espacio y tiempo entre los grupos mayances contemporáneos. Appendix to *Tiempo y realidad en el pensamiento maya,* by Miguel León-Portilla, pp. 119–167. Mexico City: Universidad Nacional Autónoma de México.

VIVAS, DAVID

1925 Mayab Kay. *Boletín de la Universidad Nacional del Sureste,* January, p. 18. Merida.

VOCABULARIO TZOTZIL

n.d. Vocabulario tzotzil de Istapa, Chiapas, Mexico. Translated by Norman A. McQuown. Microfilm Collection of Manuscripts on Cultural Anthropology, ser. 43, no. 233. Chicago: University of Chicago Library.

VOGT, EVON Z.

1966 (ed.) *Los zinacantecos: Un pueblo tzotzil de los Altos de Chiapas.* Colección de Antropología Social, vol. 7. Mexico City: Instituto Nacional Indigenista.

1969   *Zinacantán: A Maya Community in the Highlands of Chiapas.* Cambridge: Harvard University Press, Belknap Press.

1976   *Tortillas for the Gods: A Symbolic Analysis of Zinacantan Rituals.* Cambridge: Harvard University Press.

1977   On the Symbolic Meaning of Percussion in Zinacanteco Ritual. *Journal of Anthropological Research* 33:231–244.

1978   *Bibliography of the Harvard Chiapas Project: The First Twenty Years, 1957–1977.* Cambridge: Peabody Museum, Harvard University.

VOGT, EVON Z., AND CATHERINE C. VOGT

1970   Lévi-Strauss among the Maya. *Man,* n.s. 5:379–392.

WALLIS, ETHEL C.

n.d.   Names of Family Relations, Tzotzil, Zinacanteco Dialect. MS, Summer Institute of Linguistics, Norman, Oklahoma.

WASSERSTROM, ROBERT F.

1970   Our Lady of the Salt. B.A. honors thesis, Department of Anthropology, Harvard College.

WAUCHOPE, ROBERT

1938   *Modern Maya Houses: A Study of Their Archaeological Significance.* Carnegie Institute of Washington Pub. 502. Washington, D.C.

1948   *Excavations at Zacualpa, Guatemala.* Middle American Research Institute, Tulane University, Pub. 14. New Orleans.

WEATHERS, KENNETH, AND NADINE WEATHERS

1949a   *Diccionario español-tzotzil, · tzotzil-español.* Mexico City: Instituto Lingüístico de Verano.

1949b   *Jkot t'ul schi'uk stio benagro (El conejo y el venado).* Mexico City: Instituto Lingüístico de Verano.

1949c   *Segunda cartilla tzotzil.* Mexico City: Instituto Lingüístico de Verano.

1951   *Primera cartilla tzotzil.* Rev. ed. Mexico City: Instituto Nacional Indigenista.

WEATHERS, NADINE

1947a   Problem of Writing Initial Glottal Stop in Tsotsil. MS, Summer Institute of Linguistics, Norman, Oklahoma.

1947b   Tsotsil Phonemes with Special Reference to Allophones of B. *International Journal of American Linguistics* 13:108–111.

1949   Tzotzil Texts and Dictionary. In Materials on Mayan Languages of Mexico, pp. 157–215. Microfilm Collection of Manuscripts on Middle American Cultural Anthropology, ser. 4, no. 26. Chicago: University of Chicago Library.

1950   Morphological Analysis of a Tzotzil (Mayan) Text. *International Journal of American Linguistics* 16:91–98.

n.d.a   Los fonemas del tzotzil. MS, Summer Institute of Linguistics, Norman, Oklahoma.

n.d.b   Tzotzil Vocabulary of Hot and Cold Foods. MS, Summer Institute of Linguistics, Norman, Oklahoma.

WERBY, ELIZABETH A.

1971   Tzotzil Speech and Couplet Pair Formations. MS, Harvard Chiapas Project, Peabody Museum, Harvard University.

WERNER, DAVID

1980   *Bu mu'yuk jloktor: Ja' sbijubtasel hkampesinoetik boch'otik nom na'il poxtambailetik nakalike.* Translated by Jasinto Arex [Jacinto Arias]. Princeton: Science Press. (Original eds., 1977, *Donde no hay doctor* and *Where There Is No Doctor.* Palo Alto: Hesperian Foundation.)

WILSON, CARTER

1966   *Crazy February.* New York: J. B. Lippincott.

1972   *A Green Tree and a Dry Tree.* New York: Macmillan.

XEC, PATRICIO, AND GAIL MAYNARD

1954   Diccionario quiché preliminar: Quiché-español, español-quiché. Mimeographed. Quezaltenango, Guatemala.

XIU CHRONICLES

1608–1817   MS in Peabody Museum Library, Harvard University.

ZACCICOXOL

1588   Zakicoxol. Photocopy, Ayer Collection, Newberry Library, Chicago.

1800, 1824   Zakicoxol. 4 additional undated MSS, Gates Collection, Princeton University Library.

1875   Zaccicoxol. MS, Berendt Linguistic Collection, University of Pennsylvania, Philadelphia; photocopy in Tulane University Latin American Library, New Orleans.

1891   Conquista de México. MS copy of 1783 script, Erwin Dieseldorff Collection, Tulane University Library, New Orleans.

BIBLIOGRAPHY

n.d.   Sakigoxol. MS No. 3168, National Anthropological Archives, Smithsonian Institution; Washington, D.C.; transcription by William Gates (Zakigoxol Text A),
MS No. 3168:XII, also in National Anthropological Archives.

ZIMMERMANN, GÜNTHER
1956   Aus dem Brieftagebuch eines Quiché-
Gemeindeschreibers aus dem Jahre 1794.

In *Die Wiener Schule der Völkerkunde*,
edited by J. Haekel, pp. 492–503. Vienna: Horn.

ZWENG, NANCY A.
1973   An Analysis of the Structure and Symbols Used in Zinacanteco Prayers. MS,
Harvard Chiapas Project, Peabody Museum, Harvard University.

INDEX

171